W9-CCB-961

THE EMBLEMATICS OF THE SELF: EKPHRASIS AND IDENTITY IN RENAISSANCE IMITATIONS OF GREEK ROMANCE

ELIZABETH B. BEARDEN

The Emblematics of the Self:

Ekphrasis and Identity in Renaissance Imitations of Greek Romance

UNIVERSITY OF TORONTO PRESS
Toronto Buffalo London

Toronto Buffalo London
www.utppublishing.com
Printed in Canada

ISBN 978-1-4426-4346-8

Printed on acid-free, 100% post-consumer recycled paper
with vegetable-based inks.

Library and Archives Canada Cataloguing in Publication

Bearden, Elizabeth B., 1975–
The emblematics of the self: ekphrasis and identity in Renaissance
imitations of Greek romance / Elizabeth B. Beardon.

Includes index.
ISBN 978-1-4426-4346-8

1. European literature – Renaissance, 1450–1600 – History and criticism.
2. European literature – Renaissance, 1450–1600 – Greek influences.
3. Identity (Philosophical concept) in literature. 4. Ekphrasis. I. Title.

PN721.B42 2012 809.031 C2011-904281-9

University of Toronto Press acknowledges the financial assistance to its
publishing program of the Canada Council for the Arts and the Ontario
Arts Council.

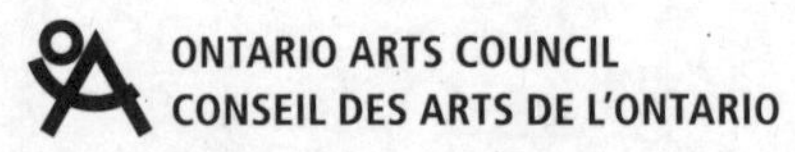

University of Toronto Press acknowledges the financial support of the
Government of Canada through the Canada Book Fund for its publishing
activities.

For Michael Harrison

Contents

List of Illustrations

Acknowledgments

I am pleased to acknowledge some of the people and institutions that have helped to make this work possible, though I realize that I cannot thank them all or thank them enough. I will start with Timothy Reiss, who advised this project's ancestor in the form of a dissertation; he is this book's inspiration, though he is in no way responsible for its blemishes. I aspire to his intellectual generosity and to the way he makes academic work speak to the world. Daniel Javitch has been a careful critic and a firm friend. Without Ernie (Ernesto) Gilman's sage advice and friendship, I might not have finished this book, or graduate school for that matter. Leonard Barkan, Gigi Dopico-Black, Salvador Martínez, and Richard Sieburth are also wonderful teachers who helped me to hone my ideas. NYU's Graduate School of Arts and Science Lane Cooper Dissertation Fellowship aided the project's beginnings significantly.

The book has become quite a different creature since my appointment to teach at the University of Maryland in 2006, and I am especially indebted to my colleagues who have read portions of the manuscript or who have provided other substantial advice. These include Professors Bauer, Cartwright, Coletti, Grossman, Hallett, Harrison, Leinwand, Mack, Ray, Richardson, Rudy, Valiavicharska, and, last but never least, Gerard Passannante. I thank them for their invaluable advice and assistance. The graduate school and my department at UMD have generously supplied a subvention for the publication of this book, for which I am deeply grateful. I am also very pleased to thank the anonymous referees and editors of the University of Toronto Press for their thoughtful comments and corrections. Chapter 2 was aided by the moral support of Vessela Valiavicharska, the helpful comments of Roderick Beaton, Larry Kim, and David Elmer, and the intellectual atmosphere of the ICAN IV Conference in Lisbon in the summer of 2008. I am also thankful to Karina Galperín for sending me her excellent work on Reinoso. A version of this chapter will appear in a collection entitled *Fictional Traces: The Reception of the Ancient Novel,* edited by Marília Futre Pinheiro and Stephen Harrison, and published by Roelf Barkhus as volume 13.1 of the *Ancient Narrative Supplementum* series. An early version of chapter 4 appeared in the May 2006 issue of *PMLA*. Regarding this chapter, Alban Forcione was responsible for my interest not only in Cervantes but in Renaissance literature more broadly. He was the first to suggest that I read the *Persiles*, and I am deeply grateful to this kind man for his good influence. I completed the research and writing of chapter 5 with the aid of a short-term Folger Shakespeare Library fellowship and a semester's leave from my department in 2008. As everyone who has a chance to work there knows, the Folger and their excellent staff (especially Georgianna Ziegler and Heather Wolfe) are a class act. Thanks are also due to Mark Riley, who generously provided me with the introduction to his and Dorothy Pritchard Huber's edition of the *Argenis* before it was in print. Catherine Connors's excellent work and collegiality I acknowledge in my chapter on Barclay itself. My chapter on Wroth benefited from comments by Nabil Matar and Cyrus Mulready at RSA in 2007. Barbara Fuchs, Brian Lockey, and J.K. Barret have also been wonderful interlocutors and have gotten me thinking about my work from new perspectives on many occasions.

Amy Merritt has been an indispensable assistant; she is one of the heroes of this story, and I am very grateful to her for being there when I and the project most needed her. I have been fortunate to work with many excellent students at UMD; to the participants of my Sidney seminar and to those of my seminar on ekphrasis go heartfelt thanks. Tim and Lara Crowley, Stephanie Graham, and Beth Martin deserve special thanks in this regard as well.

I give a general and warm acknowledgment to David Landreth and Melissa Hillier, Julia Schleck and John Dettloff, Kelly Stage, Susan Harlan, Leif Sorensen, and Lynne Shutters. They know why. Lara and Paula are the best sisters I could ask for, and Mom and Don, Bill, Adele, and my favourite cousin, Lesley, have been most encouraging. My greatest thanks go to my beloved husband Michael, who makes the wish-fulfilment of romance a reality.

Note on Editions, Translations, and Abbreviations

Note on Editions and Translations

Whenever possible, I have made an effort to cite modern, accessible editions of classical and early modern texts and so too with their translations. I have made use of the wonderful early modern vernacular translations of ancient Greek romances and their prefatory material, many of which I have consulted at the Folger Shakespeare Library. These vernacular translations would have been the means by which the early modern authors under investigation here would most likely have read these romances. Nonetheless, since it is often not possible to identify which translation a particular romancer would have used, I frequently cite the Whitmarsh and Hadas translations of Tatius and Heliodorus, because I think they capture well the vividness of the prose. Throughout the book, unattributed translations are my own, and I have modernized the use of u and v and i and j unless the early modern convention is retained in a modern edition.

Abbreviations

Ach. Tat. Achilles Tatius, *Leucippe and Clitophon*, trans. Whitmarsh. I cite book, section, and page numbers for the reader's convenience.
Cervantes: Cervantes: Bulletin of the Cervantes Society of America
CL: Comparative Literature
DQ: Don Quijote, ed. Riquer
ELH: *English Literary History*
ELR: *English Literary Renaissance*

FQ: Faerie Queene, 2nd ed., ed. Hamilton, Yamashita, Suzuki, and Fukuda
HL: Humanistica Lovaniensia
JEMCS: Journal for Early Modern Cultural Studies
NA: New Arcadia, ed. Evans. I cite book, chapter, and page numbers. The chapter numbers were Greville's addition for his 1590 edition, and I cite them here for the reader's convenience, though they are not included in the Evans edition.
NLH: New Literary History
OA: Old Arcadia, ed. Duncan-Jones
OED: Oxford English Dictionary
PMLA: Publications of the Modern Language Association
RQ: Renaissance Quarterly
SEL: Studies in English Literature, 1500-1900

THE EMBLEMATICS OF THE SELF: EKPHRASIS AND IDENTITY IN RENAISSANCE IMITATIONS OF GREEK ROMANCE

Introduction

By the middle of the sixteenth century, ancient Greek romances by Heliodorus, Achilles Tatius, and Longus had been translated widely across Europe and were received to high acclaim. They became models for a new version of prose romance that strove not only to meet moral and aesthetic criteria, but also to accommodate Europe's increasingly global purview. Eager to articulate new expressions of cultural identity, Renaissance romancers were not satisfied to imitate; rather, they emulated the vivid verbal pictures they found in ancient Greek romance – both in terms of technique and narrative function – to enliven their representations of early modern cultural identity. Whether it was Miguel de Cervantes Saavedra drawing on Heliodorus to depict a group of outlandish pilgrims on their journey to Rome or Sir Philip Sidney making Achilles Tatius's verbal pictures 'speak' to the political and gender troubles of the *Arcadia*, Renaissance imitators of the Greek romance employed ekphrasis to represent and question socially determined hierarchies of ethnic, gender, and religious difference. This study focuses on how the women, foreigners, and non-Christians of Renaissance romances create and interpret verbal pictures, and it claims that their aesthetic responses constitute identity. I call this process of identity formation in romance the 'emblematics of the self.' A short excursus on ekphrasis and on the romance identity that it illuminates frame the work that follows.

A rhetorical term originating in the grammar school exercises or *progymnasmata* of the Second Sophistic (c. first to second centuries CE), ekphrasis has been defined as broadly as vivid description, and as narrowly as the description of an extant work of visual art. Ekphrasis is defined here as the verbal representation of visual representation. Like W.J.T. Mitchell in *Picture Theory* (152), I find this definition (first articulated by James Heffernan in his *Museum of Words*) to be convenient and accurate. Though ekphrasis has been defined with various degrees of flexibility in its history, this definition avoids the pitfalls of restricting ekphrasis exclusively to the description of the plastic arts (a restriction that was not imposed by classical rhetoricians, as Ruth Webb correctly insists in her recent study of ekphrasis); it also properly emphasizes the representational and, thereby, artificial and potentially intertextual aspects of these set pieces of description as they function in narrative. It is thus a definition that balances the classical and modern limits of the form and most closely approximates what early modern writers would have recognized as the highly ornamented set-pieces of literature that were expected to be a part of the repertory of any respectable author, providing what Lucian (beloved by Renaissance writers) once called a 'chance of airing his eloquence' that no one 'whose pursuits are literary' could afford to 'miss' (12).

While ekphrasis has been the object of much scholarly interest, with numerous studies dedicated to an analysis of its form and relationship to narrative, it is worth repeating a question recently posed by Simon Goldhill, 'What Is Ekphrasis For?'[1] The answer that this book propounds is that ekphrasis provides a formal key to romance characters' impressions – it functions rhetorically to reveal ethos. Though it is well known that ekphrasis was a rhetorical tool for creating *enargeia*, or the action of vividly drawing an image before the mind's eye, this descriptive mode was also used for both guiding the ethos of an audience and illustrating varied character types. Ekphrasis had its own set of deliberative and forensic applications, which I elaborate in chapter 1, but my primary interest here is the function of ekphrasis in the representation of identity in prose narrative, specifically in Renaissance imitations of ancient Greek romance.

My ekphrastic method for reading romance identity is based on the concept of passibility. This term, with its roots in ancient philosophy, was used in early modern theology and humoral theory to define impressionable susceptibility or capacity for change.[2] Romance characters are passible to the cultural and aesthetic situations that each romancer creates. Understanding romance identity to be passible avoids some potential drawbacks of self-fashioned and performative readings of early modern identity in lyric and drama that make modern formulations of subjectivity based on individual agency the benchmark for personhood,[3] often thus excluding subaltern groups. The concept of the modern subject is reputed to have been invented by early modern figures like Montaigne, Shakespeare, and Descartes. This is problematic for many reasons, not the least of which being that it presumes a narrative of progress – a Whiggish teleology – in people's understanding of themselves as individuals. Agency is moreover a problematic term for romance characters, whose fictional lives are propelled by fate (in the ancient context) or God (in the early modern context) and who are further subjected to the trials and accidents that typify romance narratives. Romances are densely populated with subaltern characters who are not given the luxury of self-fashioning or of behaviour or language that modern critics ascribe to subjectivity, agency, and by extension, depth of character. In this sense, the structure of romance very much limits individual agency. Attending to the responses of the marginal or foreign characters of romance, their passible susceptibility to the verbal images that surround them, discloses considerable insights into the hegemonic, colonial, and cosmopolitan logics that framed European attitudes towards cultural Others in the Renaissance. Thus, while my ekphrastic approach to identity is firmly grounded in early modern aesthetics and ethics, it offers an alternative method for reading identity – what might be called a countersubjectivity – that does not make individual agency a prerequisite for personhood.

But why is the Greek romance genre so particularly suited to this ekphrastic method of reading identity? Today's readers are most familiar with Homer's use of ekphrasis to describe Achilles' shield in the *Iliad*, where Hephaestus 'blaz[es] well-wrought emblems all across its surface' (18: 559, 483).[4] Ekphrasis calls forth an image – something that is other than the narrative – before our eyes, opening a textual window onto a parallel level of discourse within the story. While the use of ekphrasis in epics like the *Iliad* often leaves the onlooker dazzled and speechless – none of Achilles' companions 'dared to look straight at the glare, / each fighter shrank away' (19: 17–18, 489), and Achilles 'thrilled his heart with looking hard / at the armor's well-wrought beauty' (19: 22–3, 489) but does not speak – Greek romances present ekphrastic passages as visually coded objects and invite both the reader and the characters within the plot to decode them. After coming across a painting of Philomela, for example, Achilles Tatius's character Menelaus, in the ancient Greek romance *Leucippe and Clitophon* (c. 150 CE), reminds his comrades, 'Interpreters of signs say that if we encounter paintings as we set off to do something, we should ponder the myths narrated there, and conclude that the outcome for us will be comparable to the story they tell' (Ach. Tat. 5, 4, 79).[5] This injunction activates a number of interpretations for characters and readers alike. Furthermore, when romance characters become interpreters of ekphrastic passages, they reveal their own perspectives and identities.

Leucippe and Clitophon opens with a lush, erotic ekphrasis describing a votive painting found in a Phoenician temple to the goddess Astarte. The framing narrator, having just washed up at Sidon after surviving a shipwreck, relates how he 'saw a votive picture, a landscape and seascape in one. The picture was of Europa, the sea was the Phoenician, and the land Sidon. On the side of the land was a meadow and a troupe of maidens; in the sea a bull was gliding over the surface, and a beautiful maiden was seated on his back, sailing on the bull towards Crete' (1, 1, 3). The narrator continues, relating the verdant seaside garden, the landlocked spectators to the marine scene, the ocean surf, the figure of bull and voluptuous maiden, and the depiction of a frolicking Cupid and dolphins in lubricious detail, as the following excerpt describes:

> The artist had also depicted the shade under the leaves, and here and there the sun gently trickled through down onto the meadow, wherever the painter had parted the thatch of the leaves. The entire meadow was bounded at its perimeter, garlanded by the leafy vault. The flower-beds had been allowed to grow in rows under the leaves of the foliage: narcissi, roses, and myrtle. Water was streaming from the middle of the pictorial meadow, some spurting up from beneath the soil, and some dribbling around the blooms and bushes. A man was pictured using a mattock to irrigate the soil, hunched over one trench and opening a channel for the stream. At the edge of the meadow, on the parts of the land that jutted out into the sea, the artist had arrayed the maidens. The maidens' mien betrayed at once pleasure and terror. Wreathes were bound around their temples, but their hair ran loose down over their shoulders. Their legs were entirely bare, with no skirts around their calves (girdles drew their skirts up to the knee), nor sandals on their feet. Their faces were wan, their cheeks set in a half-smile, and their eyes stared wide open towards the sea. Their mouths gaped a little, as if they were actually about to give out a shriek of terror, and their arms were outstretched towards the bull. They were stepping into the edge of the sea, enough for the wave to lap over their feet a little; they seemed both to desire to pursue the bull and to fear to enter the sea.
>
> The colour of the sea was twofold, reddish towards the land and deep blue towards the open sea. There was spume portrayed, and also crags and waves: the crags stood proud of the land, spume whitened the crags,

> the wave climaxed and dissolved into spume, around the crags. The bull was depicted cresting the waves in the middle of the sea, while the wave rose like a mountain where the bull flexed his bulging limb. The maiden sat in the middle of the bull's back, not astride him but side-saddle, keeping her feet together on his right. She clasped his horn with her left hand, as a charioteer would the reins, and the bull inclined a little in that direction, steered by the pressure of her hand. A tunic enveloped her upper body, down to her most intimate part; from there down, a skirt concealed the lower parts of her body. The tunic was white, and the skirt was purple. Her body was just about visible through her clothing: her navel was deep, her belly taut, her waist slender, and the slenderness gave way to broadness towards her loins. Her breasts protruded gently from her chest (the girdle that fastened her tunic enclosed her breasts, but the tunic mirrored her body). Her hands were each at full stretch, one on his horn and the other on his tail, and with these she gripped either end of her veil, which was spread out above her head, encircling her shoulders. The folds of her cloak were taut, bulging in every direction (and that was how the artist depicted the wind). She was seated on the bull as if on a ship at sea, using her cloak as if it were a sail.
>
> Dolphins were dancing around the bull, cupids were playing. You might have said that the picture was even moving. Eros was leading the bull: Eros, represented as a little boy, had unfurled his wings and strapped on his quiver, and was wielding his torch. He was turned towards Zeus, smiling surreptitiously as though mocking him because it was he who had caused Zeus to turn into a bull. (1, 1, 3–5)

I attend to Tatius's vivid word picture, bidding its rich rhetorical content to echo through my book and to draw connections between the images, texts, and characters that I examine, much as it does through Tatius's romance. Ancient ekphraseis invite receivers to respond across millennia, sometimes with the creation of a work of visual art. Here, for instance, Titian's famous painting *The Rape of Europa* (figure 1.1), part of a series of mythological paintings that he referred to in his letters as *poesie*, imitates Tatius's text in what Murray Krieger would call a 'reverse ekphrasis' (xiii). Rather than being necessarily responses to preexisting works of visual art, ekphrastic passages can generate *ut poesis pictura*, a reversal of Horace's dictum advising the poet to follow the painter's art *ut pictura poesis* (just as in painting, so too in poetry).[6] Even so, the marginal figures on the shore of Titian's lush painting can only hint at what Tatius's ekphrasis captures so vividly in the onlookers'

1.1. Titian (Tiziano Vecellio), *Europa*, c. 1560–62, oil on canvas, 178 x 205cm. Isabella Stewart Gardner Museum, Boston.

response to the maritime scene. Caught between desire and fear, the maidens on the shore 'seemed both to desire to pursue the bull and to fear to enter the sea' (Ach. Tat. 1, 1, 4). The invitation of ekphrasis draws out interpretation, awe, or even confusion, and these responses are often encompassed in the verbal artwork's frame. Ekphrastic scenes frequently contain observers or wise old interpreters whose presence stimulates the response of the receiver, or, in the case of ekphrastic passages embedded in narrative, the interpretation of characters.

Appropriate verbal responses to beautiful works of art were expected of respectable people in the Second Sophistic and beyond; they were required, in fact, to distinguish a person's good breeding and education. When faced with a hall 'whose walls are decked with the flowers of art,' for example, Lucian explains that 'the cultured observer [...] surely, will not rest content with feasting his eyes on beauty; he will not stand speechless amid his splendid surroundings, but will set his mind to work, and as far as in him lies pay verbal tribute' (12). To remain silent '[n]o man of taste or artistic sensibility, none but a dull ignorant boor' (12) could abide. Moreover, the choices that are made in these 'verbal tribute[s]' reveal the speaker's cultural background. In speaking of 'vulgar ostentation of Persian monarchs,' Lucian believes that 'the barbarian has a keen appreciation of gold: to the treasures of art he is blind' (14). In ancient Greek romances like that of Tatius, however, ekphrastic encoding of cultural messages can operate on a subtler level than in Lucian's formulation. The framing narrator's interpretation of the 'votive picture' as depicting the rape of Europa in Tatius's ekphrasis, for example, overlooks the fact that the 'sacred dedication' could easily depict the Phoenician goddess 'whom the Sidonians call Astarte' (Ach. Tat. 1, 1, 3) while she cavorts with her male consort Bal in the form of a bull, as both Daniel Selden (50–1) and Helen Morales (*Vision and Narrative* 42–8) have suggested. Culturally marking the narrator's interpretation as Greek rather than Phoenician, the choice has implications for ethnic, gender, and religious identity, since the two scenarios display different ethnic affiliations, gender dynamics, and religious beliefs.

The verbal and visual interplay inherent in ekphrasis, taken with the responses of characters to these rhetorical set pieces, creates a fecund emblematic exchange between image, text, and self. The framing narrator in Tatius's romance 'admire[s] the whole of the picture' and, revealing that he is 'under the influence of Eros,' exclaims, '"What power that boy wields over heaven, earth and sea!"' (1, 2, 5). His response elicits the rejoinder of a bystander: '"Yes, I should know! Eros has dealt me enough blows"' (1, 2, 5). Commiserating, the framing narrator persuades the bystander to tell him the whole story, which comprises the romance, the story of Leucippe and Clitophon. The attractive draw of ekphrasis, much like Eros's leading of the bull 'smiling surreptitiously' (1, 1, 5) all the while, literally draws forth the *erotika pathemata*, the love pangs that both categorize what the narrator interprets as Zeus's erotic response and name the genre of the ancient Greek romance.

Keeping Tatius's introductory ekphrasis in mind, verbal pictures of the rape of Europa were ubiquitous in Renaissance literature. Poliziano sculpts the image on Vulcan's doors (*Stanze per la giostra* bk. 1, st. 105, 106), Colonna paints it on the portico of Venus's temple (*Hypnerotomachia* bk. 1, ch. 14), Marlowe mosaics it in Venus's glass ('Hero and Leander' ll. 142–50), and Spenser weaves it into both Busirane's and Arachne's tapestries (*FQ* bk. 3, 11; 'Muiopotmos' ll. 277–96). The influence of the version of the myth found in Ovid's *Metamorphoses* is undeniable, but many Renaissance authors look to Tatius's ekphrasis specifically, as did Robert Greene, who arguably never missed a 'chance of airing his eloquence' (Lucian 12).[7] Greene imitated Tatius's ekphrasis at least twice, and in both instances the ekphrastic passage instigates the narrative and inspires a series of meaningful responses from characters. In *Morando, or the Tritameron of Love*, the following ekphrasis of a painting sparks a debate about love among the characters:

> Signior Peratio spied hanging in the parlour a table most curiously painted wherein both the sea and land was most perfectly portrayed. The picture was of Europa, the sea of the Phoenicians, and the land of Sidon. On the shore was a beautiful meadow wherein stood a troop of dainty damosels; in the sea, a bull upon whose back sat a dame of surpassing beauty sailing towards Candy, but looking to the crew of her companions from whom by sinister means she was separated. The painter by secret skill had perfectly with his pencil deciphered the feature of their faces as their countenance did seem to import both fear and hope, for seeing their peerless princess a prey to such a prowling pirate they rushed into the seas (as willing to be partakers of their mistress' misery) as far as fear of such fearful surges would permit them, but pushed back with the dread of present danger they stood viewing how cunningly & carefully the bull transported his charge, how Europa, arrayed in purple robes sat securely and safely holding in her right hand his horn and in her left his tail. About him the dolphins seemed to leap, the sirens to sing, and Triton himself to triumph. Cupid also, in the form of a little boy, was there most curiously painted, having the wings

> spread, a quiver by his side, in one hand a flame of fire, in the other a chain of gold wherewith he drew the bull as by constraint, and turning his head towards Jupiter, seemed to smile at his folly and to despite his deity, that by this means he had made such a strange metamorphosis. (5–6)

Greene's close imitation of Tatius's ekphrasis turns this 'strange metamorphosis' to the purpose of inspiring debates over love, and it leads to a discussion, in which male and female characters use the painting to emblematize their opinions.[8] Greene uses Tatius's ekphrastic convention yet again in the opening of *Arbasto*, where, just as in Tatius's romance, the shipwrecked narrator, having washed up in Sidon, comes upon a votive painting in a temple to Astarte. The ekphrasis impels the narrative, but this time Greene substitutes an emblem of Fortune for the painting of Europa. Greene thus gives Tatius's text another turn and adopts the Greek romancer's narrative technique to tie the ekphrasis (this time of the emblem of fortune) to the story to come.[9] Renaissance romancers 'repainted' the models of ekphrasis they found in ancient Greek romance, and I suggest that they frequently did so to paint character specifically.[10]

The representation of identity in early modern romance is in need of critical attention. While the seminal works of Eugène Vinaver and Northrop Frye influence my understanding of romance's artful, interlaced structures and the social relevance of its formal modes, and while Patricia Parker's insistence on the genre's ambivalence towards its own happy endings informs my view of the multivalence of its identities, the foundational work of these critics does not delve into romance's particular constructions of early modern cultural identity. A new, critical assessment of romance characterization is in order. Illustrative of the problem is M.M. Bakhtin's well-known opinion on the matter of character in Greek romance. While he affirms romance's multiple cultural and political possibilities, its hybridity and polyglossia, he mistakenly dismisses romance characterization as flat and unchanging.[11] Although the modern Western concept of persons as psychologically deep individual agents is generally alien to the classical and early modern periods and is for the most part absent from romance characterization, passionate self-expression, a stoical capacity to endure suffering, and a great talent for disguise show that these characters are by no means 'flat,' the distinction between round and flat characters being itself problematic.

More promising is Fredric Jameson's recognition of the inadequacy of modern concepts of individual agency to assess romance identity. He calls for 'the choice of some other term for [...] [its] human figuration,' but he only notes in passing that romance characterization is 'pictorial' ('Magical Narratives' 139). Jameson promises that he 'will return to this problem later' (139); yet neither the article nor the book, *The Political Unconscious*, into which the article was incorporated with the omission of this passage, elaborates upon romance characterization. Wendy Steiner's *Pictures of Romance* addresses Jameson's observation up to a point, noting the affinities between paintings and romance in her trans-historical and lyrical definition of 'literary romance,' but her claim of the 'absolute constancy of identity' and 'self-sameness of the subject[s]' (52) of pre-modern romance ultimately concurs with Bakhtin's evaluation of romance identity.[12] Nevertheless, Jameson and Steiner glance at one of the most fascinating aspects of the depiction of identity in romance. I suggest that identity in the early modern period should be conceived not in terms of individual agency, but rather as passible and adaptable within cultural situation, a distinction that calls for a more useful means of assessing identity that can perceive it in characters' responses to their environments. In Greek romance, the characters' environments are bedecked with ekphrastic descriptions of visual representations. Thus the 'painting of character,' a commonplace especially in discussions of the representation of moral virtue, is determined in part by how characters paint 'verbal tributes' (Lucian 12).

While we detect proto-modern aspects of individual agency in the increased opportunity for what Stephen Greenblatt has called 'Renaissance self-fashioning' in the early modern literary imagination, readers should resist the temptation to impose modern concepts of identity onto a period where identity was to a great extent a function of a person's situatedness in community. Describing emotional elements of pre-modern identity, Timothy Reiss avers,

> [M]aterial world, society, family, animal being, rational mind, divine, named some of the 'circles' which were a person. These circles or spheres – as Cicero, Seneca, Hierocles and Plutarch called them, cued by tradition reaching beyond Plato's *Republic*, *Timaeus* and *Statesman* – did not 'surround' a person who somehow fit into them. They were what a person was: integral to my very substance. At the same time they were public and collective, common to everyone qua human. They named existential spheres to which the person enlaced in them was in a reactive relation. (*Mirages* 2)

Rather than being a strictly active or passive relation to these 'existential spheres' that situated identity, the relation between early modern persons and their communities is passible. Passibility is a way of imagining identity that allows for adaptation and flexibility without implying that people could act as independent agents able to alter their identities freely in spite of their cultural situations within family, local, and religious communities. As Reiss puts it, '[passibility] is not passivity. Passibility names experiences of being whose common denominator was a sense of being *embedded in and acted on by* these circles' (2). If scholars insist on imagining identity in the early modern period in terms of the ways that we talk about modern identity, it should be noted that readings of early modern literature that emphasize individual agency have tended to dwell on characters who would have been more likely to take advantage of social mobility, i.e., characters who were not a part of marginalized or foreign communities. For instance, as indicated by the subtitle of the book, *Renaissance Self-Fashioning: From More to Shakespeare*, Stephen Greenblatt's seminal work focused on upwardly mobile male authors.[13] Though this work is clearly invaluable for the development of New Historicism, Greenblatt's take on early modern identity in this formulation privileges individual agency. The kind of agency attributed to authors like More and Shakespeare is, in other words, only available to a small portion of wealthy people with courtly interests. By contrast, a passible model of identity formation allows for a more sensitive approach to understanding the ways in which subaltern people could navigate the pressures of their early modern world, and it is precisely the predicaments of outsiders that Greek romance authors tend to emphasize.

The emblematics of the self thus answers Jameson's call for another term for the human figuration in romance. It speaks to the way this popular genre's women, foreigners, and non-Christians articulate their character through interactions with the verbal images that surround them. The richly ekphrastic forms of early modern imitations of Greek romance draw marginal and foreign identity as passible to new sets of cultural situations, including changing visual environs. From the genre's inception, Greek romance 'prefer[s] the marginal parts of the known world,' and their authors 'who were Romanised Greeks, or Hellenised Syrians or Egyptians or Jews, occupied a cultural space in which identity, education and language, belief systems and social arrangements were fluid' (S. Stephens 57). I suggest that ekphrasis, as a part of this multicultural romance world, is a dialogic form that is generative of identity.

Drawing on Mieke Bal's theory of visual narratology and on Bakhtin's dialogic formulation of heteroglossia, I explore the narratological, dialogic, and ideological possibilities of ekphrasis and its close relationship with ethos. Ekphrasis functions in these texts similarly to what Homi Bhabha, drawing on Walter Benjamin's concept of *abseits*, has called a 'third space' of discourse. The interrelation between identity, image, and text wedges open cultural binaries: male/female, barbarian/civilized, black/white, Christian/Jew, or Western Christian/Eastern Muslim. Each of my chapters shows how ekphrasis can unsettle these binaries.

The vivid verbal images and characters of ancient Greek romance inspired the Renaissance romances that are the focus of this comparative study. The Spanish, English, and neo-Latin texts under examination share deep affinities in their indebtedness to Greek generic models and their diverse depictions of foreign and marginalized identities.[14] They were also part of an intertextual community: Cervantes apparently read Alonso Núñez de Reinoso, and Lady Mary Wroth and John Barclay read both Sidney and Cervantes. As the early modern tradition of romance in the Greek form developed and became ensconced in the vocabulary of romance, specific sources become harder to trace, but passible renditions of identity in a multicultural world persist. My project accordingly moves beyond intertextual and source studies models to discover what these Renaissance romances contribute to our understanding of early modern genre systems, word-image exchange, and, most importantly, cultural identity.

While my formulation of the emblematics of the self is borne out in the textual analyses that follow, the opening chapter situates my methodological approach in greater historical and theoretical depth, providing readers who are less familiar with the rhetorical roots of ekphrasis and the history of the romance genre with a scaffold for understanding subsequent formal and generic arguments. The chapter addresses the reemergence and reception of Greek romance in sixteenth-century translations and treatises, and it posits that Greek romance supplanted chivalric romance because its wide-ranging depictions of peoples and places fulfilled demands for verisimilitude and avoided the pitfalls of feigned history. The Greek romance, unlike its chivalric counterpart, most often depicts its lover-protagonists as equals and eschews national affiliation in favour of global systems. It is remarkably inclusive of female and foreign points of view. Taking into account ancient and early modern ekphrastic practices, I elaborate the emblematics of the self as a method for reading identity through verbal images, and I employ genre and word-image studies with a neoformal and narratological approach to assess how early modern romance builds on ancient Greek ekphrastic modes to craft impressionable cultural identities.

The next two chapters are devoted to early adapters of Achilles Tatius's ekphrastic techniques. These chapters emphasize how encoded or hidden double meanings in verbal pictures, what Daniel Selden identifies as the ekphrastic version of syllepsis, can encode both religious and gender identity. The second chapter begins by advocating a new reading of Tatius's ancient romance, *Leucippe and Clitophon*, arguing that sylleptic ekphrastic techniques coupled with instances of cross-dressing hold the key to explaining the ancient romance's problematic ending: the first-person narrator is actually Melite cross-dressed. While the argument that the work has an encrypted female narrator may seem radical and is certainly new for present-day scholarship, it is a reading shared by Tatius's first Renaissance imitator, the exiled Spanish *converso* Alonso Núñez de Reinoso, who makes his Melite figure Isea the undisguised narrator of his romance *Los amores de Clareo y Florisea y los trabajos de la sin ventura Isea* (1552). Reinoso's is not only the first explicit imitation of the Greek romance in the Renaissance, but it also marks the first work of Spanish sentimental prose to feature a consistent female first-person narrator. Isea gives an ekphrastic voice to Spanish Jews' experiences of exile and longing for the homeland. Both romancers allegorize female narration in ekphraseis that describe painted and embroidered representations of the Philomela myth. Reinoso, however, masterfully reprises Tatius's ekphraseis to lament the Jewish Diaspora.

In the third chapter, I continue to consider the ekphrastic characterization of gender. As did Reinoso before him, Philip Sidney builds on Tatius's polysemous ekphrastic techniques. The paintings, verbal emblems, and personal *imprese* of the *New Arcadia* (1590) make Tatius's pictures speak to gendered role reversals through a visual lexicon familiar to Elizabethan readers who shared courtly expectations of verbal image literacy. Scholars have considered gender identity in Sidney's romance from philosophical, humoral, and performative perspectives, but Sidney's characters simply do not fit well into these discourses' gender binaries. Rather than reading the exchange of gender roles in the *Arcadia* as necessarily demoting masculine valour, I suggest that Sidneian romance conceives of gender as passible, constructing a 'third sex' (*OA* 3, 206), in which the gender positions of characters can best be located in generic and aesthetic terms. Hence, I analyse shifts in gender through the emblematics of the self, emphasizing Sidney's characters' facility in creating and interpreting the visual signs that bedeck the *New Arcadia*. Cross-dressed Amazons and shepherdish princesses uncouple valour from sexual distinction, and gender differences are drawn most forcibly in characters' responses to visual signs: male characters turn out to be uncomprehending onlookers to proleptic and violent images and performances, and female characters prove more apt to comprehend the messages that ekphraseis convey.

Heliodorus's use of ekphrasis to encode and then include foreign identity serves as a model for romancers in my next two chapters. I examine transhistorical and transatlantic pictographic exchange in order to assess criteria of cultural otherness in *Los trabajos de Persiles y Sigismunda: historia setentrional* (1617). Cervantes intermingles Ethiopian and American pictographic language, European alphabetism, and colonial models of barbarian identity to emphasize the ingenuity of indigenous peoples. Descriptions of paintings in the *Persiles* mirror both Heliodoran versions of Ethiopian hieroglyphs and American pictographic language to subvert European paradigms of graphic representation and challenge familiar colonial rationalizations of power dynamics in the Americas. Like Heliodorus, whom Cervantes explicitly imitates, the Spanish author uses ekphrasis first to alienate and subsequently to accept foreign characters into a ruling society. Questions of foreign or barbarian identity hinge on the power of ekphrastic interpretation as a marker of cultural identity.

When John Barclay, the author at the centre of my fifth chapter, transposes the Elizabethan court to Mauritania in his neo-Latin romance *Argenis* (1621), questions of African identity turn on interpretations of ekphraseis rather than on complexion. Heliodorus is Barclay's principal model for Greek romance, and, much like Cervantes, Barclay learns from the Ephesian how to render foreign identity ekphrastically while adapting the Greek ekphrastic model to his own cultural concerns. Barclay's work, which was widely read in his day, offers us a unique opportunity to examine a Renaissance author's published treatise on cultural identity, in the *Icon animorum* or *Mirror of Mindes* (1614), alongside the same author's masterful imitation of Greek romance. In Barclay's romance, the emblematics of the self disrupts European assumptions about African identity, and this global romance bridges what in Barclay's own time were deep cultural divides. Barclay considers European identity as passible in his *Icon animorum*, in which he crafts an early modern model of rooted cosmopolitanism. He then broadens his notion of cosmopolitan passibility for Europe into the global settings of his political romance, *Argenis*, attending in particular to the negotiation of Afro-European relations. He makes Heliodoran use of polyvalent verbal images as a visual language of sociability that defuses national divides: his emblematic depictions of African identity create chiastic cultural crossovers between Mauritania and the Elizabethan court. The *Argenis* ultimately promotes cultural and familial alliances with the help of verbal images in a global Greek romance.

Although Mary Wroth was influenced by the reception of Greek romance, my final chapter concentrates on how she subverts the idealizing norms of the genre and its ekphrastic character. In her *Urania* (1621), Wroth dashes romance expectations of political, familial, and religious reconciliation, denying the assimilation of foreigners and cosmopolitan unions. Wroth pictures her characters through a rich embroidery of enchantments, masques, and paintings. Strikingly, however, she systematically undoes the promised unions of her romance – be they marital or political – through a series of highly ekphrastic episodes that subvert the emblematics of the self. In the first volume of the *Urania*, characters negotiate a series of intricately wrought enchantments that emphasize female constancy in private relationships and female sovereignty in public spheres. Their success or failure depends on their ability to decode the highly ekphrastic enchantments that they face. Though each of these enchantments allows for the assimilation of foreigners into European social and political alliances, the lover/protagonists Pamphilia and Amphilanthus find it increasingly difficult to decipher the ekphraseis that vex them. When the action in the second volume turns farther east, where Persians and Tartars are the pieces necessary to complete Wroth's woven cloth of love, romance again fails to enable assimilation. Despite the adeptness with which Persian and Tartarian characters create and elaborate visual images that admirably express their identities and desires, Wroth's European characters are unwilling or unable to engage these images with their own interpretations. Wroth manipulates ekphrastic, geographic, and humanist conventions in her *teatrum mundi* to make lovers, Persians, and Tartars all subject to a 'tottering' romance globe.

The passibility of romance identities in these texts mirrors European anxieties about the potential for a loss of identity in what was an increasingly global early modernity, and romance responds to these anxieties by promising the assimilation of its outsiders into European communities through the very wish-fulfilment that characterizes the genre.[15] Wroth's refusal to make good on the cosmopolitan promise of Greek romance anticipates future subversions of this genre's idealizing tendencies. The release of romance from the critical debates of the Renaissance did not free it from neoclassical objections, and only in the last fifty years has the genre begun again to tender sustained critical attention. As Barbara Fuchs has suggested, romance is perhaps best thought of today as a strategy that often contaminates other texts.[16] In my conclusion, I explore how the emblematics of the self functions as a romance strategy in later works such as Aphra Behn's *Oroonoko*, Herman Melville's *Moby-Dick*, and Thomas Pynchon's *The Crying of Lot 49*, where race-based slavery, nascent capitalism, and the deconstructive power of postmodernity collide with and capsize the idealizing conventions of romance. Ultimately, I propose that we can trace romance strategies not only in romance's subversive narratival experimentation and delightful content, but also in its insistence on crafting rich depictions of cultural identity through the emblematics of the self.

1 The Romance Globe: Why the Renaissance Repainted Greek Romance

The often-told story of Heliodorus's reception by sixteenth-century humanists is also, in many respects, the success story of its genre in the Renaissance.[1] Appropriately enough, the circumstances of the *Aethiopica*'s rediscovery resemble the tales of kidnapping that typify Greek romance. During the sack of Buda by the Ottomans (1526), a German soldier spirited the beautiful Greek manuscript away from the Hungarian royal library. Again in keeping with the genre's tendencies, the abduction led to a happy reversal: the captive was removed from obscurity to an elevated status. Like its protagonists, moreover, the *Aethiopica* was subject to much wandering. From Hungary, it travelled to the press of Vincentius Obsopoeus, who published it in Greek in Basel in 1534. The romance was first translated into vernacular by the French Bishop Jacques Amyot in 1547, into Latin by the Pole Stanislaus Warschewicski in 1551, and into Italian by Leonardo Ghini in 1556. The translation into Spanish by the Hellenist Francisco de Vergara was lost, making the anonymous translation in Antwerp in 1554 the first surviving Castilian rendering. The most influential Spanish translation, and the one that Cervantes probably read, was from the Latin by Fernando de Mena in 1587. Thomas Underdowne's was the first English rendering (c. 1569). All throughout Europe, the demand for the *Aethiopica*'s translation proclaimed its wide appeal.

As Samuel Wolff avers in his study of the influence of Greek romance on Tudor literature, 'It is as if the Greek Romances were "made to order" for the entertainment of the Renaissance [...] Hardly any other kind of fiction, hardly any other view of life, could appeal more strongly to the sixteenth-century novel-reader and novel-writer than the [Greek romance's] ornate, spectacular, rhetorical, sentimental, fortuitous medley'

(235).[2] Wolff's appreciative statement in 1912 was unusual, not only for its concentration on the contribution of ancient Greek romance to the development of English literature – something that critics often overlook – but also because after the waning of nineteenth-century philological interest in the genre, twentieth-century readers, especially Anglo-American readers, tended to have little patience for the long, baroquely complicated narratives that inspired longer and, in certain cases, more intricate romances in the sixteenth and seventeenth centuries.[3] Virginia Woolf, for instance, describes the somnolent effect of Sir Philip Sidney's *Arcadia*: '[A]s the succession of stories fall on each other like soft snowflakes, one obliterating the other, we are much tempted to follow their example. Sleep weighs down our eyes. Half dreaming, half yawning, we prepare to seek the elder brother of death' (48). Woolf observes that the flurry of the *Arcadia*'s narrative can weigh heavy on the modern reader; nonetheless, the intricacy, variety, and number of these highly pictorial narrative facets illuminate her concluding remarks on Sidney's romance, in which she suggests, 'In the *Arcadia*, as in some luminous globe, all the seeds of English fiction lie latent' (49). I suggest that Renaissance romancers are drawn to precisely this dreamlike quality, these languorous tableaus and outstretched descriptive passages of the ancient genre, to paint the luminous globes of early modern Greek romance.

The renaissance of the ancient Greek romance, as scholars have termed it, surely occurred for numerous reasons, but the angle of this story that most interests me is a formal and cultural one.[4] It requires both a diachronic and synchronic critical approach to be best understood. As the history of the genre's reception reveals, early modern authors value the Greek model not only for its moral and aesthetic qualities, but also for its cultural variety, which romancers reprise to fit their own set of societal concerns. Debates in the Renaissance surrounding the Greek romance's elevation as morally and aesthetically superior to chivalric romance tell us how Renaissance humanists received and adapted the new genre. Furthermore, ekphrasis, a ubiquitous rhetorical figure in Greek romance, is a key element in these texts' representations of identity. Classical and early modern poetics and rhetoric along with narratological, new formalist, and word-image studies can illustrate the close historical and theoretical link between ekphrasis and *ethos*. Ekphrasis, as it is inherited and adapted from the ancient Greek romance, thus becomes a powerful tool for illuminating romance identities.

Chivalry vs Chastity: Moral and Aesthetic Criteria in the Romance Debate

By the second half of the sixteenth century, authors of a large group of prose romances claim to imitate or even outdo Heliodorus's *Aethiopica,* also called *The Loves of Theagenes and Charicleia*. The works of Achilles Tatius and Longus were also graced with several translations and appeared in new editions along with their own set of imitations. Early modern writers praise the Greek romance as a replacement for the books of chivalry, a genre 'de quien nunca se acordó Aristóteles' ('that Aristotle never even thought about' Cervantes, *DQ* 24). Chivalric romances such as *Le Morte d'Arthur, Amadís de Gaula, Tirant lo Blanc, El espejo de la caballería,* and the *Palmerín* series – not to mention the *Orlando Furioso* – enjoyed an unprecedented popularity and were the first 'best sellers' of the age of the printing press. Nevertheless, from its medieval beginnings, writers such as Dante and Petrarch questioned the moral content of chivalric romance, and later humanists also began to criticize the books of chivalry based on aesthetic criteria, taking them to task for their wayward structure and lack of plausibility through neo-Aristotelian arguments developed from readings of Horace's *Ars Poetica* and Aristotle's *Poetics* (after its appearance on the critical scene). These debates help to explain the appeal of the ancient Greek romance to both authors and readers of its early modern imitations.

The Greek romance differs from its medieval and early Renaissance chivalric peers, but the interpenetration and kinship of the forms is undeniable.[5] After all, Greek romances as well as their Latin cousins survived and were read right through the medieval period.[6] The trials of Amadís and Oriana in the *Amadís,* as well as the mixed chivalric and Greek themes in *Floire et Blancheflor* (which is often considered to be a medieval romance in the Greek style), testify to the interdependence of the genres, and I do not suggest that Greek romance ever fully supplanted its chivalric cousin.[7]

Nonetheless, as the chivalric romance lost prestige in the eyes of writers who adopted neoclassical principles of unity and verisimilitude, renewed interest in the Greek romance enabled a shift in the production of romance towards imitations of this ancient model. The allure of Greek romance results in a plethora of imitations. Sidney's *Arcadia, L'Astrée* by Honoré d'Urfé, Madeleine de Scudéry's *Le Grand Cyrus,* Lope de Vega's *El peregrino en su patria,* Cervantes's *Persiles,* John Barclay's *Argenis,* and Wroth's *Urania* as well as the genre's theatrical offspring by playwrights such as Shakespeare, Alexandre Hardy, and Calderón represent a small sampling of the genre's imitations.

With the exceptions of magic and transvestism (which also appear in books of chivalry), the moral contents of Greek romances (especially that of the *Aethiopica*) were more acceptable to the sixteenth-century critic than those of chivalric romance. The two romance models tend to diverge in their attitudes towards chastity.[8] The elevation of chastity in the *Aethiopica*, as noted by Diana de Armas Wilson, contrasts with 'the courtly ideology in chivalric romance' as epitomized by Chrétien de Troyes's *Lancelot*, which 'countenanced and [...] even valorized, adulterous love' (*Allegories* 16). The critics of books of chivalry, she argues, found a more appealing formulation of romantic love in the Greek romance, which, 'In its glorification of marriage, family, and domestic life,' proposes an 'implicit critique of the chivalric system' and reflects 'the ascendant idea that love could, after all, exert its powers between married people' (16).

The privileging of chastity (for both male and female protagonists) and love within marriage in the *Aethiopica* has circumvented criticisms of romance as an immoral genre for modern as well as early modern critics. Marcelino Menéndez y Pelayo, commenting on the success of the *Aethiopica* in the Siglo de Oro, asserts that its elevation of love and chastity is its best feature. He claims that its morality outweighs its story and style, which 'aunque superior a su tiempo' ('although superior for its time') are not as significant as its 'moral pura' ('pure morality' 16). While he lauds Heliodorus's privileging of love and chastity, he dismisses Heliodoran style.

Placing too much emphasis on the genre's morality in the story of its reception risks perpetuating criticism based on moral criteria, and it overlooks the fact that not all protagonists of Greek romance are chaste. Ostensibly less morally pure Greek romances such as *Leucippe and Clitophon*, which are also a part of the genre's renaissance, exert a significant influence on early modern European literature. Tatius's Renaissance translators split on whether or not to include the racier parts of the *Leucippe*, such as the debate over whether boys or girls make better lovers for men and the technically adulterous sexual intercourse between Clitophon and Melite. That many translators included these passages in part or in whole indicates that perhaps the morality of Greek romance was not its most important feature. For instance, Alonso Núñez de Reinoso (1552) expunges both the debate and the sex, William Burton (1597) expurgates nothing, and Anthony Hodges (1638) omits the debate and some of the more lubricious details of the adultery, commenting in his preface, 'by the exection of the two testicles of an unchaste dispute, and one [immodest] expression, I have so refined the author, that the modestest matron may looke in his face and not blush' (sig. A3v). Menéndez y Pelayo thus overestimates the singular importance of morality in this 'chaste dispute,' at least insofar as it relates to the whole genre.

Another morally attractive aspect of Greek romance for Renaissance writers is that its structure is easily assimilated to Christian pilgrimage. Emilia Deffis de Calvo notes that the Spanish adaptation of the Greek model features the travels of pilgrim lovers, who 'recorren todas las iglesias y santuarios que encuentran' ('visit all of the churches and holy places that they come across'), emphasizing Christian pilgrimage, which Deffis de Calvo reminds us is also a metaphor for the journey of the soul: 'La cargazón ideológica es muy fuerte e impone una relación de causa-efecto que reemplaza la decidida presencia del azar como rector del hilo de acción en los modelos clásicos' ('The ideological emphasis is very strong and imposes a cause-effect relation that reinstates the definite presence of fate as the director of the thread of action in the classical model' 126). Deffis de Calvo observes that the characters' travels are not prompted by random events; rather, the frame of the pilgrimage introduces the Christian view that these events are the manifestation of divine will. She argues that this modification of Greek romance enriches 'los cánones establecidos por Heliodoro y Tacio, en particular en lo relativo a la diversificación cronotópica y, por ende, a la matización de la imagen humana correspondiente' ('the canons established by Heliodorus and Tatius, particularly in relation to chronotopic diversification and, finally, to the shadings of the corresponding human image' 126). In the context of the Counter-Reformation, the Spanish imitation of the Greek romance can thus be viewed as emulation due in part to the cause-effect rationale that the Christian context lends to the adventures of the wanderers. Episodes become trials of Christian faith as well as tests of chastity and love. Deffis de Calvo essentially propounds that pilgrimage gives direction and meaning to the adventure-time chronotope, hinting at a corresponding increase in the complexity of characterization. Yet I note that this use of pilgrimage does not elevate Greek over chivalric models that employ the quest as an organizing structure. Nonetheless, the Christianization of the classical model is certainly significant, as is the Christianization of all ancient models in the Renaissance, and does allow questions of religious identity often to take centre stage in the elaboration of ethos in imitations of the Greek romance.

Beyond its touted moral superiority, Greek romance was also preferred to its chivalric counterpart for aesthetic reasons. In the preface to his 1547 translation of the *Aethiopica*, Jacques Amyot was the first critic to promote it as a superior model to the chivalric romance. This prologue is significant for the determination of aesthetic criteria in Renaissance debates about poetics more broadly; one scholar goes so far as to claim that 'The preface to the French translation of *Theagéne et Chariclée* is, with the translation itself, a determining event in the history of the European novel' (Fumaroli, 'Jacques Amyot' 23). Amyot does offer Greek romance – what he calls the historical prose romance – to remedy the perceived immorality of chivalric romance; but he also moves beyond moral valuations to employ aesthetic criteria based on plausibility and unity to criticize chivalric romance.[9] These aesthetic criteria become central tenets of neo-Aristotelian formulations of poetics.[10] Yet, ironically, the same aesthetic criteria with which Amyot praises Greek romance eventually become the pattern for neo-Aristotelian criticisms of all romance in debates between the Ancients and the Moderns.

By the High Middle Ages, the structure of chivalric romance usually followed the interlaced model described by Eugène Vinaver, which he likens to 'the fabric of matting or tapestry; a single cut across it, made at any point, would unravel it all. And yet it was clearly not a unified body of material: it consisted of a variety of themes, all distinct and yet inseparable from one another. Everything leads to everything else, but by very intricate paths' (72). Though Vinaver convincingly argues that chivalric interlace has its own beauty and narrative coherence, this structure was not acceptable by neoclassical standards. Chivalric romance is digressive and wayward, and owing to its chronicling pretences it usually does not begin *in medias res*. Daniel Javitch claims in *Proclaiming a Classic* that by the time of the composition of Ariosto's *Orlando Furioso*, the discontinuity of the chivalric structure becomes so pronounced that Ariosto leaves many of the narrative threads frayed or else suspends them for so long as to lose the interest of the reader. Ariosto plays with this discontinuity self-consciously, but his play is in and of itself a commentary on how wayward the structure of chivalric romance could be. Though this structure is often pleasurable and even sometimes preferable to a modern reader, it did not conform to neoclassical standards in the Renaissance.

Sixteenth-century critics favoured the Greek romance for what they deemed to be its superior narrative structure. One of the most often praised aesthetic aspects of the *Aethiopica*, for instance, is its opening *in medias res*. Amyot lauds it as follows:

> Mais surtout la disposition en est singuliere: car il commence au mylieu de son histoire comme font les poëtes hèroïques: ce qui cause de prime face un grand esbahissement aux lecteurs, et leur engendre un passionné desir d'entendre le commencement: et toutesfois il les tire si bien par l'ingenieuse liaison de son conte, que l'on n'est point resolu de ce que l'on trouve tout au commencement du premier livre, jusques à ce que l'on ayt leu la fin du cinquiesme. Et quand on en est là venu, encore a l'on plus grande envie de voir la fin que l'on n'avoit au paravant d'en voir le commencement: de sorte que tousjours l'entendement demeure suspendu, jusques à ce que l'on vienne à la conclusion, laquelle laisse le lecteur satisfaict de la sorte que le sont ceux qui à la fin viennent à jouyr d'un bien ardemment désiré, et longuement attendu.

> But above all the disposition is remarkable: since it starts in the middle of the history, as do the epic poets: which causes *prima facie* great admiration in the readers and engenders in them a passionate desire to know the beginning: and it draws them in further with its clever organization of the story; such that what is found at the beginning of the first book is not resolved until the end of the fifth has been read. And having arrived there, there is an even greater desire to see the end than there was before to see the beginning: in such a way that the mind is kept in constant suspense, until one comes to the conclusion, which leaves the reader satisfied in the same way as are those who finally come to enjoy an ardently and long awaited desire. (107–8)

Amyot praises the *Aethiopica*'s beginning *in medias res* and its well-woven episodes, and he claims that the reader's attention is held throughout and rewarded at its close. Thus the suspense that the structure creates in the reader and the satisfaction that it delivers in the end mirror the emotional experiences of the characters, amplifying the wish-fulfilment that the narrative relates. The *Aethiopica*'s narrative structure makes for a reading experience that is, according to Amyot, both pleasing and edifying.

As debates between the Ancients and the Moderns developed, some writers even claimed that the *Aethiopica* had an epic structure, elevating its status above that of romance.[11] In his *Poetices libri septem* (1561), J.C. Scaliger recommends the Greek romance to the epic poet, stating that the *Aethiopica* is a 'librum epico Poetae censeo accuratissime legendum, ac quasi pro optimo exemplari sibi proponendum' ('book that should be read most attentively by the epic poet, and that should be proposed to him as the best possible model' 144; ct. and trans. Forcione, *Cervantes, Aristotle* 66).[12] Alonso López Pinciano (El Pinciano), in his influential treatise *Philosophia antigua poética* (1596), echoes Scaliger's praise for the *incipit in medias res*, stating that an epic

> deue començar del medio de la acción, y ansí lo hizo Homero en su *Vlysea*, y ansí Heliodoro en *Historia de Ethiopía*; y es la razón porque, como la obra heroyca es larga, tiene necesidad de ardid para que sea mejor leyda; y es assí que, començando el poeta del medio de la acción, va el oyente desseosso de encontrar con el principio, en el cual se halla al medio libro, y que, auiendo passado la mitad del volumen, el resto se acaba leer sin mucho enfado.

> ought to begin in the middle of the action, and so did Homer in his *Odyssey*, and so too did Heliodorus in his *Ethiopian History;* and here's the reason why: since a heroic work is long, it needs a trick to be read more attentively. And so it is that, as the poet begins in the middle of the action, the listener proceeds desirous of discovering the beginning, which [the reader] comes upon in the middle of the book, and having passed the mid-point of the volume, [the reader] finds little annoyance in reading the remainder. (3: 206)

Not only does El Pinciano laud the *Aethiopica*'s structure, but he goes on to suggest that Heliodorus is the best at disposing the threads of his plot. Fadrique, one of El Pinciano's character-interlocutors in the text, states that 'Don del Sol es Heliodoro; y en eso del ñudo y soltar, nadie le hizo ventaja' ('A gift from the sun is Heliodorus, and in tying and untying plots, no one can surpass him' 2:86). For El Pinciano, Heliodorus's management of complicated and interlaced plot elements is thus exemplary.[13]

Despite its moral content and excellent disposition, most critics hesitated to classify the *Aethiopica* as a full-fledged epic. Even El Pinciano does not grant the *Aethiopica* epic status equal to Virgil's and Homer's works, citing its subject matter of love as being less exalted than that of the historical epic. Grand events such as war and people of the highest social status were considered appropriate to epic. Torquato Tasso also finds fault in the *Aethiopica* despite his praise for its structure in a letter to Scipione Gonzaga, in which he compares the *Aethiopica* to Virgil's *Aeneid* in its ability to hold the reader's attention.[14] As Rosanna

Camerlingo succinctly puts it, Tasso claims that the *Aethiopica* consists of 'heroic poetry whose subject matter, however, is not properly heroic' (57). Though the chastity of the *Aethiopica*'s plot elevates it above the chivalric romance, the focus on love instead of warfare ironically prohibits its elevation to epic status. Nonetheless, I suggest that the Greek romance's lack of historicity and focus on less prestigious characters helps it to encompass the increasingly global purview of European colonial and cosmopolitan discourse in the early modern period.

The Romance Globe

Although the Greek romance certainly appealed to the moral and aesthetic agendas of Renaissance writers, scholars, and critics, it also offered authors marvellous, cosmopolitan settings that were verisimilar and that accommodated a variety of marginalized and geographically dispersed peoples. As Tim Whitmarsh and Shadi Bartsch remark, 'Even in such an elevated example of the form as Heliodorus' *Charicleia and Theagenes* – suffused as it is with literary allusion and Neoplatonism – the opportunity to speak is granted to an Athenian courtesan, a commercially minded merchant, a deaf Zacynthian fisherman and a Greek nurse working in the Persian court' (238). Furthermore, unencumbered by the proto-nationalist program of many chivalric romances that sought to assert cultural dominance through feigned historical representations of *translatio studii et imperii*, the Greek romance was devoid of strict national affiliations that might limit the breadth of its representational scope.[15] These characteristics made Greek romance a popular model for imitations in the late Renaissance, and also made it a ripe source for complex figurings of cultural identity.

The positive reception of the ancient Greek romance's cultural flexibility can be traced through early modern commentaries on the need for verisimilitude and the censuring of historical pretence. The question of verisimilitude became a central issue in the debate over the status of romance relative to the epic, and it augmented the emphasis on the foreign in romances that took Greek romance as a model. Amyot certainly constructs his argument allowing for the importance of 'quelque divertissement' (105) to lighten more serious reading; nevertheless, the books of chivalry, 'dont le sujet n'est point véritable' (105), must be discarded because their marvellous and thereby unbelievable content cannot be pleasurable or useful. Amyot's opinion about books of chivalry is ultimately dismissive:

> [O]ultre ce qu'il n'ya nulle erudition, nulle cognoissance de l'antiquité, ne chose aucune (à brief parler) dont on peust tirer quelque utilité, encore sont ilz le plus souvent si mal cousuz et si esloignez de toute vraysemblable apparence, qu'il semble que ce soyent plustost songes de quelque malade resvant en fièvre chaulde, qu'inventions d'aucun homme d'esprit et de jugement.
>
> [B]esides the fact that they have no erudition, no knowledge of antiquity, nor a single thing (in brief) from which one can take something useful, they are usually so poorly composed and so devoid of all semblance of truth that they seem as if they were the dream of a sick man who suffers from a high fever rather than the inventions of a man of spirit and judgment. (107)

Drawing on Horace's *Ars Poetica*, Amyot compares the inverisimilar material of the books of chivalry to the 'sick man's dream,' and opposes them to the moral profitability of reading the *Aethiopica*, in which the reader will find

> passions humaines paintes au vif, avecques si grande honnesteté que l'on n'en sçauroit tirer occasion ou exemple de mal faire : pour ce que de toutes affections illicites et mauvaises, il a faict l'yssue malheureuse, et au contraire des bonnes et honnestes, la fin désirable et heureuse.
>
> human passions painted to life throughout, with such great chasteness that one could not possibly find an occasion or example for wrong doing: because all illicit or bad sentiments turn out badly, whereas those that are good and honest meet a desirable and beautiful end. (107)

Through the pithy discourse and believable action, a moral code is pleasurably laid down in which the good characters serve as a model for the reader. Amyot's argument implies that a book must be verisimilar to be pleasurable in the first place. By making verisimilitude a necessary ingredient for both the pleasure and profit that reading can provide, Amyot outdoes previous Christian invectives that had been launched at books of chivalry. The realism and moral depiction of character in the *Aethiopica* extends to the verisimilitude of the genre more broadly, and the depiction of character in particular becomes an interesting platform on which Renaissance imitators build. This 'painting' of character, moreover, metaphorically contributes to the emblematics of the self.

The Renaissance demand for verisimilitude also makes the depiction of the foreign in ancient Greek romance alluring to early modern romancers.[16] Advocating verisimilar-marvellous material, Tasso recommends that his contemporaries 'take matter [...] from Gothland, Norway, Sweden, Iceland, the East Indies, or countries recently discovered in the vast ocean beyond the Pillars of Hercules' (*Discourses* 50) to include marvellous material in their fiction that would, nonetheless, seem verisimilar. Ancient Greek romance provides extensive descriptions of foreign people and 'locations where Greeks (however defined) necessarily encounter non-Greeks and thus explicitly contrast ethnicities and cultural behaviours' (S. Stephens 57). This cultural variety suited the Renaissance demand for verisimilar-marvellous material admirably.

Real places that are marvellous and not necessarily known to the author also fit Tasso's injunction to imitate icastically rather than fantastically, a point that he derives from Marsilio Ficino's commentary on Plato's *Sophist*, and that also suits well the ekphrastic modes employed by Greek romance.[17] Icastic imitation, unlike fantastic imitation, imitates true things that are real or rationally intelligible. Tasso explains that the poet is 'a maker of images in the fashion of a speaking painter' (*Discourses* 31), a commonplace of comparisons between the sister arts, but goes on to explain that rather than imitating things that never existed, i.e., fantastic things, the poet should imitate icastically, 'images [...] of existing things, this imitation belongs to the icastic imitator. But what shall we say exists, the intelligible or the visible? Surely the intelligible' (32). In allowing for icastic imagination that includes the non-visible, such as 'images of Angels' (32), Tasso both allows for Christian miracle as a part of his verisimilar aesthetic and distances the work of the poet from that of the historian. As Marshall Grossman has explained, 'Although the icastic imagination imitates true things, it differs from history in so far as the true things it imitates need never have been apprehended by the senses' (15). Thus Tasso includes the foreign in his work, but rather than presenting the foreign as an eye-witness travel writer or historian might (he certainly never travelled to all the places that he wrote about), he icastically represents foreign places and people to produce what he terms the verisimilar-marvellous.

Tasso puts his theory into practice by drawing on Greek romance models. He imitates, for instance, the nativity story of Charicleia from Heliodorus's *Aethiopica* to craft the story of the virago Clorinda in his *Gerusalemme Liberata*. Both women are born white to black African queens because their mothers gaze at the painted image of a white female figure when they conceive their daughters.[18] The 'pregnant images,' Andromeda and St George's maiden, impress their complexions on Heliodorus's and Tasso's protagonists respectively. Tasso makes use of this romance strategy specifically to give his heroine a marvellous foreign identity (Ethiopian) that nonetheless enables him to assimilate this initially Muslim character to European and Christian paradigms.[19]

The multilocal settings of Greek romance depicted a wide variety of cultural identities that appealed to Renaissance romancers. European interest in foreign peoples and places amounted to an obsession by the middle of the sixteenth century, with readers avidly devouring all manner of travel accounts and relations of conquest and colonization in the Americas, Africa, and the East.[20] The chivalric romance had already shared in the discourse of colonization and conquest; but the Greek romance provided a model for icastic rather than fantastic depictions of the foreign that would employ Tasso's verisimilar-marvellous.[21] The spatial configuration of the Greek romance, rather than being strictly fantastic or strictly actual, resembles Michel Foucault's concept of heterotopia. In contrast with nonexistent utopias, heterotopias are 'countersites, a kind of effectively enacted utopia in which the real sites, all other real sites that can be found within the culture, are simultaneously represented, contested, and inverted' ('Of Other Spaces' 24). The interconnected foreign spaces function as heterotopias in that they allow for a working out of social problems that exist in the real space from which the author writes, a function of heterotopia that Foucault likens to social experiments that took place in American colonies (27). This heterotopic configuration applies to the method by which sixteenth- and seventeenth-century romance narratives constructed foreign heterotopias to work out domestic cultural concerns.

The Greek romance is, moreover, appealing to Renaissance romancers for its negotiation of history. Chivalric romance contributed to its project of proto-national ascendancy with its chronicling pretence, a pretence that Greek romance lacks.[22] Along with the inverisimilitude of books of chivalry, Amyot criticizes their pretended status as history. He believes that history is the most profitable reading possible, but that by its claim of historicity, such an inverisimilar genre as chivalric romance corruptly leads people to mistaken beliefs. Yet, while Amyot expresses concern about the effects of fiction disguised under the 'nom d'istoriale verité' ('the name of historical truth' 106), his worry is assuaged by the lack of historical pretence and excellent composition and verisimilitude he perceives in the *Aethiopica*. As Camerlingo points out, 'the criteria whereby the historical verity of the genre is criticized are primarily aesthetic' (49). The verisimilitude and unified structure of the 'ingenious fiction' thereby allows the *Aethiopica* to avoid the pitfalls of chivalric romance and supplies an author like Tasso with an icastic (intelligible) though not necessarily historical model. Yet critics like El Pinciano lament that the subject and protagonists of Greek romance do not have 'la grandeza necessaria' ('the necessary grandeur' 3: 224) to reach the perfection of Virgil and Homer, though Heliodorus's choice of locations makes the royal lineage of the protagonists possible and, therefore, believable to Spanish readers, who 'no sabían tanto de las cosas' ('don't know as much about those things') pertaining to 'Persia o Ethiopía' (2: 332), again reflecting Tasso's recommendations to use foreign places to create verisimilar marvels. The potential historicity of narratives is extremely problematic in the sixteenth century because the pretence of historicity is worse than no claim to historicity at all. It is precisely this lack of historical specificity and the subsequent exclusion from epic status, however, that make the Greek romances excellent models for crafting romance globes.

Authors such as Sidney, d'Urfé, and Barclay took advantage of the multiplicity of place and lack of historical specificity in the Greek romance to craft veiled social commentaries. In other words, the lack of a tie to national traditions makes the ancient Greek romance a model for the beginnings of the *roman à clef* and political romance tradition. According to his friend Fulke Greville, Sir Philip Sidney took advantage of the flexible relation between story and history in the *Arcadia* to craft a political and moral tale, in which Greville claims Sidney intended 'to turn the barren philosophy precepts into pregnant images of life; and in them, first on the monarch's part, lively to represent the growth, state and declination of princes, change of government and laws: vicissitudes of sedition, faction, succession, confederacies, plantations, with all other errors or alterations in publique affaires' (19). Sidney's readers frequently interpreted his work to have political significance,[23] something that the lack of historical specificity of Greek romance allows for, and many imitations of Greek romance began to be published with keys that claimed to decode the romance's alleged meaning, hence the invention of the *roman à clef*. In the preface to *L'Astrée* (1607), which takes the ancient Greek romance as a model, Honoré d'Urfé explains,

> Si tu te trouves parmy ceux qui font profession d'interpreter les songes, et descouvrir les pensées plus secrettes d'autruy, et qu'ils asseurent que

> Celadon est un tel homme, et Astrée une telle femme, ne leur reponds rien, car ils sçavent assez qu'ils ne scavent pas ce qu'ils disent.
>
> If you find yourself among those who profess to interpret dreams and to discover the secret thoughts of others, and if they assure you that Celadon is this man or that man, and that Astraea is this woman or that woman, do not answer them, for they are aware that they do not know what they are talking about. (32; 4)

D'Urfé explains that he has cleverly avoided making one-to-one correspondences that would so easily be revealed, but despite d'Urfé's cagey assertion, his romance, like many others, was quickly provided with a key.[24]

The first Renaissance romance to be specifically called a 'political romance' was John Barclay's *Argenis* (1621), a neo-Latin imitation of Greek romance. Barclay's character Nicopompus, who stands in as an authorial figure for Barclay himself, explains how this new genre can be put to work for moral and political purposes.

> Grandem fabulam historiae instar ornabo. In ea miros exitus circumvolvam: arma, coniugia, cruorem, laetitiam insperatis miscebo successibus [...] Pascam animos contemplatione diversa et veluti pictura locorum [...]. Novi nostrorum ingenia: quia nugari me credent, omnes habebo. Amabunt tamquam theatri aut arenae spectaculum. Ita insinuato amore potionis addam salubres herbas. Vitia effingam virtutesque et praemia utrisque convenient. Dum legent, dum tamquam alienis irascentur aut favebunt, occurrent sibi ipsis agnoscentque obiecto speculo speciem ac meritum suae famae. Forte pudebit eas partes diutius agere in scena huius vitae, quas sibi cognoscent ex merito contigisse in fabula. Et ne traductos se querantur, neminis imago simpliciter exstabit. Dissimulandis illis multa inveniam, quae notatis convenire non poterunt. Mihi enim non sub religione historiae scribenti libertas haec erit. Sic vitia, non homines, laedentur, nec cuiquam licebit indignari, nisi qui vexata flagitia in se turpi confessione recipiat. Praeterea et imaginaria passim nomina excitabo, tantum ad sustinendas vitiorum virtutumque personas, ut tam erret qui omnia, quam qui nihil, in illa scriptione exiget ad rerum gestarum veritatem.
>
> I will compile some stately fable in manner of a history. In it will I fold up strange events and mingle together arms, marriages, bloodshed, mirth, with many and various successes [...] I will feed their minds with divers

> [*sic*] contemplations and, as it were, with a map of places [...] I know the disposition of our countrymen: because I seem to tell them tales, I shall have them all. They will love my book above any stage-play or spectacle on the theatre. So first bringing them in love by a potion, I will after put in wholesome herbs. I will figure vices and virtues, and each of them shall have his reward. While they read, while they are moved with anger or favour (as it were against strangers), they shall meet with themselves and find in the glass held before them the show and merit of their own fame. It will perchance make them ashamed longer to play those parts upon the stage of this life for which they must confess themselves justly taxed in a fable. And so that they may not say they are traduced, no man's character shall be simply set down. I shall find many things to conceal them, which would not well agree with them if they were made known. For I, who bind not myself religiously to the writing of a true history, may take this liberty. So the vices, not the men, shall be struck. No man can take exception but those who shall reveal his own naughtiness with a most shameful confession. Besides, I will have here and there imaginary names to signify several vices and virtues, so that one who demands that everything in my writing be consistent with the facts of history shall be as much in error as one who demands that nothing be so. (*Argenis* 2, 14, 336; 337)[25]

By showing his readers this 'pictura locorum' picture or 'map of places,' which nonetheless lacks historical specificity, Nicopompus answers both Tasso's injunction to entertain with a verisimilar-marvellous use of foreign elements (in Barclay's case Africa, the Levant, and Europe) and Amyot's concerns about historical pretence. Barclay's character's explanation that his book is not a true history, 'non sub religione historiae scribenti' ('As I do not religiously write a history' 336), makes it an apt 'speculo,' a mirror or 'glass,' for moral and political reflections while having the distinct advantage of censuring his contemporaries under a protective veil. Though Barclay is said to be the first to use this format to create the political romance specifically, he was not the only one to use Greek romance to veil social commentary.

The heterotopic formulation of foreign places and chronological flexibility of Greek romance could represent a variety of cultural and political strife. Moreover, these generic characteristics could be employed by authors whose cultural status was compromised; the enforced wandering and trials that the ancient Greek romance's characters undergo were an appealing model to Iberian translators and authors who faced turmoil in their own lives. In her study of

Alonso Núñez de Reinoso, Constance Hubbard Rose argues that the Greek romance attracted the displaced and wandering peoples who had suffered exile from Spain at the hands of the Inquisition. Jews, Erasmians, *conversos*, and finally *moriscos*, many of whom had been scholars and literate members of the now dwindling Spanish middle class, settled across Europe and the Mediterranean. Rose suggests that 'perhaps the early Spanish translators of Heliodorus' *Aethiopica* were drawn to the work for the resemblance it bore to the social situation they shared with a certain portion of potential readers' (159), those readers being scattered wanderers themselves. Rose asserts that many of the Spanish translators and imitators of Greek romance in the sixteenth century were exiles, including the anonymous translator of the first Spanish version of the *Aethiopica*, published in Antwerp in 1554. Reinoso and his circle were also exiled *conversos*, and his displacement from Spain to Portugal to Italy made him quick to imitate the wanderings of *Leucippe and Clitophon*, which he read in a partial translation and then probably in its entirety before crafting his own romance.

The multiplicity of place and lack of historical specificity that I observe in the ancient Greek romance correspond with what M.M. Bakhtin classifies as the adventure-time chronotope of romance. Bakhtin recognizes what he terms the 'prenovelistic discourse' of the Greek romance and its contributions to Renaissance prose, including the romance. The heteroglossia of the Greek romance contributes to novelistic discourse, and heteroglossia results from the inclusion of other voices, a polyglot consciousness in the construction of the text that represents 'a rich world of diverse forms that transmit, mimic and represent from various vantage points another's word, another's speech and language' (50). The inclusion of the Other is decisive in the Greek romance, for 'this discourse always developed along the boundary line between cultures and languages' (50). Though I agree with Bakhtin's assessment of heteroglossia in Greek romance, I disagree with his judgment of its characterization.[26] Bakhtin asserts that the Greek romance, with its many trials, weaves a plot, the action of which is not tied to limitations of time: 'It lies outside biographical time; it changes nothing in the heroes, and introduces nothing into their life. It is precisely an extratemporal hiatus between two moments of biographical time' (90). The adventure time, in other words, is simply bracketed by the protagonists' meeting and their eventual marriage.

Bakhtin claims that this chronotope results in a paucity of character development, but several classicists have contradicted his view of romance characterization. Alain Billault, for one, convincingly argues that the adventure time of ancient Greek romance is precisely what enables the change and flexibility of its characters' identities, explaining that the characters 'change: they are not the same persons in the end as they were in the beginning of the story. The trials they have undergone, the deeds they have done have left their mark on them and shaped their nature' (127–8). Moreover, these changes are most often articulated as a response to suffering, since '[c]haracter development through suffering actually is a favourite theme,' and characters often 'pathetically recapitulate [their trials] and identify themselves with their misfortunes,' a convention that allows characters to '[construct] and [claim] an identity that results from [their] misadventures' (128). Thus the trials that compose the adventure-time chronotope, according to Billault, actually build character development, and I add that they do so through passibility – a capacity to suffer and to change – rather than through models of individual, independent agency.

The tendency to judge romance characterization as flat or unchanging in fact masks deep ideological concerns. Calling on the views of Karl Marx and Bertolt Brecht to support what he views as a misplaced critical bias, Daniel Selden suggests that the modern requirements for subjective characterization and emphasis on independent agency cause critics to overlook character complexity in the ancient Greek romance, thus commodifying character and denying social change. Selden notes that many evaluations of character in the Greco-Roman romance 'tend to be not descriptive, but judgmental.' He observes that they prefer an 'unforgettable individual,' and place a premium on 'the fullness of the portrait and the impression of psychological depth' (45). This predisposition of the modern critic not only obscures the complexity of ancient romance characterization, but also reveals inadequacies in modern ways of conceiving of personhood as well. Selden explains:

> behind the deceptively simple device of subjective characterization lies a complex literary mechanism that concomitantly exploits, advances, and mystifies the prevailing socioeconomic order. By rediscovering this strategy, however rudimentary, in ancient fiction, the academy accomplishes at least two things: it reinforces the great novelistic myth that character as such is universal, and it ensconces modern prose uncritically as the acme of literary, and by implication social, evolution [...] [which] entails an aesthetic judgment, but leaves an ideological remainder. (47)

What Selden observes as a problematic approach to assessments of character in the ancient world extends to critical evaluations of early modern characterization, where readers are sometimes frustrated by what they perceive as a lack of depth in romance characterization. Rethinking ancient and early modern identity as passible can thus make us better interpreters of romance and can account for the 'ideological remainder' of which Selden speaks.

Ekphrasis and the Emblematics of the Self

Attending to the way romance characters create and interpret ekphrastic passages provides a new method for charting flexible depictions of cultural identity in romance narratives. Ekphrasis illuminates identity for three reasons: its rhetorical association with ethos in its creation and interpretation, its multivalent function in complex romance narrative structures, and its ability to wedge open deep ideological tensions in cultural binaries. Ancient and early modern definitions of ekphrasis show that the ekphrastic mode's relation to ethos and characterization is evident from its early articulations in Western rhetorical formulations. Ekphrastic interpretation, moreover, functions as a form of expressing cultural knowledge and character. Ekphrasis relates narratologically to identity as well: romancers use ekphraseis as graphic puzzles in their complex polyglot narratives, and ekphrasis's tie to characterization becomes a platform for multiple and varied acts of ekphrastic creation and interpretation on the part of marginalized and foreign people. The relationship between ekphrasis and romance identities is a function of the numerous points of view that are included in romance narratives and serves to enliven the dialogic relation between word and image in the text. As we will see, the polyvalence of ekphrastic articulations of identity thus destabilizes ideologically determined cultural binaries.

Ekphrasis, literally *a calling forth*, was elaborated principally as a rhetorical device closely associated with ethos, or the character of a speaker or audience. Aristotle recommends ekphrastic description for its power to align the ethos of an audience and its ability to depict character type in his *Rhetoric*.[27] In reference to epideictic and deliberative oratory, Cicero demonstrates the power of vivid visual description to create commonplaces in his *Academica* and *De oratore*.[28] In his *Institutio oratoria*, Quintilian further elaborates ekphrasis's necessity in the context of forensic rhetoric by classifying *evidentia* as a type of *descriptio*, which is necessary in order to convince a jury.[29] A common feature of the recommended use of *sub oculos subiectio* (to bring [something] before one's eyes) is how these vivid descriptions affect or express character, usually through their ability to manipulate emotions.

The connection between ethos and ekphrasis was solidified during the Second Sophistic when ekphrasis was institutionalized as a part of the rhetorical curriculum in the *progymnasmata,* thus making it a tool for self-betterment in the moral education of an orator. This function was also evident in literary works of the period. The *Tabula Cebetis* presents ekphrasis as a means of revealing moral character, Lucian investigates how verbal tributes to visual art define character and declares visual *allegoresis* to be an essential rhetorical talent for any respectable orator, and Philostratus conceives of ekphrasis as a means of displaying cultural status. The ancient definitions of ekphrasis, in other words, forge links between ekphrasis and the expression of identity.

Though the word *ekphrasis* was infrequently used in the early modern period, ancient ekphrastic literature was widely disseminated, and the use of ekphrastic interpretation as a tool for expressing moral character was readily apparent to Renaissance readers. The late-Stoic text *Tabula Cebetis* (*Tablet of Cebes*), which in the Renaissance was wrongly attributed to a follower of Pythagoras and is now dated to the first century CE, illustrates the expression of character through ekphrastic interpretation. This example of ekphrastic literature became available to early modern readers in Florence in its *editio principes* (c. 1494–6) and later in Ludovicus Odaxius's Latin translation (1497). The *Tabula* narrates an old man's (Genius's) ekphrastic explanation of an allegorical painting found in a temple of Kronos that depicts the human journey through life. The painting represents an island populated by allegorical figures who manage the entrances to three concentric enclosures. Depending on the moral decisions that the traveller makes in this landscape of human life, the outcome will be happiness or disaster; hence, moral character is elaborated through a series of ekphrastic interpretations. Without Genius's ekphrasis, the painting has no meaning for the audience, who frequently interject questions and exclamations in the text.

Cebes' use of ekphrastic interpretation as a tool for moral examination was available to early modern readers through numerous translations. The Tablet was also an integral part of early modern pedagogy, making it widely read. The task of translating the Greek text was a feature of both humanist and religious educational plans. For example, it became a part of the mid-level grammar instruction of the *Ratio Studiorum*, the curriculum of the Jesuits. The prevalence of the *Tabula,* and its role as a fairly rudimentary text at beginner and mid-level grammar instruction, ensured that it would be familiar to most early modern Europeans who gained a basic education, and would most likely have been familiar to the authors examined in this book.[30]

Ekphrastic interpretation is, moreover, an expression of cultural status, as I have illustrated in my introduction with examples from Lucian's *De Domo – On the Hall*, which was widely translated in the Renaissance along with other of Lucian's ekphrastic works. But Lucian was not alone in assigning aesthetic responses ethical value. Philostratus describes a series of paintings to the ten-year-old son of his host and a group of students in Naples in his *Imagines* (c. 150 CE), which was also available to early modern readers. He does so because the boy has asked him to interpret the paintings and in order that '[the boy] might not think me ill-bred' (7). As a sign of good breeding, the *Imagines* were also written expressly 'to describe examples of paintings in the form of addresses which we have composed for the young, that by this means they may learn to interpret paintings and to appreciate what is esteemed in them' (5). Philostratus's ekphraseis were written as lectures or rhetorical exercises not only to display the sophist's talents, but also to convey cultural knowledge.

For Philostratus, then, aesthetic responses to visual art exhibit one's education and cultural position. The way that a person creates a verbal image, in other words, discloses aspects of identity, whether the image exists in reality or not. As Michel Beaujour argues, the 'picture (the fictional visual object)' conveys 'ethical messages in an emblematic sort of way' (31), affecting an audience as it had been outlined and elaborated by authors like Aristotle, Cicero, and Quintilian – which would have been common knowledge to Philostratus. Philostratus's project is pedagogical, ethical, and ideological in its scope because the images 'purport to educate the moral sense by way of the physical senses. The highly-charged fragments point to a more tightly structured – yet implicit – moral ideology, wherein the meanings of seemingly frivolous or insignificantly sensual signifiers turn into the scattered elements of an ethics, which can easily be pieced together' (Beaujour 32). Philostratus teaches the reader how to communicate not only moral character in the act of interpretation, but also moral instruction through the education that verbal images can provide. His project and the similar works of ekphrasis by his family and fellow sophists were no doubt important sources of ekphrastic technique and content for the writers of ancient Greek romance who were his contemporaries, but the cultural import of verbal interpretation of visual representation was also of key importance to the Renaissance imitators of Greek romance.

The classical functions of ekphrasis were reprised in the rhetorical handbooks of the Renaissance by authors like Erasmus of Rotterdam, and exercises in description continued to be a part of the rhetorical curriculum, guides for writing verbal images being common.[31] Moreover, by the early sixteenth century the ability to create and interpret works of art was a prerequisite of courtly identity. In his handbook of courtly manners, *The Courtier,* Baldesar Castiglione enjoins his reader to learn to draw and paint. In book 1, Lodovico Canossa argues that 'a knowledge of how to draw and an acquaintance with the art of painting itself' must 'in no way be neglected by our Courtier' (57). But an ability to interpret works of visual art through verbal description was also socially significant. As Michael Baxandall notes, '[A] fifteenth-century man looking at a picture was curiously on his mettle. He was aware that the good picture embodied skill and he was frequently assured that it was the part of the cultivated beholder to make discriminations about that skill, and sometimes even to do so verbally' (34). Pier Paolo Vergerio's *On noble behavior* (1404), as Baxandall translates it, claims that '[t]he beauty and grace of objects, both natural ones and those made by man's art, are things it is proper for men of distinction to be able to discuss with each other and appreciate' (Baxandall 34), a statement that echoes Lucian's opening of *De Domo* and was a part of Renaissance consciousness about the powers of interpretation needed for encounters with art objects. Though Baxandall supports his assertions about the social obligation to interpret well with apt examples from fifteenth-century treatises on art and its interpretation, he also observes how people with different educations and experiences interpret works of art differently: '[S]ome of the mental equipment a man orders his visual experience with is variable, and much of this variable equipment is culturally relative, in the sense of being determined by the society which has influenced his experience' (40). What Baxandall's findings necessarily exclude in this instance is an estimation of how people who were not wealthy men with the opportunity for education might have interpreted works of art. Baxandall himself acknowledges that he only attends to those 'whose response to works of art was important to the artist – the patronizing classes, one might say. In effect this means rather a small proportion of the population: mercantile and professional men, acting as members of confraternities or as individuals, princes and their courtiers, the senior members of religious houses.

The peasants and the urban poor play a very small part in the Renaissance culture that most interests us now, which may be deplorable but is a fact that must be accepted' (38–9). Baxandall's investigation is naturally abbreviated in scope to historical analyses based on limited primary sources, and as such it omits how marginalized or foreign groups might have verbally interpreted images in this period. Yet marginalized and foreign ekphrastic interpretations are precisely the kinds of views that Renaissance romancers imaginatively encompass in their works of fiction.

Significant to these writers' adaptation of ekphrastic writing was the invention of new artistic media that harnessed the tensions between the visual and the verbal to teach moral lessons and to express personal intentions. The invention of the emblem and the related medium of the personal *impresa* or device encouraged the connection between ekphrasis and ethos, the acquisition of visual literacy, and the demonstration of ekphrastic interpretation as an indicator of social standing.[32] Though Andrea Alciato is usually thought to have coined the term *emblema* in his *Emblemata* (1531), the term's etymology goes back to antiquity. As Dennis Drysdall explains (300–4), in its Latin incarnations, the word *emblema* had both literary and legal applications corresponding to mosaics and personal ornaments respectively. In the Renaissance, the definition of *emblema* as mosaic is used to describe the quintessentially humanist *stile a mosaico,* the rhetorical technique of gathering together commonplaces. Furthermore, the definition of *emblema* as personal or detachable ornament is aptly destined to fit its manifestation as the personal *impresa* that the emblem tradition encompassed. The figurative use of *emblema* before its designation as a medium that combined image and text shows that 'Alciato's invention is not simply the product of an isolated inspiration but arises in the context of one of the central problems of humanist stylistics. The process of composing by means of common-places, the "stile a mosaico," raises the obvious problem of integrating the borrowed elements into the new text, a problem of the process of imitation' (Drysdall 304). Alciato's work – a series of images paired with brief mottos and exegetical poems – popularized the word 'emblem' in its familiar form, and it accounts both for mosaic and ornamental definitions in its use. The name of the medium melds well with the mental assembly necessary in both crafting and cognitively processing pieces of mosaic into an intelligible whole, and the *emblema*'s etymology as personal ornament anticipates the individual intentionality of the personal *impresa*.

The activity of creating and interpreting both emblems and personal *imprese* became a prerequisite of any educated person's social repertory. In his *Courtier*, Castiglione describes how devising emblems was a part of courtly culture:

> I say that the custom of all the gentlemen of the house was to betake themselves immediately after supper to the Duchess; where, amidst the pleasant pastimes, the music and dancing which were continually enjoyed, fine questions would sometimes be proposed, and sometimes ingenious games, now at the behest of one person and now of another, in which, under various concealments, those present revealed their thoughts allegorically to whomever they chose [...] often 'emblems,' as we nowadays call them, were devised; in which discussions a marvelous pleasure was had, the house (as I have said) being full of very noble talents. (13)

This skill for creating emblems and *imprese* and for allegorically interpreting them was developed with the help of collections of emblems and treatises that emphasized their link to ethos. Rhetorically, the media's link to personhood was emphasized by calling the image the emblem's body and the text its soul. The link to ethos is inherent in the media's purported aims: the emblem proper was often used to convey universal truths, *imprese* were crafted to communicate specific intentions or states of mind, and both were interpreted allegorically. The fact that educated people in the Renaissance were so familiar with creating and interpreting this essentially ekphrastic mode of depicting ethos makes the use of emblematic rhetoric in literature a natural outcome.[33]

Emblems themselves and the emblematic style were closely intertwined with personal expression, and the activity of processing visual and verbal signs both to interpret moral meaning and to craft a personal ethos is precisely what occurs in the interpretation and creation of ekphrastic passages by characters in romance narratives. Hence, the emblematics of the self provides a definition of the ekphrastic characterization present in Renaissance romance using aesthetic and ethical terms that are at home in the period. All of the romances that I examine in this book include verbal descriptions of emblematic media and express character emblematically through ekphrastic renderings of objects in the text on the part of romance characters.

To take Sidney's *New Arcadia* as an example, Patrick Scanlon suggests that Sidney 'develops visual images and comparisons which, if not drawn directly from emblem literature, are at least very like it in subject matter and style' (219). He relates this emblematics to characterization, remarking that '[e]mblematic revelation of character and emotion enriches the *Arcadia*. Emotions are objectified in brief scenes and the objects included there, in memory, and in dreams. Vivid insights into Sidney's characters help us to appreciate their dilemmas, and distill from their predicaments a universal moral application' (232). Scanlon's observation about the *New Arcadia* is, I suggest, true of many Renaissance imitations of the ancient Greek romance. Renaissance romancers were doubtless familiar with the emblem model, and emblems were used as tools for conveying cultural knowledge – the educational function of emblems is well known.[34] Moreover, the reading of emblems requires the image-text-ethos relation that defines the emblematics of the self, in which a character reveals ethos through the verbal interpretation of visual representation. To be clear, I do not claim that emblems proper and ekphraseis are the same; rather, the mental process required in the emblematic interpretation of both emblems and *imprese* and its involvement with both moral teaching and personal intention beautifully encapsulate the expression of character involved in ekphrastic creation and interpretation in Renaissance romance.

Given that ekphrastic interpretation reveals ethos both in the classical and early modern contexts, I now turn to the matter of what happens when ekphrastic passages and interpretation are embedded in polyglot romance narratives. Ekphrasis functions to open up multivalent expressions of identity in these complex narrative configurations. In the ancient Greek romance, as Shadi Bartsch suggests, ekphraseis 'are no mere rhetorical showpieces but forge playful and intricate connections with the narrative and its events,' and are presented 'for readers guided by the conventions of the epoch, as illuminators of the text; they promise insight into it; they call for acts of interpretation' (6). The function of ekphrastic passages in ancient Greek romance narratives can be analeptic (looking back in the narrative), sylleptic (presenting two contrary views simultaneously), or proleptic (looking forward in the narrative), and these narratological functions add variety to the possible interpretations of ekphraseis that romance characters make. On a narratological level, attempts at description, which Mieke Bal defines as 'a privileged site of focalization' (*Narratology* 36), result in multiple verbal interpretations of visual representation.[35] Character focalizers often express their identities through their focalizations of visual representations.[36] In other words, the focalized object is that which is seen, but its presentation also discloses something about the focalizer (150, 152).

Acts of ekphrastic interpretation in the multiple plot lines of romance elucidate how Europeans imagined marginal and foreign identities in the early modern period. What Bal has observed about the potential for multiple descriptive renditions to express character is especially true in the romance genre, where the depiction of foreign places, which function as heterotopias, and the lack of historical specificity – what Bakhtin interprets as the bracketed time of adventure time – allow myriad characters to provide different focalizations of visual representations in numerous places and times. Furthermore, multiple layers and points of view in romance narrative open a verbal image to many interpretations that not only disclose aspects of the focalizer's identity but also enliven the verbal image. In novelistic discourse, according to Bakhtin, the relation between word and object (in this case a visual artifact in the narrative) is always dialogic. The polyglot depictions of an object reveal the heteroglossia of novelistic discourse itself. Bakhtin explains that objects are 'from one side highlighted while from the other side dimmed by heteroglot social opinion, by an alien word about them' (277). Thus he likens the relation between object and interpretation to 'an artistic representation, an "image" of the object,' and goes on to explain that the verbal interpretation of objects functions like 'a ray of light,' and the 'living and unrepeatable play of colors and light on the facets of the image that it constructs can be explained as the spectral dispersion of the ray-word, not within the object itself [...] but rather as its spectral dispersion in an atmosphere filled with the alien words, value judgments and accents through which the ray passes on its way toward the object; the social atmosphere of the word, the atmosphere that surrounds the object, makes the facets of the image sparkle [...] Such is the image in artistic prose and the image of novelistic prose in particular' (277–8). The dialogic relation between the word and its object is articulated here using metaphors of visuality and Renaissance models of visual perception. Bakhtin extends these visual metaphors to claim that the heteroglot relationship between word and object is the same as that of the verbal representation of visual representation in the form of a work of visual art. The word and object relation essentially enlivens a verbal image, which we can call an ekphrasis. Bakhtin's observations on the relationship between word, object, and image represent not only the multiplicity of possible interpretations in a narrative, but also the way in which these attempts at description vivify the objects they describe. The work of visual art, by extension, calls forth these varied interpretations, making the relation between word and image dialogic.

What Bakhtin defines as the dialogic relation between language and object in the creation of verbal images is, moreover, something that Renaissance romancers would have been able to perceive (albeit in different terms) in the relation between word and image represented in the emblem tradition, as I have explained above. A picture would be accompanied by a motto, and both would be explained through a description or verbal image. The verbal image enlivens the word/picture relation and makes for an intelligible moral lesson.

The dialogic relations of word and image in emblematic literature supplement what many modern theorists of ekphrasis formulate: tensions between verbal and visual representation expose culturally embedded ideologies that frame the way we think about the self. W.J.T. Mitchell explains that tensions between word and image encompass ideological problems of '"gender, race, and class," the production of "political horrors," and the production of "truth, beauty, and excellence,"' and he believes that 'The basic contradictions of cultural politics and of "Word and Image" are mutually symptomatic of deeply felt shifts in culture and representation: anxieties, on the one hand, about the centrality and homogeneity of such notions as "Western civilization" and "American culture" and, on the other, about the sense that changing modes of representation and communication are altering the very structure of human experience' (*Picture Theory* 35). Mitchell enlists triadic formulations of what he calls the 'imagetext' relation by drawing on Michel Foucault, Michel de Certeau, and Charles Sanders Peirce in order to open up image-text comparison. But the imagetext problem might also be addressed by calling upon theorists like Walter Benjamin and Homi Bhabha to present ekphrasis as a third space of discourse, which can help to unravel not only the ideologically determined relationships between image and text, but also hierarchies of cultural identity that can be read through the emblematics of the self in romance narratives.

The triadic formulation of the emblematics of the self can help to open the culturally determined binaries that are embedded in the image-text relation and that have a real impact on constructions of marginalized or foreign identities. The relation of ekphrasis, interpretation, and ethos functions to disclose culturally embedded ideology. Mitchell speaks of a triadic model of imagetext that could encompass heterology, hybridity, and 'otherness'; however, although he touches on concepts of splitting and nonoppositional dialectic formulations of the imagetext, he does not fully apply these notions to ekphrasis in *Picture Theory*. In an interview conducted by Christine Wiesenthal and Brad

Bucknell, Mitchell fleshes out his idea of the imagetext, which he calls 'the heterogeneous playing field in which agents find themselves' (17). Here Mitchell elaborates a three-part concept of the imagetext, in which the 'gap' in between image and text constitutes a kind of generative divide. In noting the 'uncanny resonance' and drawing an analogy between Foucault's analysis of the gap between Magritte's painting of a pipe and its caption 'This Is Not a Pipe,' Peirce's triadic concept of the sign, and Lacan's three-part idea of 'register,' Mitchell's argument reflects the dynamics of 'power-knowledge-desire' (*Picture Theory* 180), which he claims ekphrasis can enliven.[37]

Moreover, in an interview with Homi Bhabha, 'Translator Translated,' Mitchell asks Bhabha to resolve the issue that Mitchell himself seems unable or unwilling to tackle in *Picture Theory*: how, he asks, does Bhabha reconcile his aversion for transcendent dialectic models 'with a mobilizing of conceptual binaries like subject and object, the self and the other, and with notions of doubling, contradiction, splitting, and of course ambivalence? Are binary oppositions and conceptual pairings things you can live neither with nor without?' (33). In response to this question, which reflects dilemmas in Mitchell's theorization of the image/text, Bhabha says that the answer lies

> in learning how to conceptualize 'contradiction' or the dialectic as that state of being or thinking that is neither the one nor the other, but something else besides, 'Abseits' [...] This is where the influence of Walter Benjamin has been formative for me. His meditations on the disjunctive temporalities of the historical 'event' are quite indispensable to thinking the cultural problems of late modernity. His vision of the Angel of History haunts my work as I attempt to grasp, for the purposes of cultural analysis, what he describes as the condition of translation: the 'continua of transformation, not abstract ideas of identity and similarity.' His work has led me to speculate on differential temporal movements within the process of dialectical thinking and the supplementary or interstitial 'conditionality' that opens up alongside the transcendent tendency of dialectical contradiction – I have called this a 'third space,' or a 'time lag.' (34)[38]

Bhabha's conceptualizing of a dialectic that could be approached by a 'third space,' something *abseits*, might result in a dialectic that would not be generalizing. This model of dialectics mediated by a third space augments Mitchell's formulation of the imagetext. Indeed, Mitchell's analysis of the imagetext split occurs partly through his treatment of ekphrasis, which, I suggest, can function as one of these extra-dialectic spaces. It is not 'pure' text, not 'pure' image, but resides on the split between them.

Ultimately, ekphrasis is shown to be a hybrid medium that can subtly reveal ideologically determined binaries as precisely ideological. What better mode to use when articulating passible expressions of identity in romance narratives? As I will demonstrate in my chapters to follow, the multiple ekphrastic characterizations in early modern imitations of the Greek romance serve to wedge open the cultural binaries of male/female, civilized/barbarian, West/East that romance characters negotiate. The fact that romance gives a voice to subaltern characters, and that ekphrasis is inherently associated with ethos – it is wrapped up in social expectations for cultured behaviour and appears in a narrative that structurally highlights multiple points of view – allows for a rich field of ekphrastic characterization in the romance genre.

In sum, I have engaged Renaissance and contemporary criticism to determine the moral and aesthetic explanations for the Greek model's supplanting of chivalric romance in early modern literary criticism, proposing political and cultural reasons for the appropriation of the Greek model by Renaissance authors. Renaissance romancers embrace the Greek romance not only on the basis of moral and aesthetic criteria, but also for its capacity to articulate a vast variety of cultural and linguistic narratives. The Greek romance mode's lack of national affiliation and its ability to speak to and for a variety of marginalized and dispersed peoples appeal to writers of the late Renaissance who negotiate a variety of cultural contact zones through transatlantic cultural crosscurrents and continuing conflicts with the Kingdom of Morocco and Ottoman Empire across the Levant. Finally, as a means of examining romance depictions of passible cultural identity, I have explained how the emblematics of the self can reveal identity and widen cultural dialectics. The narratological, dialogic, and ideological function of ekphrasis enlivens the relations between image and text, makes them 'sparkle' (Bakhtin 277), and finally illuminates the romance globe.

2 *Converso Convertida*: Cross-Dressed Narration and Ekphrastic Interpretation in *Leucippe and Clitophon* and *Clareo y Florisea*

In the dedicatory epistle to *Los amores de Clareo y Florisea y los trabajos de la sin ventura Isea*, 1552, Alonso Núñez de Reinoso (a Spanish *converso* living in exile in Italy) relates how he happened upon a partial Italian translation of Achilles Tatius's *Leucippe and Clitophon* in a Venetian bookseller's shop. Expertly drawing in his reader, he explains:

> me tomó desseo, viendo tan buen nombre, de leer algo en él. Y leyendo una carta que al principio estava, vi que aquel libro avía sido escritto primeramente en lengua griega y después en latina, y últimamente en thoscana y passando adelante hallé que començava en el quinto libro. El aver sido escrito en tantas lenguas, el faltarle los cuatro primeros libros, fue causa que más curiosamente deseasse entender de qué tratava; y, a lo que pude juzgar, me paresçió cosa de gran ingenio, y de biva y agraciada invención.
>
> I was taken with the urge, seeing as it had such a good title, to peruse it. And reading a letter that was placed at its opening, I saw that the book had first been written in the Greek language, and later in Latin, and finally in Tuscan; and passing further along, I discovered that it started at the fifth book. Its having been written in so many languages and the lack of the first four books, caused me to desire to know more precisely what it was about, and from what I could judge, it seemed to me a thing of great wit, and of lively and graceful invention. (Reinoso 95)

The *mise-en-abyme* of reader, letter, and mysterious text, with its polyglot translations, locates the reader in Reinoso's cosmopolitan position and imbues the reader with his humanist 'urges' and 'desires,' all of which are satisfied with a witty and delightful Greek romance dressed up in the erotic title *Amorosi ragionamenti*.

Manuscripts of *Leucippe and Clitophon* made their way to Western Europe as early as the fifteenth century, in part because of the flight of Hellenic scholars from Constantinople after its fall to the Ottomans in 1453.[1] These manuscripts and their Latin and vernacular translations provided models for imitations that fed Europe's fascination with the ancient past and the present's discoveries. In other words, Reinoso had potentially struck gold and sought to convince the reader that in picking up his imitation, they had done so as well. His dedication turns out to be the early modern version of a book-jacket teaser, and we know now that he not only was probably familiar with *Leucippe and Clitophon* entire before he published his version, but also knew its Italian translator, Lodovico Dolce, who pens one of the dedicatory sonnets to Reinoso's romance (Reinoso 369), and about whom Reinoso writes in the dedication to Luís Hurtado de Mendoza, he is 'uno de los más excelentes autores que agora en toda Italia se sabe' ('one of the best authors that is now known in Italy' 238).[2] Reinoso thus opens his story with a playful humanist dissimulation – one critic has called it the 'historia de una mentira' ('history of a lie' Teijeiro, '*Clareo y Florisea*' 353) – that would have been evident to a careful reader and transparent to his printers.

Reinoso chooses his patrons, moreover, with an eye to benefit from the authority and allegorical potential of his work's genealogy. Luís Hurtado de Mendoza's brother Diego owned the Greek copy of *Leucippe and Clitophon* that was the basis for Annibale della Croce's Latin translation (from which Dolce's Italian translation was rendered).[3] The Mendozas were also the go-betweens for Titian and the Spanish court, and they commissioned his painting of Europa, which was probably based on the opening ekphrasis of Tatius's romance.[4] Reinoso's other dedicatee, Juan Micas, was an important patron of Spanish *conversos*.[5] It seems that he and his circle evinced an interest in the Greek romance. As Rose suggests, 'The rediscovery and vogue for the Byzantine novel among intellectuals may be interpreted, in part, as a means of expressing enforced exile, with the concomitant of endless wandering,' and in the hands of *conversos* the 'mode refers to the [Jews'] historical situation, which, temporally and geographically links the Second Diaspora with the First' (10). Thus Reinoso was able to appeal both to those captivated by antiquities and to those interested in the allegorical potential of Greek romance to represent the trials of exiled crypto-Jews like Reinoso himself.[6]

His enigmatic preface anticipates his sophisticated use of ekphrasis both to encrypt and to reveal identity, a technique that I propose Reinoso learns from Tatius's ekphrastic characterization of gender, and that he applies to his own inscription of Jewish identity. Insisting on the originality of his work – 'imitando y no romançando' ('imitating and not [simply] translating into vernacular' 95) – Reinoso writes his version of Tatius's tale, interpolating many chivalric and pastoral episodes into what becomes a generically hybrid text and elaborating upon the jilted lover Isea's story after the marriage and departure of the protagonist lovers Clareo and Florisea. Like Tatius, Reinoso swathes his plot with ekphrastic passages, disguises, and recognitions, and his alterations to the story shift emphasis to his Melite character, Isea, whom he uses at least partly as a vehicle for expressing his own experience of loss and exile as a Spanish *converso*. In fact, Reinoso's decision to narrate the story from Isea's perspective might seem to be his most significant alteration to Tatius's tale, but I believe that Reinoso is actually responding to a set of clues that Tatius embeds in the multiple instances of cross-dressing and ekphrastic description that complicate the identity of Tatius's first-person narrator. I propose that Reinoso's election of Isea as narrator constitutes a reading of Tatius's text that explains the *Leucippe*'s problematic ending: the narrator of *Leucippe and Clitophon* is actually Melite cross-dressed.

There are thus two major threads in my argument here: first, Reinoso's romance makes plain Tatius's disguised female narration, and second, Reinoso's narrator similarly disguises Jewish exile. Ekphrasis is the figure that connects these two threads. Tatius encodes the female identity of his narrator in sylleptic ekphraseis, and Reinoso, while making his female narration explicit, turns Tatius's ekphrastic technique into a means of inscribing the plight of exiled Jews. Reinoso thus employs the emblematics of the self to represent both female and Jewish identity passibly.

Beginning with Foucault's assertion that the Greek romance genre glorifies a 'new erotics' (*The Care of the Self* 228–32) and continuing with a series of works that challenge and expand upon Foucault's observations, scholars observe the social elevation of women in these texts and comment on how 'they permit women's voices to be heard, voices that would otherwise be smothered in the patriarchal environment within which the novels are set' (Whitmarsh and Bartsch 240).[7] Yet classicists have overlooked the possibility that the *Leucippe* might be narrated from a first-person female perspective. I consider this possible reading in Tatius's romance and in the way that Reinoso bears this reading out.

The ending of *Leucippe and Clitophon* has been a source of consternation for critics. The romance ends with Leucippe and Clitophon happily married and on their way to Byzantium (the last word in the text), but it opens in Sidon (the first word in the text) in a manner that seems to contradict the lovers' happy ending. At the opening, the framing narrator, who has just described the painting of Europa/Astarte, encounters a young person who is alone, forlorn, and self-identified as Clitophon. As this opening scene is set chronologically after the plot's events have taken place, one might ask, what is Clitophon doing in Sidon, and what happened to Leucippe? This apparent inconsistency has been assigned to poor authorship, possible lacunae in the text, conventions of Platonic dialogue, generic strictures on first-person narration, or a general resistance to closure in the text; but I believe that cross-dressed narration by Melite is a more elegant solution that is evident in the text itself and that hinges on gender identity and ekphrastic interpretation.[8]

The *Leucippe* employs cross-dressing to conceal identity. A simple change of clothes or boyish haircut does the trick. For example, cross-dressing masks the identity of the kidnappers of Clitophon's half-sister, Calligone. The pirates have 'eight accomplices secreted on land in advance, wearing women's clothes and with their beards shaved from their chins, each carrying a sword in the folds of his clothes,' an apparently effective disguise, as all of Clitophon's family 'thought that they were women' (Ach. Tat. 2, 18, 30).[9] Leucippe herself becomes unrecognizable when she has her hair cut off by her captors during her enslavement. Clitophon fails to recognize her, even after talking with her, and his friend Satyrus explains that her haircut, which made her look like an 'ephebe' (5, 18, 89), is probably to blame.

Most important to this explanation of the story's ending is the instance of cross-dressing that occurs between Melite and Clitophon. Melite, who has convinced Clitophon to marry her after they think that both her first husband and Leucippe are dead, switches clothes with Clitophon to help him escape from her husband when he turns up unexpectedly. After Clitophon dons her clothes, she exclaims, '"How much more handsome you have become with this clothing! [...] I once saw Achilles like this in a painting. But please take care, dearest, and keep this clothing as a memento of me; and leave yours for me, so that I may put it on and be enveloped by you"' (6, 2, 98). Melite, enveloped in Clitophon's clothes, is thus outfitted to become the *Leucippe*'s narrator. At the romance's end, she is heartbroken and alone. She will not reunite with her first husband after his shameful behaviour, condemnation by the court, and flight from justice. Leucippe and Clitophon have married and left for Byzantium.

At the romance's beginning, when the framing narrator comes across the votive painting in Sidon, he sees what he assumes is a young man affected by the picture. The presumed young man identifies himself as Clitophon and goes on to tell the story of *Leucippe and Clitophon* (1, 2, 5). The framing narrator emphasizes the bystander's youthful appearance: 'To judge by the look of you, it is not long since your initiation into the [love] god's cult' (1, 2, 5). Unless we assume that the boyish figure is actually the youthful Melite, this observation seems discordant. Clitophon was already nineteen at the story's beginning, and it is unlikely that he would look so youthful by its end.[10]

Melite's narration of the romance both resolves the discrepancies of the story's ending and fulfils generic expectations for first-person narratives in Greek romance. If Melite is indeed the narrator of the tale, Tatius's work would better fit into the generic expectations of first-person narration common to the inset stories of other Greek romances. Noting that *Leucippe and Clitophon* is unique among Greek romances for being told entirely from the first-person perspective, Glenn Most argues that it is natural that the first-person narrator of the *Leucippe* would appear forlorn at the opening, because 'there is a generic tendency within Greek erotic romances for first-person narratives to be tales of woe' (119), and, specifically, in other Greek romances, 'the [inset] first-person narrative is a lament for the misfortunes the narrator has suffered in the past and is still suffering at the time of his narration' (118). Rather than assuming that Clitophon is the narrator and is just pretending to be sad for the sake of generic convention, I argue that Melite's narration accounts both for the apparent inconsistencies of the ending and for Most's observations on the genre.

Whereas cross-dressing obscures identity in Tatius's romance, I suggest that ekphraseis and simple references to paintings provide points of alternative focalization that expose gender ambiguity. As scholars like Bartsch, Selden, and Morales have shown, ekphrastic passages are nexus of polyvalent meaning in the *Leucippe*. Moreover, these ekphraseis invite responses that elaborate the interpreters' ethos: in the *Leucippe*, a close examination of these passages discloses the inherent gender ambiguity of the narrator, and in *Clareo y Florisea*, the ekphraseis reveal allusions to exiled Jewish identity. An examination of Tatius's ekphrastic technique in his rendition of the Philomela myth and its reception in Reinoso's romance, in which Reinoso adapts female narration to address his own cultural concerns, supports this claim.

A fundamental feature of Tatius's ekphrastic technique is its sylleptic character, syllepsis being a rhetorical figure in which one word is taken to have two meanings simultaneously. For instance, the ekphrasis of Europa/Astarte that opens the *Leucippe* can be read in multiple ways that encode ethnic, religious, and gender identities in their implicit interpretations, as was mentioned in the Introduction. Daniel Selden explains that the text 'strategically accommodates both possibilities, so that depending on the reader's frame of reference, Hellenic or Phoenician, the image can be decoded in two opposing ways. This doubleness reveals that any assumption about gender, mutability, or power here is culturally contingent' (50). Selden likens this ekphrastic technique to syllepsis. The erotic ekphrasis of the votive painting in Sidon inspires our narrator to tell the story of *Leucippe and Clitophon*, a story that I suggest holds the secret of her cross-dressed identity. In fact, ekphraseis of dreams and paintings in the *Leucippe* obsessively dwell on gender ambiguities, role reversals, and even androgyny, making the aesthetics of gender ambiguity a 'permanent feature of Achilles Tatius' world' that 'causes confusion of not only sexual but also social identities,' as Romain Brethes has recently remarked (6).[11] The insistence on gender ambiguity extends to comparisons of Clitophon to cross-dressed heroes: Clitophon's comparison of himself with Hercules cross-dressed (Ach. Tat. 2, 6, 23), Melite's comment on his resemblance to Achilles cross-dressed (6, 2, 98), and Thersander's derisive likening of him to Penthius cross-dressed (6, 5, 100). All of these instances could be read as clues dropped by Melite, the narrator, about her adoption of Clitophon's identity. Moreover, in the exchange of clothing between Melite and Clitophon, Melite's observation that she 'once saw Achilles like this in a painting' (6, 2, 98) may be a play on the author's name, Achilles Tatius, which could be interpreted as an indication that the author is a woman and has taken Achilles as a pen-name. We will never know if the author's name was a cross-gendered disguise, but the possibility of female authorship is fascinating.

Although to my knowledge no other scholars have argued that Melite narrates *Leucippe and Clitophon*, at least one Renaissance reader shares this interpretation. Reinoso's story is told from the first-person perspective of his Melite character, whom he calls the *sin ventura* Isea, or luckless Isea. Both Tatius and Reinoso problematize female narration through polyvalent ekphrastic passages describing painted and embroidered representations of the Philomela myth. Where the female narration of Tatius's romance is hidden with cross-dressed disguise, Reinoso puts female narration on display in his appropriation of Tatius's ekphrastic techniques. Ekphrastic representations of Philomela allegorize the role of female narrators in both works, and in the case of Reinoso, illustrate a Renaissance author's masterful reworking of ancient ekphrastic and generic modes.

In *Clareo y Florisea*, the first-person female narration is transparent and self-conscious from the start. Isea opens the work, lamenting:

> Si mis grandes tristezas, trabajos y desventuras por otra Ysea fueren oýdas, yo soi çierta que serán no menos lloradas que con razón sentidas; pero, con todo, pienso que pues mis tristes lágrimas ablandaron y enterneçieron las duras piedras, que ansí harán a los blandos y tiernos coraçones, so pena que no siendo ansí, confesarán que son más duros que las duras peñas.
>
> Esta mi obra, que solamente para mí escrivo, es toda triste, como yo lo soi. Es toda de llantos y de grandes tristezas, porque ansí conforme con todas mis cosas y tenga el hábito que yo tengo. Cuenta fortunas agenas porque mejor se vea quán grandes fueron las mías y aún, al presente, lo son.
>
> If my great sorrows, trials and misadventures could be heard by another Isea, I'm sure that they'd be no less cried over than rightfully heartfelt; but with all that, I think that my solemn tears well might soften and make tender even hard rocks, and so too will it be with soft and tender hearts, which if not being moved under such pain, must admit to being harder than the hardest mountain peaks.
>
> This my work, which I write only for myself, is all sadness, as am I. It's all about lamentations and great sorrows, because thus it conforms with all that pertains to me and thus it has the same habitus as I have. I tell of the stormy misfortunes of others, because thus one can better see how extensive were mine, and how extensive they even are at present. (Reinoso 1, 97)

As Reinoso scholars have noted, Isea's opening draws on literary models of exile, female narration, and lamentation from Ovid's *Heroides* and *Tristia*, Boccaccio's *Fiammetta*, and possibly the narrations of Spanish nuns.[12] Self-conscious of her authorial role, Isea explains how she knows of things that happened to Clareo and Florisea before she met them. Clareo has related them to Isea himself: when she and Clareo travel by ship to Ephesus after their wedding in Alexandria, 'ívamos nuestro camino, contándome Clareo todas las cosas que con Florisea avía passado hasta el tiempo que comigo casado se avía, de la manera que atrás tengo contado' ('we went along our way, Clareo telling me all of the things that happened to him with Florisea before he married me, just as I have related them here before' 10, 131). Isea's careful justification of possible inconsistencies in her first-person narrative actually explains how Tatius's narrator Melite could have also come to learn the back story of Clitophon and Leucippe. Isea's explanation reflects how Tatius's narrator 'painstakingly, even legalistically provides narrative justifications for apparent breaches of the perspective from which the story has been told' (Most 116) and, by extension, also suggests how Melite might have told Clitophon's tale.

Along with elucidating the narration of its source, Reinoso's reception of Tatius's narrative techniques voices Reinoso's experience of loss and exile as a Spanish crypto-Jew or *converso*. Reinoso himself insists in his second dedicatory epistle, which was addressed to Juán Micas, that *Clareo y Florisea* allegorizes moral lessons, and that 'debaxo de su invención ay grandes secretos' ('beneath its composition lie great secrets' Reinoso 369). He illustrates the allegorical capacity of simple stories to render moral lessons using classical examples: giants, Midas, Actaeon turned to a stag, and Caeneus defeated by the Centaurs and transformed into a bird.[13] He follows these examples with possible interpretations of his characters' roles in *Clareo y Florisea*, and he claims that the figure of Isea demonstrates 'quán bien están los hombres en sus tierras, sin buscar las agenas' ('how happy men are in their own lands without looking for new ones' 370). Isea's story thus illustrates the trials of exile according to Reinoso.

In addition to the author's direct association of the character with the plight of exiles, Isea's name and position reflect the lamentable status of *conversos* specifically, and the work itself can be read as an allegorical lamentation for the Second Diaspora. Her name, read as a continuation of her epithet, *sin ventura* or 'luckless' Isea, sounds in Spanish like *sin ventura y sea* (luckless and shall be so). Moreover, the name may be a biblical reference to Isaiah, whose prophetic book addresses the plight of widows and Jewish exile. As we will see, Isea depicts herself as an exiled widow. Like many *conversos*, Reinoso escaped first to Portugal and then to Italy in his flight from the Inquisition. Appending episodes to the romance that trace Isea's wandering in search of a refuge, Reinoso encodes in her lamentations the heartbreak of *conversos* who fled their homeland to avoid persecution. As Rose explains, the Jewish *converso* population, 'faced with the prospect of the vicissitudes of compulsory migration or the anxiety of living in a land that might, at any moment, reject them,' experienced a 'feeling of group identity' and a 'desire to communicate the experience' using 'new modes of literary expression by which *converso* authors could relate the historical predicament in which they and their potential readers found themselves entrapped' (10).[14]

Tatius's ekphrastic passages describing the Philomela myth supply Reinoso with a means of allegorizing female narration and also provide him with a model for encoding Jewish lamentations. In Tatius's romance, Leucippe and Clitophon come across a painting of Philomela in Alexandria after Leucippe is ominously attacked by a hawk. The painting is described by Clitophon in the following ekphrasis:

> I saw a picture hanging up (for I happened to be standing next to a painter's studio), and the encrypted meaning it conveyed was a similar one. It told of the violent rape of Philomela by Tereus, who cut out her tongue. The picture incorporated the entire narrative of the drama: the robe, Tereus, the banquet. The maid was standing holding the unfolded robe; Philomela stood by her with her finger placed upon the robe, indicating the pictures woven into it. Procne had nodded her understanding of this performance: she was staring fiercely, furious at the picture. The embroidery showed the Thracian Tereus wrestling with Philomela for Aphrodite's prize. The woman's hair was torn, her girdle undone, her dress ripped, her chest half exposed. Her right hand was digging into Tereus' eyes, while her left sought to shut away her breasts with the shreds of her dress. Tereus held Philomela in his grip, pulling her towards him with all his bodily strength into a constricting, skin-to-skin embrace. This was the depiction the artist had woven into the robe. The remainder of the painting represented the women, simultaneously cackling and cowering, showing Tereus the leftovers of the feast in a basket, the head and hands of his son. Tereus was depicted leaping from his couch, waving his sword at the women and kicking his leg against the table. This was neither standing nor fallen, a pictorial indication that it was about to fall. (Ach. Tat. 5, 3, 78–9).

The story of Philomela ekphrastically described here in Tatius's romance is most famously told in Ovid's *Metamorphoses* book 6, where it follows the story of Arachne's web. It is one of the earliest myths about the origins of graphic representation. James Heffernan points out that Arachne's and Philomela's stories, while providing an 'alternative genealogy' against a 'formidable tradition of what might be called masculine ekphrasis' (46), do so at the expense of the female narrator. After all,

Philomela's graphic narration is a lamentation for her rape, not the description of arms or of heroic deeds. Nonetheless, Philomela's graphic narration of her story on cloth shows her passibility, both because it documents her suffering and because it demonstrates her adaptability and ingenuity under terrible circumstances.

In accordance with the Greek romance's ekphrastic conventions, the depiction of Philomela invites interpretations from characters and readers, and it challenges them to consider how the representation portends future events in the narrative. About the painting of Philomela in Alexandria, Leucippe and Clitophon's friend Menelaus advises, 'interpreters of signs say that if we encounter paintings as we set off to do something, we should ponder the myths narrated there, and conclude that the outcome for us will be comparable to the story they tell' (Ach. Tat. 5, 4, 79). Menelaus's advice establishes how ekphraseis function as what Harlan has called 'proleptic similes' (52) for the action to come in the narrative, and the ekphrasis thus inspires further interpretations amounting to a visual *allegoresis*. Clitophon interprets the painting as a warning that Leucippe will be captured, which does occur and which leads him to believe that she is dead.

Leucippe's story parallels Ovid's version of the Philomela myth when she is captured, held in a hut, and threatened with rape by Thersander, Melite's first husband (Ach. Tat. 6, 4, 100). Moreover, Leucippe becomes a narrator like Philomela when she writes a letter to Clitophon telling him of her woes (5, 17, 89). Her letter and Philomela's cloth are both female lamentations and both demand recompense. Leucippe is thus, at first, most comparable to the painted figure of Philomela in Tatius's romance.

Supplying Leucippe as a stand-in for Philomela is not the only way the painting can be read, and an alternative interpretation both illustrates Tatius's sylleptic ekphrastic technique and provides further textual evidence for Melite's narration of the story. Meeting cultural expectations for an educated response to the aesthetic stimulus of the painting, Leucippe requests that Clitophon explain the painting further, especially in respect to details which were apparently omitted in the initial description. Observing that 'the female of the species is rather fond of myths' (5, 5, 79) – a remark that gains a level of irony if we can assume that Melite is the adept narrator of myths putting these words into Clitophon's mouth – Clitophon further interprets the painting for Leucippe.[15] The elaboration follows:

> The nightingale, the swallow, and the hoopoe: all three humans, all three birds. The hoopoe is the man; of the two women, Philomela is the swallow and Procne the nightingale. The women came from the city of Athens. The man's name was Tereus, and Procne was his wife. It seems that with barbarians one wife will not satisfy Aphrodite's needs, especially when the opportunity to indulge in rape presents itself. Such an opportunity to display his nature was provided to this Thracian by Procne's kindly affection: she sent her husband to collect her sister. He began the outward journey still faithful to Procne, but the homeward one aflame for Philomela. On the way, he made Philomela his second Procne. Out of fear of Philomela's tongue, he gave her as her wedding present the gift of speechlessness, clipping the flower of speech. All to no avail, for artful Philomela invented silent speech: she wove a robe to be her messenger, weaving the plot into the threads. The hand imitated the tongue: she revealed to Procne's eyes what normally meets the ears, using the shuttle to communicate her experience. When Procne heard from the robe of the rape, she sought to exact an excessive revenge upon her husband. Their anger was doubled, since there were two women of a single mind: they plotted a feast more ill-starred than their marriages, blending resentment into a recipe for atrocity. The feast was Tereus' son, whose mother Procne had been before her anger: she had no memory of the birth-pangs now. Thus do the pangs of resentment vanquish even the womb: for when wives desire nothing other than to hurt the husband who has brought grief to the marriage-bed, though they themselves suffer no less pain as they inflict it, they weigh up the pain of suffering against the pleasure of inflicting. Tereus' feast was served up by the Furies: the women brought him the leftovers of his son in a basket, cackling as they cowered. When Tereus saw the leftovers of his son, his meal filled him with sorrow: he realized that he was the father of the feast. When this dawned upon him, he flew into a mad rage, drew his sword, and ran at the women. They were whisked into the air, and Tereus was lifted up with them, metamorphosing into a bird. Even now they preserve the image of their suffering: the nightingale flees, with Tereus in pursuit, retaining his hatred thus even in winged form. (5, 5, 79–80)

Clitophon's exegesis of the tale provides a platform for numerous links to the plot, and where Menelaus signals that the painting may have proleptic significance, the reader is now invited to assemble and reassemble multiple likenesses as well. Like the painting of Europa/Astarte, the ekphrasis of Philomela is sylleptic. There are at least two possible correspondences between the ekphrasis and the action to follow: first, if Leucippe is Philomela, then Melite and her husband Thersander can stand for Procne and her rapacious husband Tereus; but second, Leucippe may also be shadowed by Procne and Clitophon by Tereus, since Clitophon takes a new woman (Melite) while his first (Leucippe) still lives.[16] The latter interpretation puts Clitophon in the position of calling himself a barbarian: '[i]t seems that with barbarians one wife will not satisfy Aphrodite's needs' (5, 5, 79–80), and, if we assume that Melite is putting these words in Clitophon's mouth, the comment becomes one of the many ironic criticisms that her narrator's role affords her to make of Clitophon.

The final outcome of the ekphrasis, in which Procne, not Philomela, is turned into a nightingale (a departure on Tatius's part from the way the myth is usually told), signals the ways in which the painting's significance can be flipped. Though she does not note this particular variation on the myth, Bartsch observes that departures of this kind from conventional representations of myths are typical of Tatius's ekphrastic technique and that they are 'always crucial to the foreshadowing action of the description and to Achilles Tatius' play on the readers' expectations. [They are] precisely there to be noticed' (72). Moreover, these departures often function as clues to alternative interpretations. Since Leucippe never has sex at all in the course of the story's action – the consummation of her marriage is not narrated – and since Melite is ultimately, like Procne, the jilted lover, Tatius's choice to have Procne turned into the narrating nightingale provides more evidence that his first-person narrator could be a metamorphosed, storytelling Melite.

Emulating Tatius's representation of Philomela, Reinoso reworks Tatius's ekphrasis to make his Melite character, Isea, immediately fill the role of the *sin ventura* Philomela, the two women sharing the 'luckless' epithet. In her feminist analysis of this passage, Galperín notes Reinoso's emphasis on the connection between Isea and Philomela (234–67), and she draws links with other Iberian uses of the Philomela myth to allegorize female narration. Galperín further discusses the violence perpetrated against Philomela (254), and she notes that both Florisea and Isea suffer false decapitations that mirror the cutting out of Philomela's tongue, Reinoso having added Isea's *scheintod* in the twentieth chapter of his romance. Yet, unlike Philomela, Reinoso's female narrator does not portray herself as a victim and does not seek vindication. Isea relates how Clareo ekphrastically renders a painted image of the Philomela myth displayed in a house, but in Reinoso's version, this painting appears in a dream as follows:

> la noche antes avía visto en sueños una casa en la qual estava toda la historia de la sin ventura y mísera Filomena pintada, viéndose en aquella tela (la qual Filomena avía labrado) la fuerça que Tereo le avía fecho, y cómo la mostrava a Progne, su hermana, la qual estava triste y airada contra el marido, y cómo después le ponían las dos hermanas en la mesa la cabeça y manos del muerto hijo; y él las seguía con la espada desnuda, y a la fin todos se convertían en páxaros.
>
> Estas cosas todas que Clareo avía visto mostraron el mal que después le vino; pero con todas ellas, no pudiendo escusarse, açeptaron el yr a la nao [...]
>
> the night before he'd seen in dreams a house in which the whole story of the luckless and miserable Philomena was painted, in that cloth (the one that Philomena had worked) being seen how Tereus had forced her, and how she had shown it to her sister, Procne, who was saddened and irate with her husband, and how later the two sisters placed the head and hands of his dead son on the table; and he pursued them with naked sword, and in the end they were all changed into birds.
>
> All these things Clareo had seen showed the evil that was to come; but with all of that not being able to excuse themselves, they accepted the trip to the boat [...] (Reinoso 7, 111)

Much like Tatius's ekphrasis, Clareo's word-picture details Philomela's depiction on cloth of her rape and mutilation by Tereus, the gruesome revenge that she and her sister effect through infanticide, and the metamorphoses of all three characters into birds.[17] Though the Leucippe character, Florisea, is captured, just as in Tatius's version, Isea is immediately linked with Philomela. Along with sharing the epithet of *sin ventura* or luckless, the fact that Isea, as she often reminds the reader, is the one writing down the whole lamentable story, including Clitophon's dream, aligns her with Philomela's act of narration. Reinoso in fact omits the detail that Tereus cuts out Philomela's tongue, perhaps emphasizing that Isea is in total command of her narrative voice in this work.

Also like Philomela, Isea uses embroidery to lament graphically. At the beginning, unsuccessful stages of her attempted seduction of Clareo, Isea relates:

> me baxava a un jardín y por allí me començava de passear; pero luego mis cuydados me llevavan a otra parte y sentávame un rato, y tomando una almohadilla començava de labrar. Entre punto y punto, quedando olvidada y sospirando muy menudamente, labrava sobre debuxo la muerte de

> Leandro y de Hero, y ansí el sacrifiçio que se hizo de la sin ventura Yphygenia, y los amores de Phedra y quexas de Demophón por Phylis; y acabando de labrar de día, tornava de noche a deshazer lo labrado, porque dezía yo que, en acabando aquella mi lavor, Clareo se casaría comigo.
>
> I went down to a garden and began to walk in it; but later my cares carried me to another place and I sat myself down for a while, taking out an embroidery cushion I began to work. Lost in thought and sighing frequently between one stitch and the next, I depicted the death of Leander and of Hero and the sacrifice that was made of the luckless Iphigenia, and the loves of Phaedra and the complaints of Demophon for Phyllis, and finishing the work by day, I switched to unmaking the work by night, because it was my desire that when I finished my work, Clareo would marry me. (Reinoso 9, 123)

False deaths, uncontrollable loves, and forsaken women all depict aspects of Isea's own misfortunes, and her graphic representations of these tales on cloth reflect the narration of Philomela.[18] To this motif of female narration is added the reference to Penelope's shroud for Laertes. At this point in the romance, Isea is proving to be anything but a faithful widow, having fallen in love with Clareo after assuming that her husband had been lost at sea. Isea herself is the forestalled suitor, Clareo having deferred her attempt to marry him. This ironic allusion picks up on an undercurrent of humorous self-awareness and self-mocking on Isea's part that differentiates her narration from that of Philomela. Taking some responsibility for the trials that she undergoes, Isea has an ironic tone that can be interpreted in at least two ways, as readings of similar passages in Boccaccio's *Fiammetta* attest. While this ironic play may echo the sometimes loose allegiance between author and narrator in the *Fiametta*, if we do not read this irony as a misogynist undermining of the female narrator, Isea's ironic humour adds to our impression of her as a complex and sympathetic person.

After Isea suffers the loss of Clareo and wanders away from her homeland, she relates a dream that echoes Clareo's vision of the Philomela painting. The description of the dream follows:

> yo soñava que me hallava debaxo de unos altos álamos, riberas de un rýo que (según yo después supe) Henares se llamava. Y estando assí, me paresció que veía nueve nimphas, todas vestidas de blanco, las quales venían con los cabellos esparzidos, y me dezían:

–¡O Ysea, y quán bien empleados son en ti aquestos trabajos en que andas! ¡Y quán bueno te uviera sido tomar el consejo que en algún tiempo te dimos, y aver sosegado tu ánimo y reposado tu spíritu, tomando por tu voluntad, entonçes, el medio de la razón, antes que, agora, el remedio del tiempo!

Y diziéndome estas cosas, paresçe que me convertían en tórtola, diziendo:

–Tu vida será siempre como es la desta sin ventura ave, la qual, viéndose biuda, no possa en ramo verde, ni beve en aguas claras.

Y paresçíame, después, que me mudavan en aquellos árboles que dizen Iúpiter aver mudado a las hermanas de Phaetón quando lloravan riberas del río Eridano, las quales están siempre alli vertiendo bivas lágrimas. Yo, queriendo bolver sobre mí, pensando ya ser convertida en árboles, desperté y quedé espantada;

I dreamed that I found myself underneath some tall poplars, on the banks of a river which (as I later found out) was called the Henares. And being thus, it seemed to me that I saw nine nymphs, all dressed in white, with their hair loose, and they said to me:

'Oh, Isea, and how well you bear the trials through which you pass! And how good it would have been for you to take the advice that we once gave you, perhaps thus quieting your mind and resting your spirit, taking thus as your own choice the way of reason, before having to take now this solution!'

And telling me these things, it seemed that they changed me into a turtle-dove, saying to me:

'Your life will always be like that of this luckless bird, which seeing itself a widow, does not alight on the green branches, or drink from the clear waters.'

And it seemed to me then that they metamorphosed me into those trees, into which they say Jupiter transformed the sisters of Phaeton when they cried along the banks of the Eridanus river, the ones who are always there shedding living tears. I wanting to return to myself, thinking that I had been transformed into trees, woke up and was frightened; (Reinoso 29, 220–1)

As in Philomela's story, Isea's trials result in metamorphoses, albeit in her dream. She relates that nine nymphs 'me convertían en tórtola' ('changed me into a turtle-dove'). Though the turtle-dove differs from the nightingale into which Philomela is traditionally transformed, Clareo's ekphrasis of the images in his dreams simply stipulates that the women are turned into *páxaros*, or birds. This is intriguing, because Reinoso pointedly departs from Dolce's Italian version of the ekphrasis as well as from Tatius's here. Dolce, in a quintessentially humanist emendation, 'fixes' Tatius's ekphrasis, such that Philomela is turned into the nightingale and Procne into the swallow, as the pertinent passage of his Italian translation demonstrates:

> –Gli uccelli che tu qui vedi dipinti, gia furono creature humane, come noi siamo; cioé Progne e Philomena, che tali erano i nomi loro. Questa, dicono i poeti che fu mutata in rondine, e quella in luscigno, ambedue atheniesi e sorelle. L'huomo singono essere stato Re di Thracia, e marito di Progne, nominato Thereo, e aggiungono che in upupa fu trasformato.

> The birds you see painted here were once human creatures, as we are, that is, Procne and Philomela, these were their names. The former, so the poets say, was changed into a swallow, and the latter into a nightingale, both being Athenian and sisters. The sinister man was King of Thrace and husband of Procne, named Tereus, and, they add, was also transformed into a hoopoe. (Dolce 377)

Diverging from both Tatius's and Dolce's version of the Philomela myth, Reinoso builds on Tatius's ekphrastic variation in Isea's dream, replacing the nightingale with the turtle-dove, which was associated with chaste widows.[19] The behavioural details that the nymphs enumerate – not alighting on green branches and never drinking clear water – are commonplaces expressing the bird's loyalty and longing for its lost mate. Isea's dream of being transformed into this bird rather than the nightingale highlights a plot change that Reinoso effects in his romance; despite her best efforts at seduction, Isea, unlike her model Melite, never has sexual intercourse with Clareo, leaving her technically chaste. The reference to the turtle-dove is also religious. The Christian association of the turtle-dove with both Jesus and Mary is well known, but the bird is often also linked to exiled Jewish identity, the widowed turtle-dove perpetually suffering and lamenting for her lost mate, or homeland.[20] Most strikingly, this dream takes place in Spain along the banks of the river Henares, Reinoso's own inaccessible homeland, and expresses the theme of lamentation that pervades the romance.[21]

Though Isea is closely aligned with Philomela, her role in determining her own situation, for better or worse, is emphasized by the nymphs' comments and by her subsequent transformation into poplar trees.

This metamorphosis into poplars refers to the transformation of Phaethon's sisters into poplar trees crying tears of amber along the banks of the mythical Eridanus river. This second transformation implicates Isea as partly to blame for her own suffering, since Phaethon's sisters, the Heliades, suffer their metamorphoses for having encouraged their brother on his reckless ride. It also draws the dream's allusions away from Spain and back to the author's exiled and uncertain geography, the Eridanus sometimes being placed in the underworld and sometimes being associated with the Po river in Italy but never being fixed. Isea has fallen asleep on the banks of this illusive river, far from Reinoso's homeland of Spain.

Underscoring the emotional and geographic distance that Reinoso experienced in his exile, Isea travels to Spain after she has her prophetic dream, only to be rebuffed by a convent of nuns that she seeks to join. Ironically, in the heterotopic geography of this romance, set as it is in an uncertain and distant past, Spain is considered, as it was in the ancient world, to be the 'fin de Europa' ('at the farthest reaches of Europe' Reinoso 31, 231). Isea, who has lost everything in the course of her wandering away from her home in Ephesus, where she was once a powerful and rich woman, is turned away by the Abbess, who explains 'que quanto a entrar en aquella casa, que era menester traer mil ducados de dote, y ser de don y de buen linage' ('that in order to enter that house, it was necessary to give a dowry of one thousand ducados, and to be high-born from a good lineage' 32, 233). This anticlerical criticism reflects both the cupidity of the church and its preoccupation with *pureza de sangre* or blood purity, the reference to lineage emphasizing that *conversos* were not allowed to join nunneries. This episode, occurring so far from the rest of the story's action and anachronistically depicting aspects of the church that applied to Reinoso's own time, inscribes the Second Diaspora onto the vast geographies of the Greek romance while it emphasizes Spain's alterity for an author who once called the nation his home.

The references here, both intratextual and intertextual, are thick; Isea demonstrates her adeptness at crafting mythological narrative and at surviving her trials, and she also emphasizes her role in the events that befall her, a passibility that is reflected in her insistence on writing her story down for other women to read and pity. After being rejected by the convent, Isea, destitute and friendless, makes her way to the Ísla Pastoril, where she writes her story. In the opening of the narrative, Isea makes her purpose in writing clear: 'no pido remedio, sino piedad, si para mí ay alguna; pero yo soi çierta que en esta tierra no la ay, porque en otras ya podría ser que la hallasse y que muchos llorarían los trabajos de la sin ventura Ysea, que tan lexos agora de aquellas partes se halla' ('I don't ask for recourse but for pity, if there is any for me; but I'm certain that there is none in this land, though in other lands it may be possible that pity might be found and that many would cry over the trials of the luckless Isea' 1, 97). Unlike Philomela, Isea desires no revenge, only pity, and she seeks it by addressing a community of female readers, the 'piadosas y generosas señoras, a quien mis palabras endereço' ('pitying and generous ladies, to whom I direct my words' 1, 97). In addressing a group of female intended readers in her pointedly retrospective story, Isea seeks a community of readers that will sympathize with her exiled and lamentable state. Isea thus uses female narration for healing and comfort. The nine nymphs of her dream could represent the nine muses, and Isea's metamorphoses illustrate the transformative power of fiction-making.

In her final lament (also written from the Ísla Pastoril) Isea turns back to Spain in a gesture that both hints at the ekphrastic encoding of her exiled state and longs for a specifically Spanish audience to respond to her story. Isea exclaims:

> [e]ngañando mis trabajos con lo que escribo, como haze la donzella las largas noches con la tarea, biviendo aquí sin ser usada a estos çielos, ni a las aguas ni manjares destas tierras, sin tener persona ninguna a quien pueda contar mis males ni con quien descanse en mis trabajos, los cuales no quiero yo que en esta tierra tengan remedio, porque ansí no se detenga la muerte de mí tan deseada.
>
> Bien sé que si esta mi obra en algún tiempo aportare a las riberas del río Henares, que piadosamente será leýda, y mis penas sentidas y con razón lloradas.

> Disguising my trials with what I write, as does a girl on long nights with her needlework, dwelling here not used to these skies, nor to the food and drink of these lands, without having a single person to whom I might tell my woes or with whom I might take comfort in my trials, which I don't want to end in this land because that might delay the death that I so desire.
>
> Well do I know that if some day my story were to be carried to the shores of the Henares river, it would be read compassionately and my pains would be felt and lamented with great reason. (236)

The double entendre of *engañando* here (both distracting the speaker from her troubles and disguising a greater matter in women's work) illustrates how this woman's *tarea* (needlework), like that of Philomela, might encode her woeful story ekphrastically. As Barbara Fuchs observes, here Isea's 'repeated complaints about her wanderings and misfortunes give way to a far more direct lament for Spain' and 'strongly suggest [...] Reinoso's longing for his own unattainable homeland' (*Passing* 101). While this final reference to Spain, as Fuchs suggests, makes 'Reinoso's transformation of the Byzantine novel into a capacious fictionalization of the sorrows of exile and exclusion' (101), I add that it also reiterates the particular capacity of ekphrasis to encode the 'sorrows of exile and exclusion' passibly suffered by *conversos* like Reinoso. Poignantly, Isea's hope that her story will be carried back to Spain again emphasizes not only the speaker's (and author's) distance from that land, but also the desire that Spain attend to this lament. Perhaps this story might invoke pity because it could be read by those close to the author or those who shared his predicament, but perhaps also this turn of the intended audience from a group of receptive women at the story's opening to a specifically Spanish audience by its end reflects the Utopian wish that this romance might change the opinions of those who would expel *conversos* to the life of wandering and lamentation fictionalized in Isea's tale.

Though Reinoso's work has not yet enjoyed the same appreciation as its ancient model, *Clareo y Florisea* was popular enough to be translated immediately into Portuguese and French, and it likely influenced Cervantes's *Persiles*.[22] Reinoso's decision to translate and emulate Tatius in his romance demonstrates the substantial appeal of the Greek romance in the early modern period, and it shows an attentiveness to the possibilities of the genre to give a voice to underrepresented groups. Reinoso's astute election of Isea as narrator builds on what Tatius's text reveals only sylleptically: the cross-dressed narration of Melite reflects and echoes through the visual and verbal ekphraseis of not only Tatius's but also Reinoso's romance. Reinoso amplifies the seductive appeal of Melite with the creation of Isea, and he discloses his own set of subtle sylleptic possibilities in the ekphraseis with which he adorns his text. Ultimately, telling *Clareo y Florisea* from the perspective of the jilted lover unveils Tatius's cross-dressed narration and inscribes a new encryption in its sylleptic ekphraseis, the lamentations of Spanish *conversos*. Thus, intersections between *Clareo y Florisea* and *Leucippe and Clitophon* reveal significant developments in female first-person narration and self-representation in both ancient and early modern Greek romance.

3 Amazon Eyes and Shifting Emblems in Sidney's Greek *Arcadia*

> [S]aid Dorus smiling, 'Philoclea's hap I freely grant you; but I pray you let not your Amazon eyes be busy upon the lady Pamela, for her looks have an attractive power in them, and your heart is not of the hardest metal.'
>
> (*OA* 149)

When Sir Philip Sidney dedicated his *Arcadia* to his sister Mary Sidney Herbert, Countess of Pembroke, a writer, translator, and great patron of literature in her own right,[1] he wrote in a political environment in which a woman ruled England and invoked her kingly and princely power explicitly.[2] The women in Sidney's life doubtless influenced his female characters in the *Arcadia,* and the liveliness of their characterization, as Virginia Woolf observes, is tangible: 'Pamela and Philoclea, for all their sea-coloured satins and nets strung with pearls, are women and can love' (44).[3] Modelled in part on the female majesty embodied in Elizabeth I, the Arcadian heir apparent, Pamela 'of high thoughts' and 'majesty' (*NA* 1, 3, 76), supposedly became in turn a pattern for male monarchs. The *Eikon Basilike* related Charles I's appropriation of Pamela's prayer just prior to his beheading, emphasizing the exemplary status of Sidney's romance and ensuring its popularity with seventeenth-century royalists.[4] Even the leading man of the romance, Pyrocles, spends most of the narrative's time disguised as the woman-warrior, Zelmane.

With the *Arcadia*'s emphasis on strong female figures and cross-gender disguise, it is not surprising that the representation of gender has been of great interest to Sidneian scholars, who have considered the significance of gender identity in the romance from philosophical, humoral, and performative perspectives; but Sidney's characters do not fit well into the kinds of gender binaries that these discourses establish.[5] In a compelling reading of stoical female representation, Mary Ellen Lamb has called the valiant behaviour of female characters in the *New Arcadia* 'heroic constancy' (*Gender* 106) that 'offered its female audience a means through which they could perceive themselves as heroic' (112); but she avers that 'the cost of such heroism was high' for women and entailed the 'demise of the values of heroic valor' (106) for male characters. Attending to the *New Arcadia*'s reception of Greek romance and its ekphrastic modes can help to resolve this dilemma.

The gender positions of characters in the *Arcadia* can be located more accurately in generic and aesthetic terms. Rather than reading the exchange of gender roles as a moral problem that necessarily demotes masculine valour, I suggest that Sidney emulates Achilles Tatius's ekphrastic technique in the *New Arcadia* to represent gender identity as passible, allowing for the ambiguity of a 'third sex,' as Philoclea puts it (*OA* 206). Gender role reversals are, as the previous chapter has elaborated, a common feature of Greek romance, and shifts in gender can be traced through the emblematics of the self by examining how Sidney's characters create and interpret the ubiquitous visual signs that bedeck the *New Arcadia*.

Just as the Second Sophistic produced works that prescribed methods for writing and decoding verbal images in educational tracts, treatises on painting, and works of fiction, Elizabethans engaged in prescribed modes of visual literacy that were expected of courtiers. Ancient ekphraseis were attractive points of reprisal for Elizabethan authors, who delighted in moral emblems, heraldic devices, and personal *imprese*. Drawing on these courtly conventions to enhance what he learns from his Greek romance model, Sidney recontextualizes this ancient rhetorical mode into Elizabethan expectations of verbal image literacy. He employs ekphrasis to illuminate the passibility of his protagonists' gender identities and ultimately to emphasize female authority. This is especially evident in his *New Arcadia*, where Sidney adds vivid descriptions of paintings, *imprese*, and emblematic scenes, drawing on Tatius's romance for ekphrastic inspiration. Furthermore, he resets many of the descriptions that already existed in his *Old Arcadia* into the hands and mouths of female characters in the *New Arcadia*.

Sidney's description of dominant female figures and the increased focus on female perspectives in the *New Arcadia* corresponds with the Greek romance tradition and reflects the Elizabethan preoccupation with the rights of female princes, but Sidney's verbal images shift the gender identity of its male protagonists as well, 'conquering' them with the erotic force of these images. While Tatius's verbal pictures encode and portend gender ambiguity, Sidney's figures have their own erotic force. Focusing on ekphrastic examples from Kalander's painting gallery, a series of emblematic readings of the Hercules myth, and the emblem of Cupid, I contend that Sidney adapts Tatius's structural, proleptic, and sylleptic ekphrastic techniques and mirrors Tatius's passible figurations of male and female identity. Gender distinctions are drawn most forcibly in the tests of visual interpretation that challenge characters in the *New Arcadia*, where male characters are pictured as uncomprehending onlookers to proleptic and violent images and performances, and female characters are more apt to comprehend the messages that ekphraseis convey. Sidney eschews stable identities in favour of gender passibility to test the mettle of his protagonists – male and female alike. Yet Sidney's project remains incomplete, creating a literal aporia that can only be resolved at the hands of his 'most dear and most worthy to be most dear' sister (*OA* 1; *NA* 57), emphasizing female authority – albeit editorially – in the work.

Writing Greek Romance in English

Long stints in European cities such as Paris, Heidelberg, Venice, and Padua exposed Sidney to continental literary fashions, allowing him to address current literary debates in his *Defence of Poesy* and to access ancient works that were not necessarily available in England.[6] Sidney mentions Greek romances in his *Defence*, approving of Heliodorus's 'sugared invention of that picture of love Theagenes and Chariclea' (*Major Works* 218).[7] Sidney admired the Greek romance genre and could have easily read Latin or romance-language translations and imitations.[8] The Greek romance's themes of cross-dressed disguise and its emphasis on female characters are present from the *Arcadia*'s beginnings, but when Sidney revised his text, he abandoned the straightforward structure of the *Old Arcadia* in favour of the intricate narrative and *in medias res* beginning that characterize the *Aethiopica*. As one scholar puts it, 'Sidney has learned to write Greek Romance in English' (Wolff 353).

Though it has attracted less scholarly attention than the influence of Heliodorus, it is an accepted fact that Tatius's romance contributes to the *Arcadia*'s character models and plot content. Sidney might have read *Leucippe and Clitophon* in one of several translations.[9] He adds characters named Leucippe, Clitophon, and Clinias to the *New Arcadia*, but he was apparently familiar with Tatius's work from the *Arcadia*'s inception.[10] In both versions of Sidney's text, Queen Gynecia greatly resembles *Leucippe and Clitophon*'s jilted lover, Melite. The trial scene at the close of the *Old Arcadia* also imitates the *Leucippe*'s concluding trial scene in its characters and rhetoric. Moreover, Sidney borrows many of his plot elements in the revised *New Arcadia* from Tatius. For example, his false, staged executions both in the Cecropian Captivity episodes and in the episode of Antiphilus and Erona resemble the false deaths of the character Leucippe in Tatius's romance. The Antiphilus and Erona episode might also have been influenced by a similar trick in *Amadis de Gaula*, but the parallels warrant that *Leucippe and Clitophon* played a crucial role in Sidney's revisions.[11]

It is certain, moreover, that Sidney was closely associated with Tatius by his readers, as a translation of *The Loves of Leucippe and Clitophon* (1638) by Anthony Hodges attests. In the dedicatory material, references to and comparisons with Sidney come fast and furious. In the preface 'To the Ladies,' Tatius's text is categorized as like enough to the *Arcadia* to be a rival, and female readers are asked to 'lay by / Blessed Sidney's Arcady' (sig. A5v); Hodges proposes the translation as a story that will make the ladies 'not repent him to forsake' (sig. a3v). Furthermore, the note 'To the Translator' proclaims, 'The charming sweetnesse of your flowing quill, / Makes me hold Transmigration, and that still / Sydney's soule lives in you, else I am sure, / None could with such a pleasing grace allure' (sig. a4v), suggesting that the translator is literally a reincarnation of Sidney. Finally, in another section 'To the Translator' by a certain 'Roui,' the translation is compared with '[t]he godlike Sydneys workes' (sig. a4v). Here we have comparisons based on models of reading, translating, and writing to link Sidney and Tatius in the early modern English literary imagination.

Sidney's recasting of the *Arcadia* into the mould of Greek romance included many more amorous episodes, philosophical and political discussions, and, most importantly here, ornamental descriptions. Scholars acknowledge Heliodorus's influence in Sidney's reworking of his romance's structure,[12] but what is to be made of the increased complexity and number of the ekphraseis in Sidney's (re)vision? Tatius's *Leucippe and Clitophon*'s influence on Sidney is pivotal here.

Emblem and *Impresa*, Prolepsis and Syllepsis, or Making Pictures Speak Greek

Beyond his debt to Tatius for character and plot elements, Sidney also adopts Tatius's structural, proleptic, and sylleptic ekphrastic technique to craft his 'speaking pictures,' with an eye to creating an emblematics of gender ambiguity that impels multiple interpretations on the part of characters and historical readers. Crafted images in the *New Arcadia* – painted, woven, or sculpted – reflect similar images in *Leucippe and Clitophon*. They also demonstrate Sidney's familiarity with Elizabethan emblematic modes of ekphrastic interpretation.

Sidney engaged in a variety of early modern media that harnessed the tension between image and text to present veiled political and social critiques. He presented Elizabeth with his entertainment 'The Lady of May' in 1578 while at the Earl of Leicester's house at Wanstead, Essex.[13] The masque and other Elizabethan entertainments supply a sophisticated blend of theatrical performance, visual spectacle, and text to represent the courtiers' ambitions while venerating the monarch.[14] In this case, Sidney's entertainment may have been intended to warn Elizabeth against a proposed marriage to the French Duke of Anjou. Moreover, he invented his own personal *imprese* for politically suggestive entertainments such as 'The Triumph of the Four Foster Children of Desire,' in which he participated dressed in armour bearing a device of his own making.[15] Enacted before the queen and the French commissioners in May 1581, the three-day triumph again emphasizes Sidney's use of the image/text medium to express his views.

Delighting in books of emblems, heraldic devices, and personal *imprese*, Sidney inspired and participated in the development of these forms in England. Several books of emblems were dedicated to him and his circle, and as John Buxton argues, Sidney and his friends were responsible for popularizing continental modes of emblem and *imprese* at the Elizabethan court.[16] Sidney in fact not only commissioned emblem books but was well known for his wit and skill at creating his own *imprese*. At the end of his manual for the creation of *imprese*, which he dedicated to Sidney's brother Robert, Abraham Fraunce reproduces several examples of Philip Sidney's *imprese* as best examples of the form.[17] Posthumously praised as an ideal courtier, Sidney was skilled at painting *imprese* that certainly complied with Castiglione's recommendations in *The Courtier* that 'a knowledge of how to draw and an acquaintance with the art of painting itself' must 'in no way be neglected by our Courtier' (57). Moreover, along with his acquaintance with the miniaturist Hilliard and his familiarity with Renaissance treatises on painting, Sidney was fond enough of portraiture to think hard on which artist he would choose to paint his own portrait.[18]

No evaluation of the role of visual language in fiction should presume that an author needs a physical painting to 'paint' a verbal picture, and here it would be similarly foolhardy to assume that Sidney's stance towards actual works of art would be the same as his attitude towards verbal pictures. In fact, Sidney privileges what he calls 'speaking pictures,' as the basis of his poetics in his *Defence of Poesy*, explaining that 'Poesy therefore is an art of imitation: for so Aristotle termeth it in the word *mimesis,* that is to say, a representing, counterfeiting, or figuring forth – to speak metaphorically, a speaking picture – with this end, to teach and delight' (217). As Gavin Alexander observes, Sidney combines the principles of several ancient thinkers in an innovative manner to create his own definition of poetry, and the fact 'that the "speaking picture" of fiction appears to be the link between the author's act of representation and the teaching and delighting of the reader is an original touch' ('Introduction' lix). Sidney combines Aristotle's concept of mimesis and his emphasis on the need for vividness in the urbane style (*Rhet*. 3:10-11) with Plutarch's citation of Simonides' simile of the speaking picture ('De gloria' 500, 501), and with Horace's injunctions in the *Ars Poetica* that *ut pictura poesis* (just as it is in painting, so too in poetry) and his claim that the purpose of poetry is *aut prodesse* [...] *aut delectar* (to teach [...] and to delight). These three authorities are deeply engaged with intramedial comparisons as a basis for describing and prescribing poetry. Sidney's definition thus elevates ekphraseis or 'speaking pictures.'

The pictorial turn of Sidney's literary practice, moreover, was frequently lauded by his contemporaries and in his work's reception. Gabriel Harvey, for instance, gives Sidney the prize 'for pictorial skill exceeding that of Homer, Livy and Chaucer' (ct. Garrett 129) in a note in his manuscript of *De tribus scriptoribus epigramma*, and, later, in 'A New Letter of Notable Contents,' asks, 'Is not the Prose of Sir Philip Sidney, in his sweet *Arcadia*, the embrodery of finest Art, and daintiest Witt?' (131), thereby highlighting the pictorial vividness of Sidney's fiction. Furthermore, as Judith Dundas has convincingly argued, Sidney's work was a direct source of inspiration for Franciscus Junius the Younger's important treatise *The Painting of the Ancients* (1638).

Sidney's emphasis on the pictorial potential of language draws on literary models for its inspiration. Though Elizabethan England had a less lively painting tradition than was evident on the continent, Leonard Barkan reminds us that ekphrasis 'is passed on in an inheritance more from Homer, Ovid, and Petrarch than from Zeuxis, the Domus Aurea, and Botticelli. It is not a visual figure so much as a figure of speech, and like all tropes it is a lie. The specific figural activity is akin to prosopopoeia, that is, the bestowing of a voice upon a mute object; and the larger lie is that these pictures have a prior existence independent of the poet, who is ostensibly merely "describing" them' ('Making Pictures Speak' 332). Barkan's insistence on the rhetorical status of ekphrasis as always filling a lacuna, whether to bestow a voice on an image or to create a verbal picture where there is no image to begin with, emphasizes that ekphrasis is a trope of simultaneous absence (the physical work of art) and presence (the poetical invention), and reveals that the tension between the status of physical pictures and the creation of verbal pictures is, in fact, a fundamental aspect of crafting all verbal pictures, be they embedded in a culture that sanctions the visual arts or no. The relative lack of high visual arts in Elizabethan England simply serves to highlight the epistemological problem, and 'classical civilization [...] is nearly always the material for these exercises in visuality' (335). Elizabethan ekphrasis focuses specifically on reconstructing classical forms of visual language – such as that of Homer, Virgil, or, as I suggest, Tatius. Sidney figures forth images from antiquity through the Greek romancers who specialized in ekphrasis; nonetheless, he is not content to imitate, but pushes the sophistical form further, adapting it to Elizabethan cultural and political concerns with emblems of ambiguous gender that exert an erotic, gender-bending force and that test the viewer's powers of visual interpretation.

On a structural level, the ekphrastic amendments in the *New Arcadia* align the work's narrative more closely with that of Tatius's romance. Like *Leucippe and Clitophon*, the *New Arcadia*'s plot hinges on the viewing of a painting; it is essentially the outpouring of passion – *erotica pathemata* – that follows which drives the tale. As the reader will recall, the story of *Leucippe and Clitophon* is related after a stranger views a painting (the subject of which is later likened to Leucippe) alongside a handsome youth who is affected by the image. The first narrator asks the youth to tell his tale, and this narrative constitutes the romance. The princes similarly end up in Arcadia precisely because Pyrocles sees a painting of Philoclea, who, like Sidney's character Leucippe, makes her debut ekphrastically. In Sidney's revision, in fact, Kalander relates the *historia* of the painting, a passage that originally opened the *Old Arcadia,* but with pictorial markers to indicate the painting of the characters involved. When Musidorus sees the painting of the royal family in Kalander's gallery, he hesitantly asks about what the picture depicts. Kalander agrees to relate the tale: 'sitting down in two chairs and sometimes *casting his eye to the picture,* [Kalander] thus spake' (*NA* 1, 3, 75). The passage now includes pictorial deixis, which I emphasize, such as: 'Here dwelleth and reigneth this Prince (*whose picture you see*) by name

Basilius' (*NA* 1, 3, 75), who 'married a young princess, named Gynecia, daughter to the king of Cyprus, of notable beauty, *as by her picture you see*' (*NA* 1, 3, 76). What was the opening of the *Old Arcadia* becomes embedded in an ekphrastic description in the *New Arcadia*, emphasizing that skilled ekphrastic interpretation facilitates the decipherment of complicated social narratives.

Furthermore, Sidney adopts the Greek romance convention of inscribing ekphraseis with proleptic significance. To underscore the *Leucippe*'s ekphrastic contributions to Sidney's revision, it is appropriate that the character Leucippe makes her debut in the *New Arcadia* ekphrastically: her introduction is accomplished through a painting. Its description follows:

> The other [portrait of a woman], whose name was written Leucippe, was of a fine daintiness of beauty, her face carrying in it a sober simplicitie like one that could do much good & ment no hurt, her eyes having in them such a cheerfullness as nature seemed to smile in them; though her mouth and cheekes obeyed to that pretty demureness which the more one marked the more one would judge the poor soul apt to believe, & therefore the more pity to deceive her. (*NA* 1, 16, 159)

The ekphrasis provides clues about what will happen to the character that it depicts. Leucippe's lover, Pamphilus, eventually abandons her for Baccha, a whore, a deceit that is prefigured in the ekphrasis of her painting. Leucippe's portrait portends her tale of woe, and the antithetical imagery and rhetorical style of the ekphrasis emphasize the sophistical influence on Sidney's prose.

Most significantly here, Sidney adopts Tatius's brand of sylleptic ekphrasis to represent the mutability of gender identity. This can be illustrated in a comparison of Tatius's ekphrasis of the painting of Europa / Astarte with the first description of Sidney's character Pyrocles. As previously discussed, Tatius begins *Leucippe and Clitophon* with the viewing of a painting, a typical Greek romance convention. The ekphrasis can be read in at least two ways. In the first, Greek interpretation (that offered by the framing narrator), Europa is overcome by taurine Zeus and helplessly forced out to sea. In the second, Phoenician perspective, the marine goddess Astarte (to whom the painting is offered) assumes dominion over her consort, Bal, by riding him at sea. In the first, the male figure is dominant, in the second, the female. As I noted in chapter 2, Daniel Selden likens this ekphrastic technique to the rhetorical figure of syllepsis, a figure in which one word is taken to have two meanings si multaneously.

Syllepsis is typical of the literary style of the Second Sophistic, and it is especially apt for conveying passible identity in both ancient and Renaissance contexts. In his *Art of English Poesie* (1589), George Puttenham calls syllepsis 'Double Supply,' explaining:

> But if such want be in sundrie clauses, and of severall congruities or sence, and the supply be made to serve them all, it is by the figure Sillepsis, whom for that respect we call the [double supplie] conceiving, and as it were, comprehending under one, a supplie of two natures, and may be likened to the man that serves many masters at once, being of strange Countries or kindreds. (137)

Puttenham's definition of syllepsis not only emphasizes its versatility in conveying double meanings in the text, but relates the function of the trope to a multinational or multicultural position. The concept of syllepsis also works well to describe how a verbal image can accomplish what painted images of the Renaissance might convey through anamorphic effects. This sylleptic mode of ekphrasis serves both Tatius and Sidney well in expressing gender ambiguity.

In an ekphrastic passage reminiscent of Tatius's painting of Europa/Astarte, Sidney initially depicts Pyrocles, the young prince of Macedon, as both a brave young conqueror, like another Alexander, and a beautiful Greek youth, who 'if he were a man' is certainly in a dangerous rather than domineering position.[19] In the first book of the *New Arcadia*, Musidorus enlists the help of Arcadian shepherds to attempt a sea rescue of his cousin and best friend Pyrocles. As they approach the floating wreckage of Pyrocles' ship:

> upon the mast they saw a young man – at least if he were a man – bearing show of about eighteen years of age, who sat as on horse back, having nothing upon him but his shirt which, being wrought with blue silk & gold, had a kind of resemblance to the sea on which the sun (then near his Western home) did shoot some of his beams. His hair (which the young men of Greece used to wear very long) was stirred up & down with the wind, which seemed to have a sport to play with it as the sea had to kiss his feet; himself full of admirable beauty, set forth by the strangeness both of his seat & gesture. For holding his head up full of unmoved majesty, he held a sword aloft with his fair arm, which often he waved about his crown as though he would threaten the world in that extremity. (*NA* 1, 1, 66)

The description of Pyrocles, who has just survived a fire at sea only to be shortly picked up by pirates, sylleptically renders his pulchritude and pugnacity. His attitude and description reflect the attitude and description of Tatius's maid at sea. In spite of the destruction and gore that surround him, Pyrocles' stance is one of a young conqueror. Astride the mast as on horseback and sword aloft, he appears to 'threaten the world.' The conditional clause, 'at least if he were a man,' may imply that his stature is godlike, as is noted by the shepherds that assist Musidorus; but the clause, paired with the beauty of the young man, his long hair, and lack of britches, also indicates that he might be a woman and serves as a peek ahead to his Amazon disguise. This opening description of Pyrocles and the errant deeds that he performs before falling in love with Philoclea, Princess of Arcadia, would seem only to anticipate his subsequent effeminacy. The manly adventures that Pyrocles dared before the beginning of the *Arcadia*'s action, which he subsequently describes at length to impress Philoclea, portray Pyrocles' identity as active, adventurous, and masculine, but the fact that he tells her these stories while cross-dressed only underscores the change he has undergone.

As my analysis of Tatius's cross-dressed narration in chapter 2 illustrates, gender identity's dependence on ekphrastic signs and interpretation is a convention already present in the ancient romance. Greek romance represents the lover-protagonists as having a 'fully reciprocal passion between equals' (Konstan 33), and characters encounter images that depict the kinds of gender role reversals that often occur in these narratives. The relative equality of male and female protagonists in the ancient Greek model helps to enable the kinds of gender reversals upon which Sidney will build. In *The Care of the Self*, his third volume of *The History of Sexuality*, Foucault notes what he anachronistically deems 'heterosexual' orientations of love relationships in Greek romances, claiming that this configuration constitutes a 'new erotics' characterized by 'the existence of a heterosexual relationship marked by a male-female polarity' (228).[20] Foucault concludes: 'Thus there begins to develop an erotics different from the one that had taken its starting point in the love of boys, even though abstention from the sexual pleasures plays an important role in both. This new erotics organizes itself around the symmetrical and reciprocal relationship of a man and a woman, around the high value attributed to virginity, and around the complete union in which it finds perfection' (232). In the case of *Leucippe and Clitophon* and in the Greek romance as a whole, what Foucault reads as a switch from pederastic to heterosexual erotics is most salient in terms of its implications for the devaluing of one-sided or unequal relationships. Tatius and, I suggest, Sidney destabilize the protagonists' gender identities of woman as passive, beloved onlooker and man as active lover and author of the gaze by throwing these characters into situations that provoke behaviours that are not strictly speaking determined by their gender identity. Foucault views these trials as 'insofar as possible, symmetrical. Everything that happens to the one has its counterpart in the changes of fortune the other is made to undergo, which allows them to show the same courage, the same endurance, the same fidelity' (229). Foucault's observation is valid, as both protagonists are forced to suffer. This symmetrical suffering is meted out through an equal apportioning of reversed gender roles. Women in Greek romance endure physical torture and are brave in physically threatening situations, all with little help from their male counterparts. Men undergo emotional and psychological stress, they are forced into a situation of passible resistance when faced with an aggressive lover, and their gaze is perversely reversed such that they must become dumb or powerless onlookers to violent and threatening spectacles. The alteration in the male protagonist's purview repositions him from a conqueror of the female body through blazon and antiblazon into the position of the damsel in distress. These gender role reversals are further emphasized by disguises in the form of cross-dressing, compelling male protagonists to adopt literally the perspective of their female counterparts.

Along with Foucault's new erotics and its subsequent elaborations, recent work on formulations of the gaze in Tatius's romance also informs my understanding of the passibility of gender in these texts. In her monograph on *Leucippe and Clitophon*, Helen Morales claims that Tatius's text is 'profoundly ocularcentric' and 'a scopophiliac's paradise' (*Vision and Narrative* 9), and she explores gender formulations in *Leucippe and Clitophon* as they are mediated through the gaze.[21] Morales (32–3) investigates ancient forms of the masculine gaze of consumption (as if the beloved were food) and the gaze as objectification (seeing the beloved as art object) as two principal means by which (traditionally) male characters subject women scopically. Add to this the Renaissance colonialist gaze as a mark of masculinized superiority over feminized imaginings of colonized peoples, and Sidney has a copious metaphorics of the gaze at his fingertips both to describe visual experiences and to subvert expectations of their aesthetic responses.[22]

While I concur with Morales that formulations of the gaze are important in the construction of gender in the Greek romance tradition, I add that rhetorical strategies of ekphrastic creation and response expose passible formulations of gender identity. The emblematics of the self in these highly visual ancient and early modern texts provides me with a structural and formal means of opening up questions of cultural identity. I am most concerned here with how the viewing and interpretation of ekphraseis that encode gender ambiguity in Sidney's work evince acuteness or obtuseness of aesthetic sensitivity and, as we will see, can actually impress themselves on a passible or susceptible viewer's own gender position.

The Art of Reading Galleries

The *New Arcadia* includes a large array of mythological paintings enclosed in an ornamental garden house. Flanked by fountain and statuary, the paintings parallel the ones encountered by Leucippe and Clitophon in Pelusium. The painting of the Arcadian royal family is still the focal point of the episode as it was in the *Old Arcadia*, but in Sidney's revision, the artwork that surrounds the portrait situates the centrepiece painting's meaning and sets up a series of proleptic and sylleptic similes that foreshadow reversals of gender roles.

The ornamental house of artwork in the *New Arcadia* is adjacent to a beautiful garden that echoes the garden in Clitophon's father's house. Moreover, there are marked similarities between the statue and paintings in the *New Arcadia* and the statue and paintings that Leucippe and Clitophon encounter in a temple after their elopement. As Tomas Hagg observes in his assessment of Sidney's debt to Greek romance, 'The elaboration of these ekphraseis reveals that not only Heliodorus but also Achilles Tatius was on Sidney's reading list' (200). Sidney embellishes the garden and gallery in a style that reflects *Leucippe and Clitophon* specifically.

First, Sidney crafts a landscape to surround the gallery that resembles the garden in Clitophon's father's house.[23] Kalander's garden reflects Tatius's garden in several respects. The garden is the setting for Clitophon's first profession of love just as the garden house of Kalander is the location of Pyrocles' first pangs of love for Philoclea. Both gardens employ sophistical conceits to emphasize the location's sensuality. Both gardens are also orchards, and in both the landscaping is designed for an intertwined mosaic effect that relies on the erotically enmeshed positioning of trees, branches, flower beds, and light. The interdependence of the garden's plants, their carefully landscaped artfulness, as well as antitheses, parataxis, and other rhetorical techniques link these descriptions. Both Sidney and Tatius make use of erotic language to emphasize and foreshadow the delights of love to follow: for Clitophon, it is his encounter with Leucippe, and for Pyrocles, it is his viewing of the painted image of Philoclea.

The two gardens also share similar architectural features. They both contain a central pool that reflects the rest of the garden, emphasizing again the highly wrought ekphrasis as a work of verbal art that partakes of the visual image for its vivid effect. The description in the *Arcadia* follows: 'In the midst of all the place was a fair pond whose shaking crystal was a perfect mirror to all the other beauties, so that it bare show of two gardens; one in deed, the other in shadowes' (*NA* 1, 3, 73). In Clitophon's father's garden, 'In the midst of the flowers a fountain was spurting, and a square conduit for its stream had been traced around it by human hand. The water served as a mirror for the flowers, so that the grove seemed to be doubled, part real and part reflection' (Ach. Tat. 1, 15, 16). Both pools emphasize the artifice of the garden, while multiplying vividness through reflection, thereby delaying the erotic encounter. Clearly, the garden as *locus amoenus* is a commonplace of ancient, medieval, and Renaissance literature, but the similarities of these descriptions multiply as well.

Sidney and Tatius both include statues outside of their galleries that signal the proleptic significance of the paintings. In the *New Arcadia*,

> in one of the thickets was a fine fountain made thus: a naked Venus of white marble, wherein the graver had used such cunning, that the natural blue veins of the marble were framed in fit places, to set forth the beautiful veins of her body. At her breast she had her babe Aeneas, who seemed, having begun to suck, to leave that to look upon her fair eyes which smiled at the babe's folly, meanwhile the breast running. (*NA* 1, 3, 74)

In Pelusium, Leucippe and Clitophon enter a temple dedicated to Zeus Casius. They first find a statue of the god. Clitophon notes that

> The cult statue [of Zeus] is of a boy, looking rather like Apollo because of his similar age. His hand is stretched out and bears a pomegranate (the pomegranate has a mystic meaning). We were told that the god was an oracle, and so we addressed him in prayer [...]. Then we made a tour of the temple. (Ach. Tat. 3, 6, 47–8)

As Bartsch explains (61–2), the statue of Zeus in *Leucippe and Clitophon* is a sign that the paintings in the gallery are to be interpreted proleptically as the prophecy for which the characters pray. The 'mystic' meaning of the pomegranate foreshadows the importance of the images to follow. These paintings are the oracle that the lovers prayed for, though they do not recognize them as such.

The position and significance of the statue of Zeus Casius in the narrative of *Leucippe and Clitophon* sheds light on Sidney's marble Venus with suckling babe. The statue of Venus warns the reader that what will follow will have proleptic significance, perhaps mirroring the narratival prolepsis of the statue in *Leucippe and Clitophon*; nonetheless, instead of referring to religious rites and mythology alone, the statue of Venus and Aeneas reflects the role of images in yet another literary work of antiquity, Virgil's *Aeneid*. Venus guides her son Aeneas through his adventures (just as Love guides Pyrocles) and the subjugation of Aeneas to his fate is often demonstrated in his powerless and uncomprehending gaze when faced with proleptic images. Aeneas misinterprets the friezes in the temple to Juno in Carthage (Virgil 1, 454–93) as being favourable to his cause, exclaiming to his friend Achates, 'Solve metus; feret haec aliquam tibi fama salutem' ('Throw off your fear. This fame ensures some kind of refuge' 1, 463; trans. Fitzgerald 20).[24] Aeneas does not take into account the fact that these images appear in a temple to Juno, sworn enemy to the Trojans, and that this 'Fama' might not bode well for him and his crew. Later, he cannot fathom the meaning of the wrought images on the shield given to him by Venus that predict the future glory of Rome proleptically. Aeneas simply marvels at the arms ('miratur' 8, 619), and the shield – the texture of which is 'non enarrabile textum' ('beyond description' 625) – remains inscrutable to the hero.

Just as Aeneas is ignorant of the proleptic significance of images, Pyrocles is oblivious to what meaning Kalander's paintings have in store for him. Pyrocles, in fact, omits these marginal paintings entirely from his account of being transfixed by the painted cast of Philoclea's eye as he recounts the story of beholding her portrait and falling in love with her to his cousin Musidorus. As with the paintings in Pelusium, the decoding of these images becomes a game that is offered up to the careful reader. Hence, Sidney takes Tatius's invention and gives it a Renaissance twist, playing on his own audience's horizon of expectations with a reference to the *Aeneid*, a text that an early modern reader would have known well.

The paintings in Kalander's gallery, moreover, reflect the style and subject matter of the diptych painting that Leucippe and Clitophon encounter in Pelusium. The latter depiction is described as follows:

> a painting with two levels, signed by the artist, Euanthes. The painting represented Andromeda and Prometheus, both chained. This was the reason, I suppose, why the artist had combined the two subjects onto one canvas, but the situations depicted by the pictures were also akin in other respects: each victim had a rock as a prison; each had a beast as a torturer (his coming from the air, hers from the sea); their rescuers were both Argives, and related to each other, Heracles in the one case (who shot the bird sent by Zeus), Perseus in the other (who contended with the sea-monster sent by Poseidon). (Ach. Tat. 3, 6, 47)

Tatius's ekphrasis displays proleptic and sylleptic significance. An extension of the ekphrasis continues for several paragraphs, including details that foretell events in the romance's plot and emphasize the gender reversals that the lovers will undergo as a part of their trials. The prophecy that Clitophon and Leucippe seek by praying to the statue is contained in the paintings that they view and that Clitophon describes. Neither Leucippe nor Clitophon understands the images' significance, despite the fact that they later acknowledge the potential for paintings to function as prophecies (Ach. Tat. 5, 4, 79). The diptych painting does foreshadow the lovers' difficulties, but not before activating a number of possible interpretations by characters and readers.

Kalander's gallery in the *New Arcadia* similarly offers a group of mythological paintings that encode proleptic significance. The gallery is

> full of delightful pictures made by the most excellent workman of Greece. There was Diana when Actaeon sawe her bathing, in whose cheeks the painter had set such a colour, as was mixed between shame and disdain; & one of her foolish Nymphs, who weeping, and withal louring, one might see the workman meant to set forth tears of anger. In another table was Atalanta, the posture of whose limbs was so lively expressed, that if the eyes were the only judges as they be the only seers, one would have sworn the very picture had run. Besides many more, as of Helena, Omphale, Iole [...] (*NA* 1, 3, 74)

Mirroring Tatius's inclusion of the Greek artist's name, Euanthes, Sidney establishes the paintings' authority as being 'made by the most excellent workman of Greece.'

Furthermore, Kalander's paintings are set forth in a sophistical style reminiscent of Tatius's ekphraseis. The depiction of Diana, 'in whose cheeks the painter had set such a colour, as was mixed between shame and disdain,' and her 'foolish' Nymphs, 'who weeping, and withal louring, one might see the workman meant to set forth tears of anger,' reflects the painting of Andromeda, whose face shows multiple emotions:

> [T]he fear resided in her cheeks, while the beauty bloomed from her eyes. Yet her pallid cheeks were not altogether without colour, tinged as they were with a gentle blushing; nor were her florid eyes without anxiety, resembling as they did violets in the first stage of wilting. Such was the comely fear with which the artist had embellished her. (Ach. Tat. 3, 6, 47)

The two depictions share variegated colours and varied emotional expressions, heightened by the explicitness of these characteristics being expressed as painterly effects. Both authors also express the lifelike quality of their ekphraseis, as the Arcadian narrator describes: 'Atalanta, the posture of whose limbs was so lively expressed, that if the eyes were the only judges as they be the only seers, one would have sworn the very picture had run.' Compare Sidney's description with Tatius's painting of Andromeda: 'The rock was hollowed out enough to fit the maiden. This cleft seemed to say: "No human hand made me: this painting is the spontaneous creation of nature!" For the artist had roughened the pleats of the stone, just as it is when the earth has given birth to it' (Ach. Tat. 3, 6, 47). Both Sidney and Tatius dwell on the lifelike aspects of the paintings that they describe, calling attention to their own rhetorical skill at writing vivid prose. Finally, the last two paintings in Kalander's gallery represent adventures of Hercules as does Tatius's painting of the hero freeing Prometheus. These elements of style and content certainly suggest that the *Leucippe* may have influenced Sidney in the creation of the paintings in the *New Arcadia,* but of more importance is the fact that both sets of paintings provide a coded prolepsis for the narrative that is ignored or misunderstood by the characters. Each of the paintings in Kalander's gallery shows a scene in which goddesses or women control men and bring them sorrow or trials. These paintings provide Pyrocles with a warning of his coming feminization.

Readers of Sidney's time were attuned to the possible significance of these 'speaking pictures' as allegorical and proleptic devices in the *New Arcadia* along with their association with the verbal pictures of Tatius; this is evident from Abraham Fraunce's *The third part of the Countesse of Pembrokes Yuychurch Entitled, Amintas dale ...* (1592). This is the only part of the *Ivychurch* that was not a hybrid translation of Tasso's *Aminta* and Watson's Latin poem *Aminta*. Fraunce, a member of the Sidney circle and a recipient of both Philip and Mary Sidney's patronage, has an augmented cast of characters from the *Aminta* explicate mythological stories through ekphrasis and ekphrastic interpretation amounting to a kind of *Ovide moralisé* translated into an Elizabethan humanist system of writing and reading verbal images. *Amintas Dale* contextualizes Sidney's ekphrastic technique. In Fraunce's text, a number of interlocutors, including Elpinus, a painter of devices, discuss the 'speaking pictures' (Sidney's term) of ancient mythology including descriptions of Diana, Atalanta, and Omphale, all of which are taken from Ovidian sources and which echo Kalander's paintings. Elpinus borrows from Sidney's *Defence* directly (including his praise of the *Aethiopica* and other Greek romances). As Fraunce's text is not readily available in a modern edition, I cite the passage at length here:

> Poets and Painters (men say) may well goe together, sith pen and pencill be both alike free, and doo equally challeng the selfe same prerogative [...] When I talke of Painters, I meane not the ridiculous fraternitie of silly Wall-washers: neither doe I ever once thinke of our loftie rimers, when I make mention of Poets. Yet a wall may bee colored by an elegant Painter, but the conceite and elegancie is more then the colour: and poets (seeking as well to please, as to profit) have well made choyce of verse, yet the making of a verse is no part of Poetrie: otherwise, the sweete and inimitable poeme of Heliodorus, should be no Poeme, and every unreasonable rimer should weare a Lawrell garland. Both poetry, a speaking picture, and paynting, a dumbe poetry, were like in this, that the one and the other did under an amyable figure and delightsome veyle, as it were, cover the most sacred mysteries of auncient philosophie. Nay, Pythagoras himselfe by his symbolicall kinde of teaching, as also Plato by his conceited parables and allegoricall discourses in his bookes called, Phoedrus, Timoeus, and Symposium, may make any man beleeve, that as the learned Indians, Aethiopians, and Aegyptians kept their doctrine religiously secret for feare of prophanation, so the Grecians by their example, have wrapped up in tales, such sweete inventions, as of the learned unfolder may well be deemed wonderfull though to a vulgar conceit, they seeme but frivolus imaginations [...] the picturing, fashioning figuring, or, as it were, personall representing of things in verse after this manner, is most effectuall and avayleable, to move mens mindes, to stirre up delight, to confirme memorie, and to allure and entice our cogitations by such familiar and sensible discourses, to matters of more divine and higher contemplation. Poeticall songs are Galeries set forth with varietie of pictures, to hold every mans

> eyes, Gardens stored with flowers of sundry savours, to delite every mans sence, orchyards furnished with all kindes of fruite, to pleaseth every mans mouth. He that is but of a meane conceit, hath a pleasant and plausible narration, concerning the famous exploites of renowned Heroes, set forth in most sweete and delightsome verse, to feede his rurall humor. They, whose capacitie is such, as that they can reach somewhat further then the external discourse and history, shall finde a morall sence included therein, extolling vertue, condemning vice, every way profitable for the institution of a practicall and common wealth man. The rest, that are better borne and of a more noble spirit, shall meete with hidden mysteries of naturall, astrologicall, or divine and metaphysicall philosophie, to entertaine their heavenly speculation. That this is true, let us make triall [...] (sig. B1v–B2r)

The connections of *ut pictura poesis* between Sidney's *Defence* and Fraunce's text are obvious, Fraunce having lifted phrases and entire passages from Sidney, but Fraunce's articulation of 'speaking pictures' comes as an injunction to learn to write ekphrastically and demonstrates the sophisticated negotiation of verbal images in Elizabethan poetics. To different types of people are attributed varying abilities to interpret verbal pictures, and Fraunce's characters set out to interpret ekphraseis. Here, ekphrastic poetry is likened to the pictographs and enigmatic hieroglyphics of 'learned Indians, Aethiopians, and Aegyptians' (sig. b1v) as a pictorial allegorical mode that is adopted by 'Greek' poets and encodes hidden meanings in visual signs. Fraunce's *Amintas Dale* helps us to understand the Elizabethan reception of Sidney's Arcadian 'speaking pictures,' not only because Fraunce was a member of the Sidney circle, but also because he was a close reader of the *Arcadia* – both in its manuscript form (*Old Arcadia*), as is evident from his having written his *Arcadian Rhetoric* (1588) based on exempla from one of the *Old Arcadia* manuscripts, and also in its published form (the *New Arcadia*), as is shown by his having dedicated *Amintas Dale* to Sidney's sister after the 1590 *New Arcadia* was in print.

Fraunce's characters render – among many others – the mythological verbal pictures of Atalanta, Diana, Helen, Omphale, and Iole that make their painted appearance in Kalander's gallery. Moreover, one of the 'speaking pictures' that Elpinus explicates is taken from Achilles Tatius's *Leucippe and Clitophon* specifically. Explaining the myth of Syrinx and Pan in painterly terms (Pan being described in detail), Elpinus says, 'The tale is told by Ovid, and Achilles Statius' (sig. D1r). The story of the pan pipes is figured in the final book of the *Leucippe*. Fraunce's use of this exemplum supports my view that *Leucippe and Clitophon* was an authoritative source and model for crafting such mythological ekphraseis and for prescribing the verbal images' reception through a sophisticated method of humanist Elizabethan image-reading.

The mythological paintings in Sidney's text alongside Fraunce's guide for reading ekphrastically show that Elizabethans were engaging in an ekphrastic mode of humanist allegorical reading that, while it encompasses the medieval tradition of *allegoresis*, reaches back to ancient sources for its rhetorical figures and style. This ekphrastic brand of *allegoresis* may, in fact, be an integral aspect in the writing and reading of romance from the Second Sophistic through Western romance traditions, the ekphrastic aspect of which adds another level of possible meaning to narratival complexity and emblematic characterization. Illuminating romance characters' identity by means of their reactions to the fictional pictures and world that surround them demonstrates that identity in the early modern period is very much a function of community, including the environs of the visual and verbal art in which characters are embedded and the signs which they must learn to interpret.

Furthermore, Sidney uses ekphraseis in his *Arcadia* to contemplate gender specifically. In a monarchy ruled by a woman who nonetheless emphatically invoked her kingly power, male aristocrats were constantly asked to interpret the often complicated self-representations that Elizabeth presented to her followers. A poor interpreter of these signs might end up politically defeated, as did Sidney himself on several occasions. All of the Ovidian painted myths in Kalander's gallery depict powerful women or goddesses who have subjected the men around them, with the exception of the painting of Atalanta. Of course, the story of a defeated Amazon does not signify a happy ending for Pyrocles, as he adopts the costume of an Amazon. Each myth depicted has at least one corresponding episode in the *New Arcadia*'s plot, and each painting invites a series of interpretations and possible meanings.

Cross-Dressed Hercules and the Emblematics of the Self

The gender trouble in Arcadia begins in earnest when Pyrocles is 'conquered' – as he puts it – by viewing Philoclea's painting (*NA* 1, 13, 141). Pyrocles sees the canvas portraying the Arcadian royal family (minus Pamela), with King Basilius, his wife Gynecia, and Philoclea. In recounting how 'were [his] eyes infected' (*NA* 1, 13, 140), Pyrocles describes his passible response to the image's erotic influence. At first he resists the knowledge of his love, and feigns an interest in the skill of the painter as an explanation for his fixation, as he recalls to Musidorus:

> Yet did I not, poor wretch, at first know my disease, thinking it only such a wonted kind of desire to see rare sights, & my pity to be no other but the fruits of a gentle nature [...] Desirous I was to see the place where she remained, as though the Architecture of the lodges would have been much for my learning; but more desirous to see herself, to be judge, forsooth, of the painter's cunning – for thus at the first did I flatter myself, as though my wound had been no deeper. But when within short time I came to the degree of uncertain wishes and that those wishes grew to unquiet longings; when I could fix my thoughts upon nothing but that within little varying they should end with Philoclea; when each thing I saw seemed to figure out some part of my passions [...] then, indeed, then I did yield to the burden, finding my self prisoner, before I had leisure to arm myself, & that I might well, like the spaniel, gnaw upon the chain that ties him, but I should sooner mar my teeth than procure liberty. (*NA* 1, 13, 140–1)

The desire to see 'rare sights' aligns with the colonialist gaze mentioned earlier, but Pyrocles knows that his desire to conquer is only a pretence. Interest in 'the painter's cunning' is another rationalization on his part, but this cunning quite literally does affect the young prince, causing his subjugation.[25]

Pyrocles' 'disease' is figured in Neoplatonic terms and refers to early modern medical and philosophical ideas about the symptoms of falling in love. The infection, moreover, enters through his soon to be Amazon eyes, emphasizing the role of viewing in the passibility of gender. Having 'yield[ed] to the burden' of love and 'finding [him]self prisoner, before [he] had leisure to arm [him]self' is an image of being unmanned, and this destabilization happens precisely through his aesthetic susceptibility. No longer a young prince ready to conquer the world, Pyrocles has been reduced to a captive spaniel, a frequent motif in love emblems. His overthrow leads Pyrocles to cross-dress as the Amazon Zelmane to gain access to the princess, after which point he is referred to as 'she,' imprinting the gender shift in the narrative. Seeing sexy sights induces metamorphoses frequently in Greek mythology – the myth depicted in Kalander's gallery of Actaeon and Diana, for example – and erotic marvels can also induce gender transformations, as is the case in Ovid's version of Tiresias's story in the *Metamorphoses*, in which the sight of two snakes copulating in the woods 'viro factus (mirabile) femina septem egerat autumnos' ('from a man made him (a marvel to behold) into a woman for seven years' 3, 324–5).[26] Encounters with erotic verbal images also change gender identity in the *New Arcadia*.

The paintings of Hercules with Omphale and Iole in Kalander's gallery are significant to the emblematic situation of gender in Sidney's romance.[27] The brooch that Pyrocles wears in the *New Arcadia* depicts Hercules' enslavement to Omphale, pinning down his disguise and providing a lynchpin for his metamorphosis. In a sumptuous description of Pyrocles/Zelmane's new attire – in which coronet resembles helmet, doublet resembles buckler, and stockings resemble greaves – Pyrocles' Amazon disguise is described sylleptically in terms that reflect the anamorphic or curious perspective of art.[28] The two descriptions of Pyrocles' costume are almost identical in the *Old* and *New Arcadia*. One significant exception is that Musidorus, instead of helping Pyrocles into the disguise of Cleophila as he does in the *Old Arcadia*, finds Pyrocles/Zelmane already cross-dressed in a grove, altering the narrator's description in the *Old Arcadia* into a rendering charged with the voyeurism of Musidorus's gaze in the *New Arcadia*, thereby feminizing Pyrocles further.[29] Musidorus sees

> the hanging of her hair in fairest quantity in locks, some curled & some as it were forgotten, with such a careless care & an art so hiding art that she seemed she would lay them for a pattern whether nature simply or nature helped by cunning be the more excellent: the rest whereof was drawn into a coronet of gold richly set with pearl, and so joyned all over with gold wires and covered with feathers of divers colors that it was not unlike to an helmet, such a glittering show it bare, & so bravely it was held up from the head. Upon her body she ware a doublet of sky-color satin, covered with plates of gold, & as it were, nailed with preciouse stones that in it she might seem armed, the nether parts of her garment was so full of stuffe & cut after such a fashion, that though the length of it reached to the ankles, yet in her going one might sometimes discerne the small of her leg, which with the foot, was dressed in a short pair of crimson velvet buskins, in some places open, as the ancient manner was, to show the fairness of the skin. Over all this she ware a certain mantle made in such manner, that coming under her right arm and covering most of that side, it had no fastening on the left side but only upon the top of her shoulder, where the two ends met and were closed together with a very rich jewel (*NA* 1, 1, 130–1)

Drawn 'with more curious hand,' each of Pyrocles' garments is sylleptically rendered to resemble a piece of armour, emphasizing her Amazon identity, but also underscoring her double-gendered status.[30]

Sidney shifts the device of Pyrocles' pin from an *impresa* of dove and eagle in the *Old Arcadia* to an intratextual allusion that firmly establishes the importance of the paintings in Kalander's gallery as proleptic devices in the *New Arcadia*. Sidney makes an explicitly Greek reference in the crafting of this pin in his revision, anchoring Pyrocles/Zelmane's vestments and emblematizing the gender shift that he/she has undergone. The *impresa* depicts Hercules' enslavement to Omphale, as alluded to in Kalander's gallery.[31] The device is described as follows:

> A Hercules made in little form, but set with a distaff in his hand, as he once was by Omphale's commandment, with a worde in Greek but thus to be interpreted, 'Never more valiant'. On the same side, on her thigh shee ware a sword which, as it witnessed her to be an Amazon, or one following that profession, so it seemed but a needless weapon, since her other forces were without withstanding (*NA* 1, 12, 131)

The pin can be viewed as a *mise-en-abyme*. Just as the cross-dressed Hercules has relinquished his club in favour of doing women's needlework, the once valiant sword that Pyrocles had 'held aloft' has become a 'needles weapon.'[32] The Elizabethan spelling of 'needles' in Sidney's original is standard and a pun on needle-work. The brooch functions as a personal *impresa*. According to Renaissance traditions, personal *imprese* were said to have a body (the image) and a soul (the motto), and, coming from the word *imprendere*, they were devised to express the intentions of the wearer. As Samuel Daniel's translation of Giovio explains, 'this figure & mot together is called an Impresa, made to signifie an enterprise, wherat a noble mind leveling with the aime of a deepe desire, strives with a stedy intent to gaine the prise of his purpose' (sig. A6r). Fitting Daniel's advice, Zelmane's *impresa* has 'a posie which is the soule of the body, which ought to differ in language from the Idioma of him which beareth the Impresa' (sig. B3v). The soul in the Hercules *impresa* is ambiguous – so too the gender of the cross-dressed body of Hercules. Should the motto 'never more valiant,' whose Greek original is omitted, be interpreted as valiant never more, or never had he been more valiant? The poem that Pyrocles sings, 'Transform'd in Show, but more transform'd in mind' (*NA* 1, 12, 131), follows the description of his Amazon costume and transforms the description into a verbal emblem, a difference between *imprese* and emblems being the requirement of an explicatory poem accompanying image and motto. The poem, nonetheless, only serves to emphasize the ambiguity of Pyrocles' condition, amplifying the sylleptic quality of the *impresa* rather than resolving it. The choice of the Hercules *impresa* implies that Pyrocles was more impressed by the full array of paintings in Kalander's gallery than he conveyed to Musidorus, but also that he has ignored their warnings. How should this feminization of a hero be viewed? As an admirable sacrifice to love or as serious folly? This episode of Hercules' life, after all, is a penance for one of his murderous rages.

Images of Hercules cross-dressed with Omphale were popular in Renaissance paintings and in emblem books, some of which Sidney doubtless knew. Katherine Duncan-Jones remarks ('Sidney and Titian' 7) that Zelmane's Hercules device echoes Sidney's telling of the Hercules and Omphale story in the *Defence*, and she suggests that Sidney might have crafted this description based on a painting by Bartholomäus Spranger (figure 3.1), which he could have seen as ambassador to the court of Emperor Rudolf in Vienna in the spring of 1577. A physical source in the form of a particular painting is less important than the significance of the figured story itself for the *New Arcadia*'s plot, but the Spranger image with its early mannerist style is certainly striking.

A similar representation of Hercules' enslavement in *Leucippe and Clitophon*, though not the description of a painting, demonstrates the exchange and subsequent reversal of gender roles implied in the device. Clitophon speaks his first words of love to Leucippe in his father's garden, stating, 'a certain one of the gods has sold me into servitude to you, as Heracles was sold to Omphale.' Leucippe cleverly replies, '"Are you referring to Hermes? It was to him that Zeus entrusted the sale of Heracles." (She said this with a laugh.)' Clitophon, put off by her cleverness, replies, 'Hermes? What is this nonsense? You know very well what I mean' (Ach. Tat. 2, 6, 23). Here Leucippe flirts, but she also proves Clitophon's avowal by showing that she is his rhetorical master. Clitophon, of course, refers to Eros, but Leucippe teases him by reminding him that it was Hermes who was commissioned with the sale.[33] Thus, Leucippe proves that she is not only a better flirt, but also a better reader of the myth.

Interpretations of this *impresa* by the characters that surround Pyrocles also emphasize questions of gender in ekphrastic creation and interpretation, for female characters are depicted as better interpreters of images than men. Unlike Pyrocles, Queen Gynecia is an apt interpreter of signs.

3.1. Bartholomäus Spranger, *Herkules und Omphale*, c. 1585, copper, 24 x 19 cm. Kunsthistorisches Museum, Vienna.

When Pyrocles/Zelmane kills the lion, 'Gynecia swore she saw the very face of the young Hercules killing the Nemean lion' (*NA* 1, 19, 180). Gynecia's acute observation probes deeper than Zelmane imagines, and it is Gynecia who first identifies Zelmane the Amazon as a cross-dressed man. King Basilius, on the other hand, is a poor interpreter of signs. Not only does he misinterpret the prophecy of the oracle at Delphi, which leads him to sequester his family far from the Arcadian court, but he cannot decipher Pyrocles/Zelmane's cross-dressed device. The painting of Iole in Kalander's gallery prefigures Basilius's ignorance and impotence, but even in the *Old Arcadia* Basilius expresses his love to the cross-dressed Pyrocles in Herculean terms, crying,

> 'O Hercules,' answered he, 'Basilius afraid! Or his blood cold that boils in such a furnace! [...] O let me be but armed in your good grace, and I defy whatsoever there is or can be against me! No, no, your love is forcible, and my age is not without vigour.' (*OA* 456)

The 'O Hercules' is simultaneously an oath and a possible epithet for Zelmane, a double meaning which again evokes the Hercules myth for the reader, but in this case, Basilius has unwittingly compared himself to Iole. In the *Old Arcadia,* in fact, Basilius gets into bed with the cross-dressed Pyrocles thinking she is Gynecia, as Pyrocles has devised:

> [H]e came lifting up the clothes as gently as I think poor Pan did, when, instead of Iole's bed, he came into the rough embracing of Hercules; and laying himself down, as tenderly as a new bride, rested a while with a very open ear, to mark each breath of his supposed wife. (*OA* 494)

Basilius is duped in much the same way as Pan was tricked into thinking that he was getting into bed with Iole, whereas his bedfellow was actually Hercules.[34]

This emblematic exchange, while it emphasizes the passibility of Pyrocles in his feminization, also demonstrates the susceptibility of his beloved through an equal reapportioning of gender roles. Sidney modifies the centrepiece of Kalander's gallery in his revised version, augmenting Philoclea's role in its creation and, thereby, giving her a more dominant role in her conquest of Pyrocles. In the *New Arcadia,* Philoclea commissions her own picture as a testament to the injustice of her captivity, which she views as resulting from a suspicion of her chastity. Kalander explains that the painting 'was made by Philoclea, the younger daughter of his prince who also with his wife were contained in that table, the painter meaning to represent the present condition of the young lady, who stood watched by an over-curious eye of her parents' (*NA* 1, 3, 74). Philoclea's commission of the painting emblematizes the text that she has inscribed on a marble stone (*NA* 2, 4, 241), but the meaning of the visual and verbal texts shifts by book 2 of the romance. Rather than protecting her chastity, the painting attracts Pyrocles. When Philoclea comes upon the stone, the narrator explains that 'a few days before Zelmane's coming, [she] had written these words upon it, as a testimony of her mind against the suspicion her captivity made her think she lived in' (*NA* 2, 4, 241). Complementing her intentions in her commission of the painting, Philoclea writes the vow as a testament to her chastity. Nevertheless, just as the painting's chaste intent transforms into a powerful and seductive cast of Philoclea's painted eye, the force of which pierces the painting's frame to 'conquer' Pyrocles' 'infected eyes,' once Zelmane enters Arcadia, the poetry written on the marble stone has faded and smudged: the 'ink was already foreworn, and in many places blotted' (*NA* 2, 4, 242), testifying that Philoclea's thoughts are no longer chaste. The vow of chastity has bled and exceeds the limits of its prescription, and now functions as a proof of Philoclea's powerful passions' triumph over her vow. As Philoclea exclaims, '"Alas" said she, "fair Marble, which never received'st spot but by my writing, well do these blots become a blotted writer"' (2, 4, 242). Philoclea is able to read the change in her own emotional state in the decay of her vow, both in its now blurred image and in the irrelevance of its intent. Though Philoclea composes a poem on the spot that depicts her 'woman's hand' as weaker than the 'constant stone' (2, 4, 242), she 'could not see means to join as then this recantation to the former vow' (*NA* 2, 4, 242), perhaps for lack of a writing implement, but also, certainly, because her self-image no longer fits in the frame of chastity that she had previously emblematized. It is not the white marble which has conquered her vow (though it does endure); rather it is the working of nature, implying that it would not have been natural for Philoclea to remain a virgin until death.

As Zelmane enters the picture the text on the stone blurs as do gender boundaries. Philoclea's susceptibility is figured scopically, for she bemoans how 'the sight of this strange guest invaded my soul' (2, 4, 242), and this 'strange' sight, much like Tiresias's *mirabile* (a wonder to behold) metamorphoses, would seem not only to have altered her views on chastity but has, much like Pyrocles' experience of viewing

Philoclea's image, shifted her gender position as well. By the episode of the blotted vow of chastity, which marks the point at which both Pyrocles and Philoclea have inwardly acknowledged their desires, 'as Zelmane did often eye her, she would often eye Zelmane' (2, 4, 239). Philoclea's affection for Zelmane has moved beyond her desire to imitate the Amazon as a model for womanly behaviour and sisterly affection and becomes categorically sexual in nature.[35] In assessing her feelings for Zelmane, who she does not suspect is a man, 'grown bolder, [Philoclea] would wish either herself or Zelmane a man, that there might succeed a blessed marriage betwixt them' (2, 4, 239). Philoclea's sexual desire becomes explicitly masculine. Zelmane's look is described as 'submissive, but vehement,' whereas Philoclea's gaze is 'piercing' (2, 4, 239). The passibility of gender identity is pictured through the characters' interactions with verbal images, and the turns of the plot continue to task them with Herculean trials.

Cecropia, in weaving her plot to usurp her brother-in-law Basilius's kingdom from him by kidnapping and forcing one of his daughters to marry her son Amphialus, gives her own final interpretation of the Hercules myth in order to manipulate her son's moral and political decisions, and her interpretation reveals her vile character. The depiction of Iole in Kalander's gallery foreshadows Cecropia's plans. She explains to her son that

> Iole had her own father killed by Hercules, and herself ravished, by force ravished, and yet ere long this ravished and unfathered Lady could sportfully put on the Lion's skin upon her own fair shoulders, and play with the club with her own delicate hands: so easily had she pardoned the ravisher that she could not but delight in those weapons of ravishing. (*NA* 3, 17, 533)

Cecropia perversely conflates the two aspects of the Hercules myth discussed above in order to convince Amphialus to rape Philoclea, whom Cecropia has captured. Though she can manipulate the myth, she ultimately cannot control her son: Amphialus rejects violence. The Iole story marks the darker side of the Hercules myth and reveals Cecropia's villainy.

The episode in which Cecropia takes Pamela, Philoclea, and the cross-dressed Pyrocles prisoner illustrates the stoical strength of female characters and underscores the inability of male characters to interpret visual signs accurately. Faced with torture, the princesses prove their strength through eloquent stoical speeches and a refusal to bow to their aunt's threats. The gruesome spectacles which Cecropia calls a 'new play' (3, 21, 557) force Pyrocles helplessly to watch both Pamela and Philoclea suffer horrible staged deaths, which he believes to be real. Moreover, these spectacular episodes echo Tatius's predilection for falsely gutting and beheading Leucippe.

As the captivity persists, the view that 'its revaluation of femininity does not completely remove the stigma of effeminacy for males' (Lamb, 'Exhibiting Class' 60) seems possible, since neither Musidorus's siege outside the castle walls nor Pyrocles' plots from within (Achilles' and Odysseus's *modi operandi* respectively) have broken Cecropia's advantage. But, before the revision terminates, Musidorus and Pyrocles (still in his Amazon disguise) are on their way to victory, and Pyrocles regains his name and masculine pronoun as well. The final conflict demands that Pyrocles, Pamela, and Philoclea escape the clutches of a villain named Anaxias and his two brothers. As Zelmane, 'she' tricks the youngest, disarms him, and nearly manages to 'cut him asunder' (*NA* 3, 28, 590). As Zelmane, 'she' disarms, vanquishes, and denies mercy to the second, in the fashion of Aeneas's killing of Turnus (the final act being inspired by Philoclea's bracelet rather than Paris's belt) (3, 28, 592). But when faced with her final foe, the hero-heroine is Pyrocles:

> Pyrocles, whose soul might well be separated from his body but never alienated from the remembering what was comely, if at the first he did a little apprehend the dangerousness of his adversary (whom once before he had something tried, and now perfectly saw as the very picture of forcible fury) yet was that apprehension quickly stayed in him, rather strengthening than weakening his virtue by that wrestling, like wine growing the stronger by being moved. So that they both, prepared in hearts and able in hands, did honor solitariness there with such a combat as might have demanded, as a right of fortune, whole armies of beholders. But no beholders needed there, where manhood blew the trumpet, and satisfaction did whet as much as glory. (*NA* 3, 28, 593)

Moved by the 'picture of forcible fury,' Pyrocles regains his masculine identity. Though Sidney never finished this battle, his narrator assures that there are 'no beholders needed there, where manhood blew the trumpet.' This final shift from Zelmane back to Pyrocles in no way diminishes the female valour that Pyrocles as the Amazon Zelmane has blazed. Whether Hercules or Omphale, Sidney's hero is valorous.

A fitting emblematic source for the conflict and ambiguity of Sidney's romance, the Hercules myth was used in English educational plans for moral instruction. Hercules *in bivium*, Hercules at the crossroads, for instance, was the preferred emblem for figuring a moral choice. Though romance's capacity for moral instruction was certainly a preoccupation for Renaissance romancers, mostly in reaction to the genre's historical vilification, didactic estimations of the genre have their limits.[36] I believe that Sidney's romance does accomplish Horace's injunction that literature *aut* [...] *prodesse aut delectare*, should instruct [...] and should delight, but we should judge the lessons on Sidney's terms. He advocates in his *Defence* the sweetness of literature – a 'medicine of cherries' (227) – for moral instruction. Since poetry 'nothing affirmeth' (235) in Sidney's schema, it is not appropriate to judge how well it teaches based on how well it fits on to the scaffold of institutionalized early modern pedagogy; his lessons are more lively in nature and draw naturally on the popular emblem and *imprese* traditions. The Omphale and Iole paintings in Kalander's house would have signalled to an Elizabethan reader the gender ambiguity and reversals to come in the narrative, and 'glad would they be to hear the tales of Hercules' (227).

Drawing to a Close or Closing in a Draw?

The crowning glory of ekphrastic invention in the *Arcadia*'s verbal and visual play is the emblem of Cupid, which is introduced as a device of the poet Dicus in the *Old Arcadia,* and is subsequently given to Miso in the revision. The problematic Cupid epitomizes the sophistical style and proleptic and sylleptic significance of ekphrasis that Sidney has mastered. In the *Old Arcadia,* the emblem articulates a male tirade against Eros. Couched in a poetical debate over love that takes place in the eclogues, Dicus's painted emblem and his corresponding poem are represented as a part of his armour. Dicus 'did more detest and hate love than the most envious man doth in himself cherish and love hate' (*OA* 57). His heraldic device is thus described:

> [A] painted table, wherein he had given Cupid a quite new form, making him sit upon a pair of gallows, like a hangman, about which there was a rope very handsomely provided; he himself painted all ragged and torn, so that his skin was bare in most places, where a man might perceive all his body full of eyes, his head horned with the horns of a bull, with long ears accordingly, his face old and wrinkled, and his feet cloven. In his right

> hand, he was painted holding a crown of laurel, in his left a purse of money; and out of his mouth hung a lace which held the pictures of a goodly man and an excellent fair woman. And with such a countenance he was drawn as if he had persuaded every man by those enticements to come and be hanged there. (*OA* 57).

Dicus gives Cupid an alternate birth myth: Cupid is here born of Io (while in the form of a cow) and Argus.[37] He is half-human half-beast, old, and ugly. The painting of Cupid is emblematically accompanied with a poem. Dicus has composed the verse, which tells of the poets' and painters' conspiracy to represent a counterfeit Cupid in the form of a young blind babe, emphasizing Cupid's true nature and background as the withered and old half-beast offspring of Io and Argus. In the context of Dicus's presentation, the emblem warns against love that is motivated purely by the senses. The physical attraction that Basilius and Gynecia have for Pyrocles would fall into this category, but the emblem may also indicate that the princes' abandonment of all decorum for love (Musidorus's willingness to abandon his social position and Pyrocles' willingness to don a female identity) is also a certain way to 'come and be hanged.' Dicus's emblem is misogynous, presenting the physical act of love as a danger to men specifically, but the emblem is open to other interpretations.

In his revision, Sidney shifts the interpretation of the Cupid emblem from a warning against physical love to a promotion of sexual pleasure. As Clare Kinney emphasizes, the 'picture and poem are not original to the *New Arcadia;* what is new here is the marginal female voice which re-presents them' (144). In contrast to the all-male composers (including the man in disguise as an Amazon) of the *Old Arcadia*'s eclogues, the 'fair ladies' of the *New Arcadia* – including the Arcadian princesses Pamela and Philoclea, Zelmane (the cross-dressed Pyrocles), the Princess Pamela's witch-like 'governess' Miso, and Miso's daughter, Mopsa – gather and discuss tales of love in book 2. Miso is introduced by Kalander in his initial explanation of the state of affairs in Arcadia as 'so handsome a beldame, that only her face and her splay-foot have made her accused for a witch' (*NA* 1, 3, 77). Kalander sets the ironic tone for false praises of Miso's charms. Listening to their stories, Miso exclaims that they are

> full in your tittle-tattlings of Cupid: here is Cupid & there is Cupid. I will tell you now what a good old woman told me, what an old wise man told

> her, what a great learned clerk told him, and gave it him in writing; and here I have it in my prayer-book. (*NA* 2, 14, 307).

Miso tells how she came to possess the story of Cupid, explaining how she had been 'admired' as a 'young' lass in her town:

> I was a young girl of a seven and twenty years old, & I could not go through the street of our village but I might hear the young men talk: 'O the pretty little eyes of Miso': 'O the fine thin lips of Miso': 'O the goodly fat hands of Miso': besides how well a certain wrying I had of my neck became me. Then the one would wink with one eye, & the other cast daisies at me. I must confess, seeing so many amorous, it made me set up my peacock's tail with the highest (*NA* 2, 14, 307–8)

Verging on the status of an old maid, Miso nonetheless believed that the false compliments that the young men paid her were well intended and without irony. This passage establishes Miso as a poor interpreter of signs and prepares the reader to take what she presents sceptically.

An alternative to Dicus's interpretation of the Cupid emblem arises when this artifact of Sidney's *Old Arcadia* appears in a new context. Miso's striking looks and unmarried status capture the attention of a Celestinesque figure, whom Miso calls 'the good old woman' and who from the location and notoriety of her house, which 'stood in the lane as you go to the barber's shop; all the town knew her' (*NA* 2, 14, 308), one can surmise must either be a witch herself or perhaps an old prostitute turned procuress.[38] Miso continues:

> 'Minion,' said she, (indeed I was a pretty one in those days, though I say it) 'I see a number of lads that love you. Well,' said she, 'I say no more; do you know what Love is?' With that she brought me into a corner, where there was painted a foul fiend I trow, for he had a pair of horns like a Bull, his feet cloven, as many eyes upon his body as my grey mare hath dapples, & for all the world so placed. This monster sat like a hangman upon a pair of gallows. In his right hand he was painted holding a crown of Laurel, in his left hand a purse of money, & out of his mouth hung a lace of two fair pictures of a man & a woman, & such a countenance he showed as if he would persuade folks by those alurements to come thither & be hanged. (*NA* 2, 14, 308)

The old bawd shows Miso a Cupid like the one painted by Dicus. A reader of the manuscript of the *Old Arcadia* could chuckle over the fact that Dicus's emblem had ended up in the house of a prostitute in Sidney's revision. Here is a concrete example of how Sidney imagines a lower-class woman's ekphrasis in contrast to that of an Arcadian shepherd. Moreover, the significance that this bawd lends the emblem is quite different from that of Dicus. She explains, 'this same is even Love: therefore do what thou list with all those fellows one after another, & it recks not much what they do to thee, so it be in secret; but upon my charge, never love none of them' (*NA* 2, 14, 308). This new presentation of the Cupid emblem emphasizes that only physical love is desirable and that spiritual love is dangerous. Like a figure of Alcibiades, the 'good old woman' brings the discussion of love down to the physical level, but also like Alcibiades, the woman's interpretation is only part of the story.

The text accompanying the image of Cupid has a promiscuous provenance and significance. Miso relates that the old woman 'gave [Miso] this Book which she said a great maker of ballads had given to an old painter, who, for a little pleasure, had bestowed both book and picture of her' (*NA* 2, 14, 308). The poem is a slightly altered version of Dicus's poem in the *Old Arcadia* and contains the same mythological background for Cupid. The opening stanza assures that the conventional Cupid is a counterfeit:

> Poor Painters oft with silly Poets join,
> To fill the world with strange but vain conceits:
> One brings the stuff, the other stamps the coin,
> Which breeds nought else but glosses of deceits.
> Thus Painters Cupid paint, thus Poets do,
> A naked god, blind, young, with arrows two. (*NA* 2, 14, 309)

Unlike the counterfeit work of 'poor' painters and poets, the poem claims to tell the true story of Cupid. Sidney's Cupid is exiled from Olympus because of his scandalous conception. Jove charges this Cupid: 'In this our world a hangman for to be / Of all those fools that will have all they see' (*NA* 2, 14, 310). The poem reveals that both Dicus's avoidance of all love and the injunction of the 'good old woman' to enjoy sex without emotional attachment are only partial readings of the emblem. The poem warns against being seduced by appearances, but the love lesson is inconclusive.

In both versions of the painted emblem, Sidney's Cupid is figured in alchemical terms. There was an alchemical laboratory at Wilton (where

Sidney probably started composing the *Arcadia*), and Sidney's sister Mary, Countess of Pembroke, was, along with Philip, apparently interested in alchemy.[39] A long European and Eastern tradition used alchemical symbols to represent to the learned observer different steps in the alchemical process. These symbols could also enrich the meaning of a painting: particular articulations of alchemical images could essentially be a recipe for an alchemical creation. Eros can symbolize the driving force behind all alchemical processes. The double-gendered pair of portraits on a lace hanging from Cupid's mouth represent the hermaphrodite and the melding of male and female, sun and moon, and sulphur and mercury. The gallows could symbolize the *negrito* or death phase of the process in which the opposites are fully separated. The alchemist needed divine intervention (represented as Cupid, Mercury, or a dove) to combine opposite substances (often figured as a man and a woman) through a magical hierogamy into gold or the philosopher's stone, or in the case of spiritual alchemy, into knowledge of the *prima materia*.

In the *Old Arcadia*, alchemical conventions may provide the ingredients for a love potion spoiled by a heavy hand in its administration. When Gynecia falls for the cross-dressed Pyrocles' ruse, making an assignation with him only to end up sleeping with her husband Basilius, who has fallen for the same trick, she brings with her what she was told was a love potion. When morning comes and the royal couple recognize each other and realize that they have both unsuccessfully tried to commit adultery, Basilius hastily quaffs the entire potion, unaware of the cup's contents. This causes him to fall into a death-like sleep which culminates in the *Old Arcadia* in the trial and accusation of Pyrocles, Musidorus, Philoclea, Pamela, and Gynecia as murderers. The potion in the *Old Arcadia* creates an imbalance that helps drive the plot, but it is a proleptic potion that melds the protagonists in the union of marriage. Indeed, before his transformation is complete, as is cited in the epigraph at the beginning of this chapter, Dorus says to Pyrocles: 'Philoclea's hap I freely grant you; but I pray you let not your Amazon eyes be busy upon the lady Pamela, for her looks have an attractive power in them, and your heart is not of the hardest metal' (*OA* 149). The emblem, therefore, could be viewed as a key to understanding the many trials that the lovers undergo in the *Old Arcadia*. Out of contraries comes the synthesis that is all the more potent for having been tested.

But what of the *New Arcadia*? The Cupid emblem's ambiguity and the characters' androgyny go unresolved. Pyrocles, after all, is still cross-dressed at the revision's end, and the characters are never melded into marriage. I have suggested that the reapportioning of gender roles in the *New Arcadia* represents gender as a passible category, in which both sexes are capable of behaving valiantly, and in which the lessons of morality are taught sweetly. Sidney's sister appended the fourth and fifth books of the *Old Arcadia* in her 1593 edition, essentially becoming a storyteller and giving the *Arcadia* a female frame.[40] Pembroke's publishing of her brother's romance is emblematic of the increased attention given to women in Sidney's revision as storytellers and stoical heroines and of their corresponding abilities to interpret its 'speaking pictures.'

Inspired by Tatius's rich model, Sidney swathes the *Arcadia* with ekphrastic passages and interpretations that offer proleptic and sylleptic devices to characters and Elizabethan readers. He partakes in humanistic ekphrastic writing and reading practices, which authors like Fraunce exemplify and echo, with Tatius's rendering of such readings as an authority. The adoption of ekphrastic techniques from the *Leucippe* aids Sidney in his shifting of gender roles, but Sidney emulates Tatius in his use of early modern visual media and in his portrayal of verbal images as having their own erotic force. Like Tatius, Sidney never resolves gender ambiguities conclusively, but the Countess of Pembroke's invention in the form of the 1593 hybrid edition suggests that this resolution is possible, and her woman's hand in the work affords a means of moving forward even as she has kept the ambiguities of the text plain and open to investigation. Ultimately, the incomplete text is buoyed by its many proleptic pictures; readers are left to imagine a text to complete Sidney's alchemical emblem of love.

4 Painting Counterfeit Canvases: Heliodoran Pictographs, American *Lienzos*, and European Imaginings of the Barbarian in Cervantes's *Persiles*

In the *Siglo de Oro*, Spain faced the challenge of governing a sprawling empire with territorial holdings from Naples to Lima. Not only did the colonial enterprise seek to run this global economy smoothly, but the rulers of Spain were committed to govern these lands and their inhabitants under the banner of Christianity. These goals brought about brutal policies of forced exclusion – the exile of Jews and, later, *moriscos* from the homeland – and inclusion – the monumental conversions of colonized peoples and their incorporation into colonial governments and legal systems. The project of both rejecting and assimilating such diverse peoples and cultures under the auspices of the government and religion of the metropole stretched the fabric of Spanish society to the tearing point and ultimately failed in its grand and terrible scope.

The Greek romance genre became a platform for working out the consequences of these social changes. As I elaborated in chapter 2, Alonso Núñez de Reinoso makes recourse to the sylleptic ekphrastic techniques of Tatius to represent the passibility of exiled *converso* identities. For Miguel de Cervantes, the discovery of the Americas presented new formulations of cultural identity and communication, and Heliodorus becomes his ekphrastic, romance model for assimilating foreigners. As Fuchs observes, while Reinoso transforms 'the Byzantine novel into a capacious fictionalization of the sorrows of exile and exclusion' (*Passing* 101), Cervantes 'charts a centripetal movement from the far confines of the northern world to Rome, concluding his own narrative of sorrowful wandering with a broad welcome into the fold of the Church and into a metaphorical and universalized Spain' (102). This movement from 'exclusion to inclusion [...] powerfully re-imagines the discriminatory and repressive practices of Cervantes's Spain' (102).

If Cervantes's best-known character, Don Quijote, melancholically longs for the lost world of chivalric romance, his last work, *Los trabajos de Persiles y Sigismunda: historia setentrional* (1617), looks back to the earlier, kindred fictional world of the Greek romance as inspiration to weave a story of acceptance and union through trials of adversity and cultural difference.[1]

Here the emblematics of the self exposes passible formulations of 'barbarian' identity, heavily inflected as American identity, that question familiar European standards for cultural Otherness and welcome foreigners into European society. The *Aethiopica* functions as Cervantes's explicit model for ekphrastic narratives of assimilation that rely on hieroglyphic painted tokens of recognition. Focusing on transatlantic tensions and cultural exchange, I propose that Cervantes caps Heliodorus's ekphrastic inclusions of foreigners by introducing Mexican pictographic language into the European imaginary in order to question the Othered status of his half-*bárbaro* character, the young Antonio. As my analysis of three Cervantine *lienzos* or painted canvases will demonstrate, the *Persiles* uses ekphrasis explicitly to render shifts in foreign identities, providing a space for countercolonial discourse and acceptance of cultural difference.

Advertising the *Persiles* (which he viewed as his *magnum opus*), Cervantes proclaims in the prologue to his *Novelas ejemplares* that the *Persiles* would be a 'libro que se atreve a competir con Heliodoro' ('a book that dares to compete with Heliodorus' 65). He was most likely familiar with the 1587 translation of the *Aethiopica* into Spanish by Fernando de Mena, and the *Persiles* incorporates many of the conventions of Greek romance such as the *in medias res* beginning and skilfully interwoven narratives that complement the trials of the two lovers, Persiles and Sigismunda, while shifting the Greek romance into a distinctly colonial and Counter-Reformation frame.

Scholarly interest in the *Aethiopica* as a source for Cervantes has focused mainly on his adoption of the *in medias res* opening and the conversion of the journey into the motif of pilgrimage,[2] which makes sense because these were also focal points of early modern critics who praised the *Aethiopica* as a new sort of romance, as I have discussed in chapter 1. However, this critical interest often ignores or oversimplifies what Heliodorus had to offer Cervantes in terms of ekphrastic modes, characterization, and cultural critique, elements of Heliodorus's work that classicists rightly celebrate. Cervantes's exploration of foreign or marginalized identities, while it has been recognized as a feature of the

Persiles, has not been directly linked with the cultural models provided by Heliodoran ekphrasis.[3] For example, while William Childers explores the 'transnational' elements of the *Persiles*, aptly arguing for its 'more porous, less exclusive concept of national identity, compatible with a certain cosmopolitanism' (xi), he dismisses the influence of Heliodorus on Cervantes's cultural concerns, arguing that the *Persiles* 'derives little more than its external structure from Greek romance' (126–7). For Childers, the world of the Greek romance is 'homogenous,' subject to 'a single tone and obeying a single set of laws,' with variations only of 'content introduced by spatial distribution,' and he dismisses 'ups and downs in the situation of the hero and heroine,' which he attributes to 'a shallow diversity of "dangers"' (127).[4] This is not to take away from Childers's analysis of the *Persiles* itself, but to suggest that even in the best of recent scholarship on the *Persiles*, there is room for a more nuanced understanding of what Cervantes takes away from his Greek romance model.[5]

The *Persiles* employs ekphrasis to question standards of cultural Otherness, an ekphrastic strategy that Cervantes borrows from Heliodorus, but to which he gives his own colonial twist.[6] Heliodorus's *Aethiopica* is above all a narrative of cultural assimilation. The Princess of Ethiopia, Charicleia, is born white to her black royal parents. Queen Persinna gazes at a painting of the white Andromeda during Charicleia's conception, and this marks Charicleia with white skin, which the queen fears will be interpreted as a sign of illegitimacy. Persinna, therefore, orders the child to be exposed, but not without an elaborately embroidered and blood-stained cloth showing the story of her true identity. The cloth's pictographic images and its description are signs of Charicleia's exile and wandering, but they also restore her to her status as the Princess of Ethiopia.

Charicleia's true identity is discovered by Calasiris, who, as Mena translates it, procures the 'pintado y esculpido' ('painted and embroidered' *Historia etiópica* 152) cloth from Charicleia's foster-father, Charicles, and describes the hieroglyphic cloth as a 'lienzo, todo esculpido de letras etiópicas, no de las vulgares y plebeyas, sino de las reales, que son semejantes a las que los egipcianos llaman sanctas y sagradas' ('a cloth, all wrought with Ethiopian characters, but not the vulgar and plebian ones, rather the royal ones that are similar to those that the Egyptians call sanctified and sacred' 152).[7] It is through Calasiris's interpretation of this *lienzo* that Charicleia and the *Aethiopica*'s historic readers first learn of her true identity. Marked with her mother's blood and embroidery, the pictographic cloth tells the story of Charicleia's miraculous birth and her exposure. Only accessible to a select few who are capable of decoding its symbols, it is also a key piece of evidence at Charicleia's trial in Ethiopia, in which she convinces her royal parents of her true identity by showing the testimony depicted on her mother's *lienzo* (154), thereby avoiding the fate of human sacrifice, a punishment reserved for foreigners. After all of their trials, the white Charicleia is embraced by her black Ethiopian parents, is declared to be the rightful heir of the Ethiopian throne, and marries her lover, Theagenes. They become members of not only the royal family, but the royal priesthood as well. The embroidered cloth and its various ekphrastic renderings help to determine Charicleia's identity along the way, proving to be a key means of depicting and altering passible identity in the narration, a use of the emblematics of the self that Cervantes cleverly adopts in the *Persiles* to figure the shifting identity of his half-Spanish, half-barbarian character, Antonio the younger.

An apparent outsider like Charicleia, Antonio must undergo a series of trials before he is accepted into European culture, makes an aristocratic marriage, and is confirmed in his Catholic faith in Rome. Also like Charicleia, Antonio the younger carries with him a quiver, bow, and arrows, and he repeatedly must defend his chastity from unsavoury characters who would seduce him. Rather than pirates and bandits, however, Antonio defends himself against an English temptress and a *conversa* witch. Most strikingly, Antonio's identity is elaborated through a series of ekphrastic renderings of paintings in the text; but in Cervantes's romance, these ekphraseis borrow not from Egyptian hieroglyphics, but rather from the tradition of Mexican pictographic painting that was a relatively recent discovery for the colonizing Spaniards.

In her examination of colonial contact zones, Mary Louise Pratt raises the question, 'How does one speak of transculturation from the colonies to the metropolis?' (6). In assessing American influences on Cervantes, many Cervantistas point to the time that Cervantes spent in Sevilla, which, as the major Spanish port of commerce with the Americas, was a window onto the New World.[8] Cervantes was fascinated by the prospects of the colonies, having vigorously sought a colonial post. Inventories of Cervantine references to New World authors, American peoples, products, and customs make the influence of the American colonies on Cervantes and his fiction undeniable. Numerous texts that would have been accessible to him on the topic of encounters, conquest, and colonization include detailed descriptions of Mexican painting practices, though it is also possible that Cervantes could have seen examples of American art that had been brought home and could have learned of indigenous artistic practices through acquaintances that had themselves been to the Americas.[9] Pratt reminds us that 'the entity called Europe was constructed from the outside in as much as from the inside out,' and I believe that this is also true of Europe's 'modes of representation' (*Imperial Eyes* 6). By incorporating reflections of American peoples and artistic practices into a work that focuses on the inclusion of foreigners into European culture, Cervantes surpasses a distanced cataloguing of the Americas, providing a platform for critiques of both European and American cultures and their intermingling, and he does so specifically through the role of visual art in the *Persiles*.

Building on Heliodoran ekphrastic practice, Cervantes includes a series of fictional *lienzos*, or painted canvases, in the narrative of the *Persiles* that, although not created in Mexico, borrow attributes of Mexican iconic paintings to engage colonial discourse. The *Persiles* recounts a group of foreigners' pilgrimage from a septentrional (i.e., northern) barbarian isle, across northern Europe and the Mediterranean to Rome; but I suggest that it also charts the peregrination of the Mexican *lienzo* into the literary imagination of Europe.[10] Antonio the Younger is born on the barbarian island to a barbarian mother and a Spanish father.[11] As the island has striking similarities to descriptions of the New World, the young Antonio analogically adopts the identity of the mestizo; moreover, he ekphrastically declares the meaning of the *Persiles*'s *lienzos*.[12] In translating the *lienzos* into words, Antonio hybridizes their visual medium while enmeshing the Cervantine artifact simultaneously into an Amerindian iconic tradition and a colonial institutional frame: the *lienzos* themselves become artistic mestizos. Ekphrasis thus blurs boundaries of cultural identity in Cervantes's text, breaking down categories of European and barbarian, civilized and savage. Cervantes manipulates the figure of the barbarian as an interpreter of images, drawing revealing comparisons with European models of iconic interpretation and vexing concepts of the speaking self and silent Other. Ultimately, the episodes in the *Persiles* involving *lienzos* question European paradigms of the visual arts, cultural identity, and the right to self-rule.

To make these transatlantic connections clear, I briefly describe Mexican painting traditions and their role in the conquest and in subsequent colonial encounters. I next outline rhetorical and religious aspects of the European reception of the pictographic languages of the New World. Ekphrastic renditions of three *lienzos* in the *Persiles* are particularly salient here: the canvas commissioned as a memorial of the first two books, the painted backdrop of Clodio the satirist, and the canvas of the counterfeit captives.

The Barbarian's Art of Memory

From the moment that Moctezuma's emissaries painted the conquistadors in order to bring the image back to their ruler as a warning of the European threat, American canvases contributed to transatlantic discourse. A history of American pictorial production in pre-conquest Mexico would be impossible to recount within the confines of this chapter and is indeed impossible to reconstruct entirely, owing to the destruction suffered at the hands of the colonizers. Serge Gruzinski summarizes the most powerful linguistic and cultural groups, explaining that the 'Nahuatl-speaking peoples dominated in the center, in the valleys of Mexico the Toluca and Puebla, in the semi-tropical Morelos and part of Guerrero. The Purepecha occupied Michoacan, while in the southeast the Zapotec and the Mixtec shared the mountains of Oaxaca' (*Conquest* 6). These groups had their own highly developed pictorial languages and traditions. While emphasizing the variety of Mexican artistic production, Gruzinski outlines how Mexican peoples used painting to convey and preserve cultural information and knowledge, explaining: 'If they knew no form of alphabetical writing before the Spanish conquest, they none the less expressed themselves in various media – paper of amate and agave, deerskin – which could take the form of either elongated and narrow leaves that were rolled or folded in accordion pleats, or else large surfaces that were spread out on walls to be viewed. On these surfaces the Indians painted glyphs' (10–11).

Similarly to Egyptian hieratic script, these *lienzos* functioned as mnemonic devices and records for teachings about the gods, histories, or contractual agreements. For instance, figure 4.1 shows a folio from the Mixtec pre-Columbian codex of Zouche-Nuttall, which records their history and was painted on deerskin and folded like an accordion. It is one of the few such codices that survive. Figure 4.2 comes from the *Lienzo de Tlaxcala*, which was painted by Tlaxcalan artists in the sixteenth century to record their alliance with Cortés in the conquest. It illustrates how traditional paintings incorporated European painting techniques and content. A version of the *Lienzo de Tlaxcala* was sent to Spain with Muñoz Camargo's *Historia de Tlaxcalla* probably to argue for Tlaxcalan rights.[13]

4.1. Prehispanic Mixtec painting, the *Codex Zouche-Nuttall*, folio 17, c. 1200–1521 C.E., Codex (screenfold manuscript book) comprising 47 leaves, written on deer skin, 19 x 23.5 cm. © Trustees of the British Museum, London.

4.2. 'Tonatiuh Yuestziyan' (c. 1531), plate 73 of a lithograph copy of the post-conquest *Lienzo de Tlaxcala*, ed. A. Chavero, Mexico City: Oficina Tipografica de Secretaria de Fomento, 1892. Manuscripts, Archives and Special Collections, Washington State University Libraries, Pullman, WA.

Europeans would have been familiar with American painting by reading chronicles of the conquest of the New World.[14] For example, one of the first American *lienzos* that Francisco López de Gómara notes in his *Historia de las Indias* is a painted message carried by Moctezuma's emissaries. When Cortés's troops perform military exercises, Moctezuma's representatives bring the Aztec leader a painting depicting the Spaniards' horses, weapons, and numbers. Gómara notes that the emissaries 'carried a painting, very lifelike, representing a horse with a man on it, the Spaniards' arms and cannon, as well as the number of bearded men. Teudilli had already sent a painting of the ships as soon as he had seen them, showing how many and how large they were, everything represented very naturally on cotton cloth, for Moctezuma to see' (58). The chronicle avers that the Spaniards are so impressed with this means of communication that Cortés himself exchanges messages with native peoples in pictorial form. Gómara describes Cortés receiving a painted message from his allies in Chalco, who ask him for military support, 'sending him a painted cotton cloth representing the towns and [the numbers of] men who were advancing against them, and the routes they were taking' (256). This painting serves as a record and depicts strategic geographical details that a written message cannot easily accommodate.

In their initial exposure to American paintings, Spaniards often did not understand painted images to be language at all, destroying the vast majority of images that they found. According to Gómara (86), Cortés and his party at first cannot relate treasured Mexican paintings to their own understanding of worth, being unable to conceive of comparable objects in Spain. Europeans only appreciate the value of American painted languages after relating the pictorial narratives of New World populations to ancient and Renaissance models of hieroglyphics and the art of memory.

Paradigms of visual art in Spain were not purely Eurocentric by Cervantes's time. Artistic cultural hybridization – or what Gruzinski terms 'cultural *mestizaje*' in which American art hybridizes European models occurred when Spanish missionaries co-opted Amerindian iconic painting as an inroad to proselytizing. By the 1560s Franciscan friars taught Christianity to Native Americans in New Spain with the help of images.[15] As Gruzinski remarks, they 'explicitly acknowledged the decisive importance of images in the context of a strategy of conquest and colonization, with chroniclers and friars alike demonstrating a precise knowledge of the capacities of images' ('Images' 55). Teaching doctrine in America iconically reflected the medieval technique of using stained glass, sculpture, and paintings in cathedrals to instruct illiterate congregations. The co-opting of images did, however, go both ways, and like the insinuation of grotesques into European art and architecture, indigenous artists often hybridized Christian religious images with non-Christian sacred symbols of their own.[16]

Instances of contact between American and European pictographic representation can illustrate how hieroglyphics, Mexican pictographs, and the art of memory were linked in the European imagination. For example, Fray Diego Valadés, a mestizo Franciscan missionary, synthesized pictorial and textual learning in his *Rhetorica Christiana,* a manual of sacred oratory published in Perugia, Italy, in 1579. As a highly educated humanist with a personal stake in the representation of native peoples, Valadés defends Mexican iconic languages. Averring that the *Indios* have no alphabet, he nonetheless likens their painted language to Egyptian hieroglyphics (150), and he observes that 'memoria [artificial] era usada por los indios occidentales' ('the [art of] memory was used by the occidental Indians' 226), a rhetorical method that when tried 'sirve mucho, tanto para los letras como para las figuras' ('works just as well for letters as it does for figures' 226). Valadés esteems Mexican pictographs and suggests that Europeans can benefit from Amerindian methods of visual learning and communication. This assertion opens theories of the spatialization of the early modern European mind to influences beyond the advent of print and the popularity of ancient formulations of the *ars memoria,* and thus reveals transatlantic cultural crosscurrents in the development of verbal and visual systems of learning in the Renaissance. Moreover, it demonstrates that the European association of these media easily translates into Cervantes's linking of Heliodoran hieroglyphs, memory canvases, and American pictographs as ekphrastic modes for depicting identity in the *Persiles.*

Notwithstanding the Franciscans' interest in iconic proselytizing, the rise of the theocentric paradigm of art-making contributed to the missionaries' growing anxiety about the images of native divinities in hybridized *lienzos.*[17] Though many missionaries viewed the American paintings as a harmless means of teaching theology, when faced with the cultural *mestizaje* of European icons in the form of Native American hybrid images, with a few notable exceptions they later eradicated indigenous painted artifacts, fearing their ability to perpetuate local religion. Just as hybridization of religious imagery in the Americas threatened to destabilize European religious control, I propose that literary encounters with American *lienzos* in the *Persiles* also provide a point of countercolonial discourse. In the *Persiles*, Cervantes crafts a series of *lienzos*, which are paired with *bárbaros* as a means of critiquing European cultural institutions. Rejecting a theocentric theory of painting, Cervantes emphasizes the limits of the pictorial representations that he inserts into the text in order to problematize the boundaries of artistic activity. Each painting that Cervantes depicts in the *Persiles* engenders multiple counterfeit images, which in the narrative endure neither fictional tests of accuracy as mnemonic devices nor trials of efficacy as evidence; moreover, the paintings are subjected to multiple ekphrastic readings, making for a multistable effect that highlights the shifting lens of interpretation as ephemeral. Hence, instead of assuaging heterodox views, Cervantine ekphrasis serves as a wedge to pry open Eurocentric concepts of fiction, history, and cultural Otherness.

Painting a Peregrination in Words

The first Cervantine *lienzo* that I examine appears with the authority of traditional European narrative painting. After his arrival in Lisbon, Persiles/Periandro orders 'un famoso pintor [...] en un lienzo grande, le pintase todos los más principales casos de su historia' ('a famous painter [...] to paint on a large canvas all the major incidents in their story' 3, 1, 437; 197–8).[18] The prestige of the Portuguese painter alongside the fame of the city of Lisbon – the Christian perfections of which are praised by Antonio senior (3, 1, 432–3; 195) – prepares the reader for an idealized European work of art. The narrator's extensive ekphrasis promises a replete representation of the pilgrims' travels, in which 'no quedó paso principal en que no hiciese labor en su historia, que allí no pintase, hasta poner la ciudad de Lisboa y su desembarcación en el mismo traje en que habían venido' ('there was no important step along the way of their story that was not there painted, down to putting in at the city of Lisbon and their coming ashore wearing the same clothing in which they'd traveled' 3, 1, 439; 197–8). Yet the painting will prove to be hybridized, unreliable as a record of events, and ultimately a tool of subversion against European artistic and cultural paradigms.

The *lienzo* appears to conform to humanists' rules for painting mnemonic devices, incorporating the episodes of the first two books of the story into a pictorial narrative as Giovanni Battista Della Porta and others suggest.[19] The insertion of the *lienzo* into the middle of the four-part narrative and its subsequent use as a mnemonic device should, therefore, provide a metafictional portrait of the characters' personal histories.[20] But the perspective shown by the canvas proves suspect. Periandro, who has already come under scrutiny as an unreliable narrator, directs the painter to depict his version of the pilgrims' trials: 'No se olvidó de que pintase verse empedrados en el mar helado, el asalto y combate del navío [...] las fiestas de Policarpo, coronándose a sí mismo por vencedor en ellas' ('He didn't forget to have himself and his men painted like gems set in the frozen sea, the assault and combat on the ship [...] Policarpo's festivities and himself pictured with the winner's crown' 3, 1, 438–9; 198).

As the narrator describes in the extended ekphrasis, Periandro includes his most glorious chivalric moments; but the events are not depicted chronologically, nor is there any differentiation between real and dreamed – or potentially false – episodes, such as Periandro's dream island (3, 1, 438; 198). The selective and distinctly male gaze of the painting as it is crafted by the Portuguese painter, male protagonist, and narrator is, moreover, quickly broken down in the hands of its official interpreter, whose hybrid mestizo gaze creates a curious perspective, revealing gaping holes in the narrative that the painting presents.

By giving the younger Antonio the task of declaring the meaning of the painted canvas, I suggest that Cervantes refers to the Mexican messengers whom López de Gómara among others describes. As a mestizo, Antonio functions as a translator between cultures and, here, as a translator between the visual and the verbal. The narrator explains, 'Este *lienzo* se hacía de una recopilación que les escusaba de contar su historia por menudo, porque Antonio el mozo declaraba las pinturas y los sucesos cuando le apretaban a que los dijese' ('This canvas was used as a summary to save them from having to tell their story repeatedly in minute detail, for the young Antonio would simply describe the pictures when people asked them to tell about the events' 3, 1, 439; 198).

Antonio describes the painting on several occasions, and each of his ekphrastic performances links him and the memory *lienzo* to colonial imaginings of the Amerindians while providing a hybrid perspective that vexes Eurocentric expectations of barbarian and European behaviours and institutions. Just as Lisbon, the *lienzo*'s city of origin, is one of the major European trading cities and points of departure for the Americas, or as the elder Antonio puts it, 'desde ella, se reparten por el universo' ('it is the universal point of departure' 3, 1, 433; 195), the *lienzo* also contains the Western and barbarian portion of the pilgrims' travels and projects them forward into the narrative.

The first episode that features Antonio's description of the *lienzo* also criticizes the Spanish justice system. In chapter 4 of book 3, the pilgrims come across a dying man outside of Cáceres, Spain, and then are arrested by the patrolmen of the Holy Brotherhood, who assume that they have murdered the man. The young Antonio exacerbates the situation by shooting one of the officers in the arm with his bow and arrow as the pilgrims are forcibly removed to Cáceres, where the governor (a literate Knight of Santiago) eagerly threatens them with torture. The pilgrims present their defence by showing their papers and 'el *lienzo* de la pintura de su suceso, que la relató y declaró muy bien Antonio el mozo' ('the canvas with the painting of the things that had happened to them and which were recounted and described very well by the younger Antonio' 3, 4, 467; 214). Antonio's ekphrastic evidence resembles Native American testimonials in New World courts, in which indigenous peoples were encouraged to present traditional *lienzo*s as evidence in their cases,[21] and which often demonstrated the Native Americans' adaptability in using their pictographic languages in a colonial context. Despite the fact that 'cuyas pruebas hicieron poner en opinión la ninguna culpa que los peregrinos tenían' ('these proofs made it clear the pilgrims were entirely without fault in the matter' 3, 4, 467; 214), the judge rejects the pilgrims' evidence. Antonio's ekphrastic rendition of the *lienzo* has no merit in the Spanish justice system, nor do any of the proofs that the foreign pilgrims offer.

Furthermore, when Antonio's barbarian mother, Ricla, tries to pay a solicitor to help them in their case, she only reveals the corruption of the system: 'en oliendo los sátrapas de la pluma que tenían lana los peregrinos, quisieron trasquilarlos, como es uso y costumbre, hasta los huesos' ('when the foxy pen-pushers smelled that the pilgrims had money, they not only wanted to fleece them out of it but to put the bite on them right down to the bone, as is their usual crafty style' 3, 4, 467; 214). The actions of Antonio and Ricla serve to reveal the violence and corruption of the Spanish justice system. Antonio's hasty reliance on his bow and arrow finds a parallel in the governor's eager threats of torture; Ricla's attempt to hire the solicitor discloses underlying corruption. Only after a friend of the dead man comes forward to name the murderer are the pilgrims freed, but not before the culprit escapes justice. The illegitimacy of Antonio's evidence in the eyes of the 'pen-pushers' does not, however, preclude his ekphrastic rendition from having entertainment value, for after the pilgrims are freed, 'volvió Antonio el mozo a relatar el lienzo [...] dejando admirado al pueblo' ('the younger Antonio again described the events painted on the canvas [...] leaving the whole town amazed' 3, 4, 469; 215). The economy of justice leaves a murder unpunished and denies the historical and evidential value of the *lienzo*.

As the narrative progresses, Antonio distances himself from his role as ekphrastic translator and finally abandons the painting with his Spanish grandparents. He is the first to point out the canvas's shortcomings, and, contradicting the narrator's initial praise that in the canvas 'no quedó paso principal' ('there was no important step' 3, 1, 439; 197–8) that was omitted, Antonio complains to his grandfather that the canvas

> faltaba allí de pintar los pasos por donde Auristela había venido a la isla bárbara, cuando se vieron ella y Periandro en los trocados trajes: ella, en el de varón y, él, en el de hembra, metamorfosis bien estraño.

> needed a picture of how Auristela had come to be on the Barbarous Isle when she and Periandro had found themselves dressed in opposite clothing, she in a man's outfit and he in a woman's, (a very strange metamorphosis). (3, 9, 524; 245)

The feminine side of the story – Sigismunda / Auristela's story – is neglected in the canvas. Only Antonio notices this deficiency and the provocative fact that the two protagonists' first appearance together takes place in cross-dress.[22] Suddenly, when viewed from Antonio's perspective, the canvas tells a different, more problematic story in which female characters are underrepresented, and in which the male chivalric gaze that governed its creation is questioned. Moreover, the canvas freezes the foreigners at their moment of arrival in Lisbon 'en el mismo traje en que habían venido' ('[in] the same clothing in which they'd traveled' 3, 1, 439; 197–8), which bars Antonio's family from shedding their barbarian animal skins (the clothes that they wear in the painting) in the eyes of their European observers. Antonio's repudiation of the canvas also dismisses its colonial gaze, which denies his family's assimilation.

In *(A)wry Views*, David Castillo claims that Cervantes's writing is anamorphic (73–4). It is a commonplace to claim that Cervantes's work is perspectival, but Castillo's assertion is not based on the wavering between illusion and disillusion as is suggested by Leo Spitzer's 'linguistic perspectivism,' or the undoing of ideologically determined perspectives by relativism as is suggested by Américo Castro (40). As Ernest Gilman explains, '[Anamorphic devices] use the rules of perspective, rigorously applied, to parody, almost to subvert, the purposes perspective is supposed to serve' (37–8). The anamorphic image reveals multiple images that depend on a shift in perspective, but that perspective is itself contrived. If this is the case with Cervantine ekphrasis, then the shift from the initial imperialist and chivalric ekphrastic rendition of the memory canvas to Antonio's interpretation might be called a hybridized anamorphic perspective. It is also reminiscent of the sylleptic ekphraseis of Greek romance that offer differing views of gender dynamics. The polyvalence of Cervantes's ekphrastic representations in the *Persiles* emphasizes the inadequacies of patriarchal and Eurocentric perspectives on what was a rapidly changing colonial world.

Furthermore, after its painting, the *lienzo* ceases to function as an up-to-date record. If, as Castillo asserts, 'Cervantes focuses on "the incomplete" in order to rethink the nature of representation (literary and otherwise) and to challenge the reader to reflect on the arbitrariness of commonly held beliefs about the world' (*[A]wry Views* 17), then how can the incompleteness of ekphrasis be read in this instance? By giving Antonio the role of ekphrastic interpreter, Cervantes opens a third space of discourse in which the mestizo becomes an arbiter between the visual and the verbal and provides a check on the painting's distinctly male and colonialist gaze. Moreover, the insertion of the painting into the midpoint of the *Persiles*'s narrative intertextually reflects the appearance of the first volume of *Don Quijote* within the narrative of its second volume. The ekphrastic interpolation of the canvas allows Antonio and the other characters to criticize metafictionally their own representation and, as is illustrated in an encounter with a playwright on the road, invites others to do the same.

When faced with the prospect of basing a play on the story of the pilgrims as seen in the *lienzo*, the playwright confronted the greatest trial of his own life because

> venirle a la imaginación un grandísimo deseo de componer de todos ellos una comedia; pero no acertaba en qué nombre le pondría: si le llamaría comedia, o tragedia, o tragicomedia, porque, si sabía el principio, ignoraba el medio y el fin, pues aún todavía iban corriendo las vidas de Periandro y de Auristela, cuyos fines habían de poner nombre a lo que dellos se representase.

> his mind was filled with an immense desire to write a play based on them; but he couldn't make up his mind what to call it – or whether he would call it a comedy or a tragedy, or tragicomedy – because while he did know the beginning, he didn't know its middle or end, for Periandro and Auristela's

> lives were still running their courses, and the ends to which they came would later determine what their story would be called. (3, 2, 443; 200)

In discovering the diverse episodes of the canvas as a source for *inventio*, the playwright in his frustration articulates writerly concerns over the proper construction of narratives in the Renaissance and may reveal Cervantes's feelings about the difficulty of his own fictional endeavour. Commentaries on Aristotle's *Poetics* and the lingering authority of Horace's *Ars Poetica* influenced Cervantes's last work, as has been investigated by Alban Forcione and E.C. Riley,[23] and the playwright's comments raise questions of unity and digression, reminding us that as an imitation of Heliodorus's *Aethiopica* and a product of the early baroque, the parts of Cervantes's romance sometimes risk outshining the work as a whole, thereby threatening its unity. Viewed as a digression, the memory canvas is a framed object, but it is also a distorted reflection of the story at hand. Conscious that the canvas is an artistic representation, the playwright nonetheless views it as a work in progress and does not know where the narrative will lead. As the playwright-artist looks on at the unfinished story that the canvas represents alongside the 'real life' models that it depicts, a complex perspectival situation emerges that is worthy of a Velázquez. In sum, the playwright's comments undermine the painting's authority further, but in this instance – albeit playfully – through the discourse of the Ancients and the Moderns.

The pilgrims agree with Antonio's disparagements of the canvas. After he hears Auristela's story, Antonio's grandfather suggests that they add it to the painting, but

> todos fueron de parecer que, no solamente [no] se añadiese, sino que aun lo pintado se borrase, porque tan grandes y tan no vistas cosas no eran para andar en lienzos débiles, sino en láminas de bronce escritas

> everyone felt it shouldn't be; what's more they'd have liked to see what was already painted there erased, because such great and unheard-of things shouldn't be carried around on flimsy canvas, but rather should be engraved on tablets of bronze. (3, 9, 525; 245)

This criticism moves beyond the inadequacies of the particular canvas and disparages all painting as lacking permanence. Alluding to the paragon of the sister arts, the pilgrims elect writing for its relative durability, an argument that of course elevates the author, Cervantes.[24]

After all, the pilgrims' complaint emphasizes that these *no vistas cosas*, or unseen events, are part of a written, not a painted story.

Moreover, the faults of the canvas extend beyond its drawbacks as a historical and evidential record, as it does not comply with theocentric ideals of art-making. The painter leaves Auristela's image 'abreviada' – cut short, incomplete, or insufficient – because 'a la belleza de Auristela, si no era llevado de pensamiento divino, no había pincel humano que alcanzase' ('unless sprung from divine thought, no human artist's brush could ever come close to expressing Auristela's beauty' 3, 1, 439; 198). The canvas is not divinely inspired, and as the narrative progresses, the faults of paintings multiply. A series of unauthorized portraits of Auristela spin out of the original memory canvas's frame, the counterfeit images being copied from her depiction. The uncommissioned images of Auristela cause tremendous strife later on in the plot; nevertheless, the memory canvas serves as a generative device: the counterfeit images that it propagates become a part of the trials that will prove the young lovers' faithfulness to one another, a principle of all imitations of Greek romance.

Staging Barbarian Ekphrasis

The second painting to be examined here represents conflicts between barbarians and conquerors through allusions to Spanish theatrical performances and juridical debates about the rights of Native Americans. Clodio the English satirist contributes a new ekphrasis of a barbarian *lienzo* that provides a shifting perspective on indigenous testimony and human rights. Cervantes sets the opening of the *Persiles* on a barbarous island that is a hybrid of European and barbarian cultural identities.[25] Its location is nebulous. Its people and customs closely resemble accounts of the Mexican and the septentrional American *bárbaros*; but in this case, the barbarians, like Spaniards, have imperial desires. A captive describes the island:

> La cual es habitada de unos bárbaros, gente indómita y cruel, los cuales tienen entre sí por cosa inviolable y cierta, (persuadidos, o ya del demonio o ya de un antiguo hechicero a quien ellos tienen por sapientísimo varón,) que de entre ellos ha de salir un rey que conquiste y gane gran parte del mundo. Este rey que esperan no saben quién ha de ser, y para saberlo, aquel hechicero les dio esta orden: que sacrificasen todos los hombres que a su ínsula llegasen, de cuyos corazones, (digo, de cada uno de por sí)

> hiciesen polvos y los diesen a beber a los bárbaros más principales de la ínsula, con expresa orden que el que los pasase, sin torcer el rostro ni dar muestras de que le sabía mal, le alzasen por su rey; pero no ha de ser este el que conquiste el mundo, sino un hijo suyo.
>
> [It] is inhabited by barbarians, a savage and cruel people who hold as a certain and inviolable truth (being persuaded either by the Devil or by an ancient sorcerer they consider the wisest of men) that from among them a king will come forth who will conquer and win a great part of the world. They don't know who this king is that they await, but, in order to find out, the sorcerer gave them the following order: they must sacrifice all the men who come to their island, grind the hearts of each of them into powder, and give these powders in a drink to the most important barbarians of the island with express orders that he who should drink the powders without making a face or showing any sign that it tasted bad would be proclaimed their king. However, it wouldn't be this king who'd conquer the world, but his son. (1, 2, 137–8; 21)

In humorously conflating the barbarian and the imperialist, Cervantes parodies the Spaniards' imperial efforts. Diana de Armas Wilson remarks that Cervantes's 'parody of the discourses of Iberian expansionism in the *Persiles* engages not only the texts, but also the authors and readers of the chronicles of the Indies, disrupting some heavily providential modes of discourse and breaking up many long established schemata' (*Cervantes, the Novel* 180). The depiction of *bárbaros* in the *Persiles* is inflected by representations of New World peoples in historical and artistic representations of *Indios* that Spain experienced after the conquest.

The American inflection of the *Persiles,* moreover, has precedents in Cervantes's earlier work, to which it alludes intertextually. In the *Quijote,* book 2 chapter 11, Don Quijote and Sancho meet members of the acting troupe of Angulo el Malo, an actual contemporary of Cervantes, who are on their way to perform an *auto sacramental* entitled 'Las Cortes de la Muerte' ('The Parliament of Death' 1557).[26] The distinction of this *auto* is, as Wilson explains, that Indios 'appear on the Spanish stage for the first time in history. A scene represents them as coming to court with their *cacique* to complain of the injuries received at the hands of the Spaniards. The complaints of the *Indios* recall the position of Bartolomé de las Casas, whose pamphlets of some five years earlier had defended the Indians' (23). However, the *auto*'s *Indio* protagonists are missing in *Don Quijote*: the costumed actors that Don Quijote and Sancho encounter include no

Indios. Wilson writes, 'We are left with a tantalizing allusion, nothing more, to a morality play in which *Indios* lament their lost liberty' (*Cervantes, the Novel* 23). I propose that the missing *Indios* of the troupe of actors finally make their debut in the *Persiles* in the guise of the Englishman Clodio's imagined barbarian canvas.

Before the protagonists reach Lisbon and the memory canvas is painted, Clodio imagines a scene in which Antonio senior and his family travel to Spain and argue for the rights of native peoples with the aid of a canvas backdrop. The canvas in question does not exist except in the ekphrasis. Clodio criticizes Antonio senior and his barbarian family, stating that if 'este nuestro bárbaro español, en cuya arrogancia debe estar cifrada la valentía del orbe' ('this Spanish barbarian of ours, whose arrogance is an abridged version of all the pride in the world') makes it back to Spain,

> [H]a de hacer corrillos de gente, mostrando a su mujer y a sus hijos envueltos en sus pellejos, pintando la isla bárbara en un lienzo, y señalando con una vara el lugar do estuvo encerrado quince años, la mazmorra de los prisioneros, y la esperanza inútil y ridícula de los bárbaros y el incendio no pensado de la isla, bien ansí como hacen los que, libres de la esclavitud turquesca, con las cadenas al hombro, habiéndolas quitado de los pies, cuentan sus desventuras con lastimeras voces y humildes plegarias en tierra de cristianos. Pero esto pase, que, aunque parezca que cuentan imposibles, a mayores peligros está sujeta la condición humana, y los de un desterrado, por grandes que sean, pueden ser creederos.
>
> He'll have people lined up to see his wife and children wrapped in their animal skins, with the Barbarous Isle painted on a backdrop and him pointing out with a stick there – where he was captive for fifteen years – and here – the prisoners' dungeon. He'll be talking about the vain, ridiculous hopes of the barbarians for their future, and the unexpected burning of the island – just like those people who, freed from Turkish slavery and in Christian lands again, take their chains off their feet and hang them over their shoulders to tell the story of their misfortunes with pitiful voices and humble appeals. But let's not be too hard on them, although it may seem that what they're telling is impossible, the human condition is subject to incalculable dangers and those suffered by the banished – no matter how extreme – may well be believed. (2, 5, 309–10; 120)

Clodio's description of the barbarians with their backdrop results in a double perspective that neatly encapsulates English attitudes towards

Spain's colonial enterprise.[27] Insofar as Antonio senior is a 'Spanish' barbarian, he is arrogant and has enough pride to fill the world (or perhaps to conquer it). Nevertheless, Clodio's allowances resemble sixteenth-century debates over the human rights of native peoples. Doubts about the justness of the conquest of the New World had already come to a head in the debates at Valladolid and Salamanca and in the writings of Bartolomé de las Casas and Francisco de Vitoria, writings that were ransacked by English and Dutch proponents of the black legend. Clodio may thus be voicing English alignments with countercolonial discourse aimed at criticizing Spain's colonial policies. The reference to 'the vain, ridiculous hopes of the barbarians for their future, and the unexpected burning of the island' represents a transumptive slide from the history of champions of the *Indios* like de las Casas and the burning of Tenochtitlan to the literary representation of Cervantes's barbarians. Clodio finally advocates clemency for the barbarians, whether or not the details of their story are true. The staging of Antonio's half-barbarian family as both Spanish and barbarian, both Christian and somehow captive of the 'Turk,' as both truth-tellers and liars, both civilized and savage, undoes criteria that the reader may have for interpreting or in fact identifying these characters based on traditional distinctions of Otherness. Thus ekphrasis works here to unsettle these cultural binaries.

Counterfeiting Captivity with a Counterfeit Canvas

The final canvas to be analysed appears in the episode of the counterfeit captives. The seed for this episode is found in Clodio's speech above, in which he compares the plaintive *bárbaros* to mendicant ex-captives of the Turks. Comparisons between the West Indies and the Ottoman-controlled Mediterranean abound in literature and historical documents of the *Siglo de Oro*. Fray Diego de Haedo observes in his *Topografía* that Barbarosa outfits a corsair for his son, who along with his multiethnic Muslim crew having heard 'a la fama de las riquesas de Argel deseaban pasar alla como los españoles a las Indias' ('of the fame of its riches wished to go to Algiers just as the Spaniards wish to go to the Indies' 210). This comparison, which refers to the renegade piracy along the Spanish coastline, implies that Spaniards fall victim to the Muslim pirates in the same way that the Native Americans fall victim to the Spaniards, but to complicate matters the *conquistadores* also often compare the Native Americans to Turks, Moors, and Jews, especially when the *Indios* trick the Spaniards, and, as Haedo makes clear in a list of corsairs and their captains (89), the majority of the corsairs were led by renegades with an extremely diverse geographical and religious background.[28] The unstable borders between these groups of foreigners illustrate the role of the subaltern as being more a question of circumstance than necessarily of race or religion and add another possible level of meaning to the tale of the counterfeit captives as a commentary on the plight of the *Indios*.

In the tale of the counterfeit captives, in which two drop-out students pretend to be escaped captives of the Turks, the forgiveness of their fraud by two mayors frees beleaguered peoples from the 'truth' of historical accounts and affirms analphabetic government.[29] The pilgrims come upon the captives in a small square the name of which, like the birthplace of Don Quijote, is not revealed. The obfuscation of locus foreshadows the eventual destabilization of the economy of the captives' tale, and the captives' reliance on the *lienzo* to fabricate identity eventually unmasks them. The pilgrims observe

> dos mancebos que, en traje de recién rescatados de cautivos, estaban declarando las figuras de un pintado lienzo que tenían tendido en el suelo. Parecía que se habían descargado de dos pesadas cadenas que tenían junto a sí, insignias y relatoras de su pesada desventura.

> two young men who, dressed in the clothes of recently ransomed captives, were explaining the pictures painted on a canvas they'd spread out on the ground. They'd apparently relieved themselves of the weight of two heavy chains they had next to them, which were like badges testifying to their burdensome misfortune. (3, 10, 527–8; 246)

The counterfeits try to authenticate their experience with props: the canvas, a whip, chains, and costumes. They stage their story according to the art of memory. One of the captives describes their trials in Algiers, pointing out in the canvas their alleged likenesses and location in a galley through a long ekphrasis of the *lienzo*:

> 'Esta, señores, que aquí veis pintada, es la ciudad de Argel, gomia y tarasca de todas las riberas del mar Mediterráneo, puesto universal de cosarios, y amparo y refugio de ladrones, que, deste pequeñuelo puerto que aquí va pintado, salen con sus bajeles a inquietar el mundo [...] Este bajel que aquí veis, reducido a pequeño, porque lo pide así la pintura, es una galeota de ventidós bancos, cuyo dueño y capitán es el turco que en

> la crujía va en pie con un brazo en la mano, que cortó a aquel cristiano que allí veis, para que le sirva de rebenque y azote a los demás cristianos que van amarrados a sus bancos [...] Aquel cautivo primero del primer banco, cuyo rostro le disfigura la sangre que se le ha pegado de los golpes del brazo muerto, soy yo, que servía de espalder en esta galeota; y el otro que está junto a mí es este mi compañero, no tan sangriento porque fue menos apaleado.'
>
> 'Señores, you see painted here the city of Algiers, the most insatiable glutton on all the shores of the Mediterranean, a universal haven for pirates and the shelter and refuge for thieves who, from this little harbor painted here, set out in their ships to trouble the world [...] This ship, which you see reduced in size here because the picture requires it, is a small galley with twenty-two benches whose master and captain is the Turk standing on the center runway between the two lines of oarsmen; he's holding in his hand an arm he's cut from the Christian you see over there in order to use it as a whip and lash for the other Christians tied to the benches [...] That first captive on the first bench, whose face is stained by the blood that has stuck to it from the blows with the dead arm, is I myself, who acted as the stroke [rower closest to the stern] on this galley, and the other man next to me is my companion here, who isn't so bloody because he'd been beaten less.' (3, 10, 528–30; 247)

Like Antonio, the captives declare the events of a painted canvas that supposedly depicts their tale. Algiers itself functions analogously to the barbarians' isle in the *Persiles* and to the island's depiction in the memory canvas as a place of conquering and imprisonment from which the teller has escaped. Unlike Antonio, however, the counterfeits take advantage of the inherent difference between painted image and reality to tell a story that is not their own, explaining that differences between their canvas and reality occur 'porque lo pide así la pintura' ('because the picture requires it').[30] This is a statement of the requirements of perspective that scale the size of the objects portrayed, but it also opens to investigation the narrator's formulation of *ut pictura poesis et historia* to follow. The narrator states, 'La historia, la poesía y la pintura simbolizan entre sí y se parecen tanto que, cuando escribes historia, pintas, y cuando pintas, compones' ('History, poetry, and painting resemble each other and are so much alike that when you write history you're painting, and when you paint you're composing poetry' 3, 14, 570; 268). Through its relationship to fiction and history, painting exacts necessary adjustments to reality that provide an opening for misrepresentation in its sister arts. All three arts are potentially false owing to their being tied to a singular and limiting perspective. The supposedly historical account of the captives is revealed to be fictional by the two town mayors.

Tension builds between fiction and history when one mayor remembers his own personal history of the events that the painting and captives describe and says to his co-mayor, 'yo iba dentro desta galeota y no me acuerdo de haberle conocido por espalder della, sino fue a un Alonso Moclín, natural de Vélez Málaga' ('I was on that galley and don't remember his being the stroke, but rather a certain Alonso Moclín, a native of Vélez-Málaga' 3, 10, 531; 248). Though the canvas may be a legitimate record of events, the mayors do not assume that the captives' relationship to the canvas is legitimate.

The mayor interrogates the captives about the galleys depicted in the painting, the way in which they were taken prisoner, and finally asks about the number of entrances, freshwater fountains, and wells there are in Algiers. Fashioned to the art of memory, this last question ought to have been easy for the students to answer, but because it was not a part of their prepared story and was not included in the depiction of Algiers on their canvas, they fail the mayor's test. The specificity of their places in the galley does not extend to an understanding of the specifics of the locus or place where they were supposed to have been imprisoned.

Having attempted to seem historical in the depth of their story's detail, the captives desperately retreat into the oblivion of fiction in the hopes that their mistakes will also be forgotten:

> '¡La pregunta es boba!' respondió el primer cautivo: 'Tantas puertas tiene como tiene casas, y tantas fuentes que yo no las sé, y tantos pozos que no los he visto, y los trabajos que yo en él he pasado me han quitado la memoria de mí mismo.'

> 'That's a dumb question,' replied the first captive; 'there are as many entrances as there are houses, so many fountains I don't know the number, so many wells that I haven't seen them all, and the trials I've undergone there have even taken my memory away.' (3, 10, 533; 248)

The '*boba*' question is the most cunning that the mayor could have asked, and despite the captive's excuse that *los trabajos* ('the trials') he has suffered have robbed him of his memory, recollection is the only test of veracity that the mayor makes. One might ask why the mayor did not simply say that the stroke on the galley was not the captive, but it would seem that history is not always the most reliable of judges, and a memory question that involves the type of local memory that was practised by students in the sixteenth century and that is based on ekphrastic evidence is the method that he chooses to undo the captives' tale.

The captives confess that they are drop-out students from Salamanca who were heading to the Italian war front and decided to invent a way of making a living en route. They reveal that they had met other captives who 'tan bién lo debían de ser falsos' ('were also probably false') and that they 'les compramos este *lienzo* y nos informamos de algunas cosas de las de Argel, que nos pareció ser bastantes y necesarias para acreditar nuestro embeleco' ('bought this canvas from them and obtained information about some things having to do with Algiers we thought would be necessary and sufficient to lend credibility to our fraud' 3, 10, 535; 249). Not only is the canvas and their ekphrasis of it an illegitimate representation of the counterfeits' tale, but the manner in which they obtained it implies that it may have been employed as an accomplice in many such a ruse. After the mayors threaten to send them to the galleys, the captives argue for clemency, stating:

> [A]penas granjeamos el mísero sustento con nuestra industria, que no deja de ser trabajosa, como lo es la de los oficiales y jornaleros. Mis padres no nos enseñaron oficio alguno y, así, nos es forzoso que remitamos a la industria lo que habíamos de remitir a las manos, si tuviéramos oficio.
>
> We scarcely make enough to earn a miserable living by our wits, which takes as much work as the jobs of tradesmen or day-laborers. Our parents didn't teach us any trade, and so we're obliged to live by our wits rather than our hands. (3, 10, 537; 250)

Since the counterfeits live in the impoverished Spain of the sixteenth century and identify themselves as members of the struggling middle class, they stand next to Cervantes, who also had little family fortune to support him, and who after his studies became a soldier fighting against the 'Turks.' Though Cervantes's Algerian captivity was real, he too presents his audience with a fictional tale replete with evidential canvases.[31]

Forgiving the captives, the second mayor exclaims, 'les quiero dar una lición de las cosas de Argel, tal, que de aquí adelante ninguno les coja en mal latín en cuanto a su fingida historia' ('I'll give them a lesson on things about Algiers, so that from now on no one will catch them making mistakes in their Latin, I mean, in their made-up story' 3, 10, 538; 251). Truth and falsehood are reduced to a matter of decorum, a question of not making mistakes in one's 'Latin.' The counterfeit captives' lie becomes just a 'made-up story,' implying that storytelling itself is a harmless lie, and is in fact a form of lying that gives us pleasure without too much sacrifice.

The trial of the counterfeits next turns to the *lienzo* that the pilgrims abandoned: '¿traéis algún lienzo que enseñarnos? ¿Traéis otra historia que hacernos creer por verdadera, aunque la haya compuesto la misma mentira?' ('Do you, too, my good pilgrims, have some canvas with you to show us? Did you also bring with you some story you'll want us to believe is true, even though it may have been made up by Falsehood itself?' 3, 10, 539; 250). Instead of describing a *lienzo*, in a culminating gesture to the play of verbal and visual language in the *Persiles*, Antonio now bears the pilgrims' documents of safe conduct, which he presents to one of the mayors, claiming,

> Por estos papeles podrá ver vuesa merced quién somos y adónde vamos; los cuales no era menester presentallos, porque ni pedimos limosna, ni tenemos necesidad de pedilla y, así, como a caminantes libres nos podían dejar pasar libremente.
>
> These papers will show Your Grace who we are and where we are going even though we weren't obliged to present them since we're neither begging nor do we have any need to. So as free travelers you could have let us pass by freely. (3, 10, 539; 250)

The letters of authorization hark back to *requerimientos*, documents that conquistadors presented to native peoples that were supposed to certify their rights to free travel and to affirm the status of the *Indios* as vassals of the Crown.[32] In this case though, a barbarian mestizo uses the same medium to secure his rights and the rights of his own band of companions.

Antonio's development into a logocentric figure makes him an unexpected foil to the mayors, who, like the *Indios* to whom the conquistadors presented *requerimientos*, cannot read the papers. Upon being presented with the documents, 'Tomó el alcalde los papeles y, porque no sabía leer, se los dio a su compañero, que tampoco lo sabía' ('The mayor took the papers, but since he didn't know how to read he gave them to his companion, who didn't know how either' 3, 10, 539; 251).

Having adapted after his experience with the governor of Cáceres, Antonio has managed to turn the tables, but the mayors in this case are quite different from the previous judge and demonstrate Cervantes's respect for the simple country folk of Spain.

The tale concludes with an interchange of cultural stereotypes, in which the *bárbaro* is the purveyor of written authority, and the European ruler relies on an iconic, analphabetic system of rule. The idea that literacy is not necessary for individuals to be good governors extends intertextually back to the *Quijote*, where Sancho surprises all with his good sense in his governance of the Island of Barataria, despite his being illiterate. The story of the counterfeit captives evokes comparisons between the simple country folk of Spain and the native people of the New World, and the association of analphabetic learning with the side of the ruling party in this case sheds a positive light on the ability of native peoples to govern themselves.

Antonio's final participation in the Spanish judicial system is reminiscent, moreover, of Charicleia's negotiation of her trial at the hands of her Ethiopian parents. Charicleia's parents, who do not recognize her, slate her for sacrifice, a traditional fate for foreign captives in Ethiopia. Making clever use of the pictographic testimonial that her own *lienzo* provides, Charicleia too demonstrates that she can quickly adapt to the imposition of a new legal system, exclaiming to her father, Hydaspes,

> sacrificar los extranjeros por ventura la ley lo permite, mas degollar los hijos ni la le ni la mesma naturaleza lo conceden, señor padre. Y que sois mi padre, los dioses lo mostrarán hoy, aunque vos más lo neguéis. Todas las causas, poderoso Rey, que vienen en juicio suelen fundarse principalmente en dos maneras de pruebas y de argumentos: en la fe de las escripturas y en la confirmación de los testigos. Entrambas os las mostraré para ser conocida y declarada por vuestra hija. Y para los testigos, no presentaré a ningún hombre común, sino al mesmo que tiene de determinar la causa porque es grande ayuda al que litiga, para comprobación de lo que dice, el testimonio del mesmo juez. Y para la otra prueba, yo os daré aquí la escriptura donde está contenida la narración de mi fortuna y a lo que a vos os toca della. Y diciendo esto, sacó debajo de sus ropas el lienzo que había sido echado con ella, el cual traía siempre consigo a raíz del estómago, y descogiéndole, le presentó a la reina Persina.

> The law may enjoin that aliens be killed; but neither the law nor nature, father, permits the killing of your own children. And though you deny it

> the gods will this day prove that you are my father. Every suit and every case at law, your majesty, recognized two principal kinds of proof: written affidavits and the oral testimony of witnesses. I shall advance both kinds to prove that I am your daughter. As witness I call no ordinary man, but my judge himself; a defendant can acquire no greater credit than when the judge himself has knowledge of his claims. As affidavit I produce the narrative of my fortunes – and yours.' So saying she brought forth the ribbon which had been exposed with her and which she wore around her waist, unrolled it, and handed it to Persinna. (*Historia etiopica* 388–9; *An Ethiopian Romance* 254)

Charicleia uses Ethiopian pictographic language, a language that she cannot read, to help prove her case and restore her to her rightful place as the heir of the Ethiopian throne, the wife of Theagenes, and a member of the priestly class. Thanks at least in part to Antonio's passibility to European models, the *Persiles* similarly closes with his own happy marriage to a member of the nobility and confirmation in the Catholic faith.

Ironically, the appreciation of pictorial language in Europe as seen in the *Persiles* coincides with the domination of the pictorial by alphabetic language in the New World, where native peoples were forced to curtail and assimilate their painted languages to phonetic and alphabetic European forms.[33] As Cervantes writes his barbarians into the text of the *Persiles*, the *Indios* of the Americas learned to write alphabetically, which nonetheless resulted in a new mixture of American and European painted and written expression. Indigenous Americans appropriated European alphabetic forms into a mixture of painterly techniques, incorporating European writing, perspective, shading, and arrangement intermittently in traditional painted codices in order to paint and write their own histories of the conquest.[34]

The association between painting and *bárbaros* in the *Persiles* fractures stereotypical images of *Indios* in Cervantes's time by providing a shifting perspective that includes the vantage point of the *bárbaros* alongside the images that represent them; moreover, the canvases generate a commentary in the narrative on the limits of fictional and historical representation per se. The status of Painting as an equal of History and Fiction emphasizes the imperfections of both of its sister arts, and Cervantes's fiction, like his concept of history and visual art, glories in the lie that it creates. As Alban Forcione suggests in his fundamental work on the *Persiles*: 'If in the *Quixote* Cervantes depicts life repeatedly shattering the mirror of art, in the *Persiles* he reconstructs the mirror, and the result is a work of widely ranging tonalities and immense literary variety' (*Cervantes' Christian* 154). If the *Indios* in the *Quijote* are only present in their notable absence, the *bárbaros* of the *Persiles* are multiple and changing, rendering new negotiations of the painted fabric of Cervantes's literary world.

5 *Pictura Locorum*: Heliodoran Hieroglyphs and Anglo-African Identity in Barclay's *Argenis*

Grenovicum pervetusta regum Britannicorum domus est, milia IIII sub Londino, ad Tamesis ripas. Mons imminet regiae, modico supercilio subiectum oppidum fluviumque despiciens. Brevibus tumulis in illum ascenditur, verticemque deinde ingenti ambitu planities extendit. Forte in eum bene mane conscenderam, et solitudo circum erat ut nemo interpellare posset cogitationum ludum dulcissima libertate errantium. Sed memorabillis amoenitas paene sitius animum quam oculos diffudit aspectu non Britannia tantum, sed fortasse tota Europa pulcherrimo.

Greenewich is an ancient seat of the Brittaine Kings, her situations by the Thames side, foure miles from London. A hill there is, that over tops the palace, and at a moderate distance of height, takes a faire survey both of the towne, and river. You ascend to the top of it, by other little hils; upon the summit of the high hill, is a flat of great circuit. In a morning, by chance I ascended thither; noe man was neere me, to disturbe the recreation of my thoughts, which wandred about with delicious freedome. But the wonderfull pleasure of the place had almost sooner ravished my minde, then filled mine eyes, with the fayrest prospect, not onely in Brittaine, (but it may bee) in all Europe.

(Barclay, *Icon* 2, 24–5; *Mirrour of Mindes* 2, 36–7)

In his *Icon animorum* or *Mirrour of Mindes* (1614, trans. 1631), John Barclay commences his appraisal of European national identities from atop a hill in Greenwich Park.[1] From this vantage, he views the Thames, the countryside, and finally London, in all its variety. Though England may be the starting point for his ethnographic discourse, Barclay's perspective has everything to do with the insight of his being removed, outside the city limits; his is the perspective of the wandering cosmopolitan. Like his treatise on the character of nations, Barclay's life was cosmopolitan. Born to a Scottish jurist and French noblewoman in Lorraine, he travelled from France to England, where he served James I as a Gentleman of the Bedchamber for ten years and was sent on diplomatic missions to France, Hungary, Switzerland, Germany, the Netherlands, and Poland. Barclay finally left England and settled in Rome, where he died before his magnum opus, the *Argenis*, was printed in Paris. Throughout his travels, Barclay maintained his Catholicism, supported absolute monarchy, and published political fiction.[2]

The legacy of this 'thoroughgoing cosmopolitan' and 'illustrious citizen of the European Republic of Letters' (Fumaroli, 'A Scottish Voltaire' 17) is significant. The *Icon animorum* served as a cosmopolitan model of the 'character of nations' in Barclay's time; his political writings, along with those of his father, were influential; and his fiction, both the picaresque novel *Satyricon* and the romance *Argenis* that constitutes the focus of this chapter, were reprinted and translated at an unprecedented rate.[3] As is the case with so many neo-Latin texts, his works' having been written in Latin, which made them accessible to a transnational audience during Barclay's time, has resulted ironically in their being less known today.

Yet, as Catherine Connors has averred, Barclay's work, particularly the *Argenis*, is immensely appealing 'for its engagements with issues that are central concerns these days in early modern studies,' both 'for its sophisticated allusions to, and transformations of, classical texts,' and because 'it operates within, and reveals the operations of, ideological assumptions about race, gender, religion and ethnicity that were and are crucial for establishing and maintaining the power structures of Europe and the West' (247). Heliodorus is Barclay's principal model for Greek romance, and, much like Cervantes, Barclay learns from the Ephesian how to render foreign identity ekphrastically while adapting his ancient model to his own cultural concerns. Barclay's work fits particularly well in this study. He models his romance on Heliodorus's *Aethiopica*, he doubtless read and was influenced by both Sidney and Cervantes, and he offers a unique opportunity to examine a Renaissance author's published take on cultural identity alongside a masterful imitation of Greek romance. In the *Argenis* the emblematics of the self disrupts European assumptions about African identity, and this global romance reconfigures and bridges what in Barclay's own time were deep cultural divides.

I first consider how Barclay describes European identity as passible in his *Icon animorum*, a treatise that crafts an early modern model of rooted cosmopolitanism. Next, I investigate how he broadens his notion of cosmopolitan passibility for Europe into the global setting of his political romance, *Argenis*. Barclay makes Heliodoran use of polyvalent verbal images as a visual language of sociability that defuses national divides. Specifically, his romance focuses on emblematic depictions of African identity to create chiastic cultural crossovers between Mauritania and the English court in the shadowings of his romance plot. Ultimately, the *Argenis* promotes cultural and familial alliances with the help of verbal images in a global Greek romance.

Mirroring Minds

The *Icon Animorum* or *Mirrour of Mindes* develops the 'character of nations' tradition that emerged in the sixteenth and seventeenth centuries to surpass classical ethnographies by authors like Herodotus, Julius Caesar, and Tacitus.[4] In the Renaissance, Castiglione, Juan Huarte, Jean Bodin, and others described national characteristics for the education of the courtier, for negotiation of international political affairs, or for nationalist propaganda. As Fumaroli explains, 'The topic of national characters was valuable not only for diplomats, but also for statesmen working out their approach towards foreign courts, or for political philosophers desirous of explaining or evaluating the different regimes of the peoples of Europe' ('A Scottish Voltaire' 16). Yet these differing national characteristics, often explained through humoral theory, inevitably caused conflicts.[5] Though these ethnographic texts could perpetuate intolerance, Barclay's emphasis on the value of variety and his belief in the capacity for human flexibility propose a cosmopolitan solution to these potential European conflicts that provides both 'a source of official eloquence and a principle of the art of prudence' ('A Scottish Voltaire' 16). Building on early modern assessments of national character, Barclay's work advocates the use of his information for 'consortii' ('commerce or conversation' *Icon* 2, 42; 61) specifically.[6] Rather than plainly enumerating a list of stereotypes, Barclay's text emphasizes the diversity of human identity and locates it within sets of social circumstances other than geographical region alone – such as the ages of man, time periods, economic factors, education, and intellectual capacities – a position that ultimately holds out hope for conversation across national divides.

Barclay's contribution to this ethnographic tradition foregrounds human diversity. After opening his work with a discussion of how people change over the course of their lives in an examination of the ages of man, Barclay enumerates cultural differences in the context of his great appreciation for the variety of the world. As he delightedly looks out on to the view presented to him from Greenwich Hill, he asks himself:

> Quid esset quod incogitantem rapuisset; unde ille aspectus sic placeret; quae occulta vis, quae ratio meam mentem tetigisset? Num ipsa urbs, num fluminis cursus montesve, an campi, an imago silvarum? Horum omnium nihil unum, sed tantarum varietas rerum et veluti naturae suas opes explicantis industria. Subiit inde cogitatio: nihil esse in mortalium rebus ad suam pulchretudinem sic exactum quod tandem non fatiget contemplantem, nisi ad hunc quem intuebar modum diversarum dotium beneficio in aliam aliamque venustatem mutetur, semperque lassatos improvisa novitate reficiat.

> [W]hat should it bee, that thus unawares had ravished mee? why should this prospect soe wonderfully please, what hidden force, or reason, had thus wrought upon my mind? was it the City of London? the course of the river? the mountaines? or the prospect of the fields; and woods? None of all these; but soe faire a variety, and the industry (as it were) of Nature, displaying her riches. I began then to thinke with my selfe, that there was nothing in the world soe exactly beautifull, but at last would glut and weary the beholder, unlesse after that manner (as this place was) it were beautified with contrarieties, and charge of endowments, to refresh continualy the wearied beholder with unexpected novelties. (*Icon* 2, 27–8; 41–2)

Affected by the beautiful view, he seeks the cause for its appeal. The aesthetic experience demands a response, and the beauty of variety is the inspiration that impels his narrative. This appreciation for the diversity of the world broadens Barclay's earlier discussion of the changes that an individual undergoes in the course of a lifetime to a consideration of the diverse qualities of places and nations, and of the vicissitudes of time.

What impresses Barclay most is the great variety of human beings within this diverse world. He explains:

> [s]ed ille cuius gratia ceterarũm rerum ornatus institutus est, ille ad divinitatis memoriam specimenque homo compositus, pręcipue nascitur in

huius varietatis venustatem. Nam non modo diversos in corporibus habitus sortiti mortales sunt; sed et animos adeo multis simul rebus idoneos, ut nulla pictura pluribus coloribus possit, aut lineis, delectare intuentes, quam quas in hominibus fata duxerunt. Quae virtutum aut vitiorum series, quae artium sublimitas, quodve calliditatis ingenium, non est in hoc sapientiae penetrali a Natura reconditum?

But man created after the image of the deity, and for whose sake especially, all other ornaments of the world were framed, is the greatest instance of this beauty of variety. For men have not onely in their bodies a difference of habits, and proportions; but their mindes are fitted for soe many things, that noe picture can with more colours, or lineaments delight the eye of the beholder, than are drawne by the fates, in the mindes of men. What orders, or rankes of vertues and vices? what excellencies of Artes? what subtleties of wit has not Nature stored up in this Magazen of wisedome? (*Icon* 2, 29–30; 44)

The great variety of the world is only surpassed by the diversity of its people. Depicting the scope of human character in painterly terms, Barclay commences a highly emblematic rendition of character that will populate his map of Europe.

Barclay's portrayal of human diversity characterizes individuals as passible; people are susceptible to their circumstances (including regional characteristics) and are capable of change. Barclay's notion of personhood privileges the geohumoral consequences of birthplace, and the majority of the text is organized according to his descriptions of people from different European countries. Native geography makes a strong impression on a person's character according to Barclay, who suggests '[e]s praeterea cuilibet regioni proprium spiritum qui animos in certa studia et mores quodammodo adigat' ('that there is a proper spirit to every region, which doth in a manner shape the studies and the manners of the inhabitants, according to itselfe' vii; 2, 36).[7] These regional 'spirits' are rooted in a person's constitution, their *studia et mores*, and Barclay expands on the influence as follows:

ille nimirum spiritus, qui singulis regionibus proprius, nascentibus hominibus patriae habitum et cupiditates statim ingenerat. Nam ut iidem cibi pro condientium arte saporem quidem mutant, ceterum interna vis alendi aut nocendi nullis blandimentis in totum corrumpitur; ita in omni gente per æstus succedentium saeculorum mores animosque mutantium, hęret quaedam vis inconcussa, quam hominibus pro conditione terrarum in quibus nasci contigerit, sua fata diviserunt.

> Namely, that spirit which being appropriate to every region, infuseth into men, as soone as they are borne, the habit, and affections of their owne country. For, as the same meates according to the various manners of dressing, may bee changed in tast, but the inward quality of nourishing, or hurting, can by noe qualification be altogether lost: soe in every Nation among all the tides of succeeding ages, which alter the manners and minds of men, one certaine never to bee shaken off, which the fates have to every man, according to the condition of the place, wherein hee was borne. (2, 37–8; 54–5)

Barclay does put his concept of this regional spirit in material terms. This is exemplified by his culinary metaphor and his subsequent observations that different regions produce different humoral constitutions: 'ut istic naturalis levitas populos agat, turbidisque incerta consiliis; illic pingues, gravesque animi tristi superbia, tanquam specie arcanae sapientiae, ferociant' ('heere, the people are naturally light, unconstant, and wavering in their resolutions: there, the grosser and graver mindes, are naturally swelled with a melancholy pride, under the shew of hidden wisedome' 2, 38; 55–6). Nevertheless, Barclay is less concerned with the physicality of geohumoral factors than with their effects on desires and social mores. His outlook is not strict regional determinism, and this geohumoral assertion comes in the midst of his discussion of other key factors in the constitution of character.

Barclay next focuses his discussion on the quality of a person's disposition, which, like regional *spiritus* before it, is presented as a rooted quality. He explains:

> Quippe singulis mortalibus praeter patriae suae indolem adhuc proprium aliquid natura concessit, prorsusque ingenti miraculo per tot saecula et nomina populorum unicuique hominum sua lineamenta invenit, quam tam frontis quam animi habitum a reliquorum corporum mentiumque similitudine distinguerent. Hunc illius mirabilem ludum, tot hominum affectibus animisque variatum, haud quis facilius cogitando assequetur, quam pictor suis tabulis omnium corporum species atque formas incluserit. Licet tamen, tamquam eminentes in condendis silvis arbores, praecipua ingeniorum et affectuum genera intueri, quibus homines agi solent, ac propemodum componi; simulque a ceteris insigni discrimine separari.

For Nature hath granted, besides the Genius of their native Countrey, something proper to every man: and by a great myracle, among so many ages, and names of people, hath found out for every man his owne lineaments, that may distinguish the habite of his visage and minde from the likenesse of other mindes and bodies. From hence can no man sooner by contemplation finde out the wonderfull play of nature, varied in the minds and affections of so many men: than a painter in his tables can include the formes and similitudes of all bodies. Yet let it bee lawfull for us to survey, as eminent trees in a thicke Wood, the chiefe kinds of dispositions and affections, of which men use to be composed, and by them wholly swayed, and notably distinguished from other men. (10, 211–10; 3–4)

Here Barclay uses physiognomy as a template for his view of variable *ingeniorum et affectuum*, which can be translated as wits and passions, and he employs the language of the painting of character to illustrate its diversity. The quality of a person's mental disposition receives almost as much attention in Barclay's treatise as does regional *spiritus*, and unlike some other geohumoral treatises, Barclay's text does not link wits and passions strictly to regional influences.

Barclay is quick to note that not all individuals conform to the physical predispositions of their region or to the wits and passions that their physiognomy entails; in Barclay's formulation, people are susceptible to change. Observing first that physical traits do not always conform to a region's norms, Barclay goes on to suggest that intellectual and emotional characteristics are also variable:

Veluti sub iis sideribus, quae multo frigore, humentive aëre, solent candidos caeciosque populos educare, nonnulli haud secus quam in vicinia solis fusco vultu inumbrantur; In iis autum plagis quae nimio sole flagrantes plerumque spissiori sanguine subiectas gentes tingunt, quorundam hominum candor a patria ferrugine recedit. Ita in humanis populis quaedam asperae mentes regent; aliae de patria barbarie nihil habent; crassae aliquae in tenui caelo mentes, tenuesque in opaco: Nec ulla est regio, tam prosperis, aut malignis illustrata sideribus, quae non omnium vitiorum examen, simulque virtutum, in suis alumnis exceperit.

As under those Climates, which by reason of much cold, and moist ayre use to produce people faire and gray ey'd, yet some notwithstanding, as if neere neighbours to the Sunne, are of duskie visages: and in those Regions, which being scorched with the Sunnes violence, set a blacke and thicker tincture on the bloods of their inhabitants, the fairenesse of some men differs from the usuall tawninesse of their Country: So amongst humane people some mindes are rude and rugged, others partake nothing of their countries barbarisme. There are some grosse mindes in a cleare ayre, and some cleare mindes in an obtuse climate: Nor hath any region the influence of such happy or malignant starres, but that she may finde a patterne of all vices and vertues in her inhabitants. (10, 210–11; 2–3)

Having allowed for flexibility within his formula of regional traits for the vicissitudes of the aging process and for the influence of the historical era and place into which a person is born, in the course of his discussion of the qualities of men's wits Barclay extends the spheres of circumstance that mould a person's character to economic and educational factors, arguing that relative penury or wealth as well as level and quality of schooling all play a role in determining character.

The influence of one's regional *spiritus* and one's wits and passions, while presented here as particular and evident from birth, may be subject to change, and this holds out hope for personal improvement. Barclay explains his ethical reasons for presenting this *Icon* or image of different characters as follows:

Neque superflua cogitatio erit eo modo percensentis diversissimas hominum classes; in quibus se unusquisque inveniet, et qualis esse velit, aut timeat, tanquam ex sequestra et aliena imagine, deprehendet. Ac praeterea cum nullius ingenii species, tam lubrico, aut vicino vestigio in vitia propendeat, quae non facile prudentiae habenis intra rectum flecti posit; nihil quoque tam cognatum virtutibus, quod non pravitas utentium corrumpat; iuvabit affectus, impetusque mortalium suis bonis malisque stipatos contemplari, et quatenus aut noceant aut prosint vestigare; ne deinde aliquos immodice laudemus, vel supra fas et aequum aversemur.

Nor shall it bee a superfluous meditation to recount, and examine so many different rankes of men; in which every one may finde himselfe, and see as it were in a sequestred mirrour, what himselfe would eyther wish or feare to bee. And since no kind of disposition is so neare bordered upon vice, and leaning to it, but by the raines of prudence may be restrained, and kept in the right way: and none so neare a kin to vertue, but by ill usage may bee corrupted; it will be good to contemplate the affections of men as they are

> attended with good or ill, and search out how farre they may be hurtfull or availeable; lest we be missed immoderately to praise some; and too unjustly to undervalue others. (10, 112–13; 4–5)

Here the exemplary aspect of the *Icon* is clear. Not only do the virtues and vices to which Barclay calls attention potentially serve as a moral mirror, but they also provide an image of self-betterment. The *Icon* will appeal to the prudence of moderation and justice.

With its simultaneous emphasis on the beautiful *varietas* of the world to which people are susceptible and the regional *spiritus*, wits, and passions that are particular to a person from birth, the concept of passible identity that Barclay elaborates in his *Icon* resembles what Kwame Anthony Appiah has called rooted cosmopolitanism. A cosmopolitan appreciation for both universal humanity and local custom, 'two strands that intertwine in the notion of cosmopolitanism,' can be problematic, as Appiah acknowledges: 'there will be times when these two ideals – universal concern and respect for legitimate difference – clash' (xv). Nonetheless, as Barclay's work anticipates, cosmopolitan conversation and exchange can speak across these divides. Appiah proposes 'the simple idea that in the human community, as in national communities, we need to develop habits of coexistence: conversation in its older meaning, of living together, association. And conversation in its modern sense, too' (xix). This is why 'the model' to which he returns 'is that of conversation – and, in particular, conversation between people from different ways of life' (xxi). Barclay's work captures the principles that Appiah has recently recovered: though people are fundamentally shaped by where they are formed physically, Barclay's emphasis on variety allows for a passibility of nature that makes for adaptability within new social circumstances. Barclay destines his work precisely to facilitate social exchange, both in terms of the reader's self-recognition in traits that Barclay describes, and in the application of what the *Icon* offers to *consortium*, or the co-habitation that Barclay's cosmopolitan world-view idealizes.

Perhaps most importantly here, Barclay repeatedly describes human nature in ekphrastic terms. He claims that the variety of human nature outdoes 'pictura pluribus coloribus possit, aut lineis' (2, 30) a 'picture' possessing a variety of 'colors' and 'lineaments' (2, 44), and he likens the difficulty of his task of delineating all of this variety to the impossibility that a painter could include 'suis tabulis omnium corporum species atque formas' ('in his tables [...] the formes and similitudes of all bodies' 10, 212; 3–4). The treatise itself, moreover, is framed as an aesthetic response to the view from Greenwich Hill. Like a character from Greek romance, Barclay's narrator reacts to the ekphrastically rendered panorama, and his response demonstrates his own cosmopolitan point of view.

Nevertheless, Barclay's perspective in the *Icon* is limited. The *Icon* gives little attention to peoples outside of Europe, and though he considers both Muslims and Jews, his views of these people in the *Icon* are not at all tolerant or inclusive. For Africa, he wonders, 'Nam Africam qui hodie praeter mercatores adeunt, in ipsis littoribus, aut si forte nonnihil ulterius a flumium ostiis in regionem invehuntur, cum incolis subita, nec ad amicitiam valida pacta iungentes?' ('For who but Merchants goe into Affrick, and there upon that shore, or by chance, by river, somewhat farther into the country, doe traffique suddenly, or make bargains of noe great trust or friendship?' 2, 42; 61). Persia, India, China, and Tartaria all apparently also fall outside the scope of Barclay's treatise, as do the Americas.[8] Ultimately, Barclay explains that a close examination of these regions 'minus fuerit ad consortii usum, quam ad curiosam voluptatem' ('were more for the curiosity of pleasure, than the profitable use of commerce or conversation' 2, 42; 61). Nonetheless, he expands the borders of his ethnographic interests in his final work, the political romance *Argenis*, which focuses particularly on Africa.

The Argenis, or 'pictura locorum' ('a map of places')

What Barclay elaborates for Europe alone in the *Icon animorum* he expands into a 'greater Globe' (*Argenis* 78)[9] in his *Argenis*, where African and European communities are reconciled with a Greek romance vision of the world. Barclay charts the cultural attitudes of his characters through a series of highly emblematic statues, fountains, gardens, and architectural details. The cross-cultural references in the *Argenis* come fast and furious. His fiction elides the English with the Mauritanian, the French with the Sicilian, and the Spanish with the Sardinian courts, and his shadowings are often polysemous. The kinds of national characteristics that Barclay outlines in the *Icon* mix into a universal romance globe.

A much condensed and simplified sketch of the complex plot will be helpful to the reader. *Argenis* tells the story of the eponymous Princess of Sicily. The action starts *in medias res* with the arrival of Archombrotus, a Mauritanian prince, to the shores of Sicily, where he offers aid to the Gaul Poliarchus, who has wrongly been accused of treason and set upon by rebels. The Sicilian King Meleander's rule is threatened by a series of would-be usurpers, and his daughter Argenis is plied and menaced by a series of suitors (would-be usurpers and suitors at times overlapping). The knot at the centre of the intricate plot's action is that Archombrotus (who falls for Argenis even though he knows that Poliarchus loves her) is, unbeknownst to anyone but Queen Hyanisbe of Mauritania (his aunt and foster-mother), actually the son of Meleander and a now-dead Mauritanian princess (Hyanisbe's sister Anna). In the end, Argenis weds her beloved Poliarchus and becomes Queen of Gaulia, and Archombrotus marries Poliarchus's sister, becoming heir apparent to the Kingdom of Sicily. Gaulia, Sicily, and Mauritania are finally bound by political and familial ties.

The romance imitates Heliodorus's *Aethiopica*, as was noted by Renaissance readers and translators of both Barclay's and Heliodorus's work. For example, in his translation of the *Argenis* into Castilian, José Pellicer compares the two works as follows:

> O quán bien compiten la bellísima Cariclea y la divina Argenis sobre la mayoría de sus trabajos, dando a entender, que pudieron padecer iguales fortunas; una errante por paramos, por naufragios desde Grecia A Etiopía; y otra encerrada con los regalos decentes a Princesa en los dorados palacios de Trinacria, pues frequenta la desgracia tanto desiertos como ciudades. De la cortesía de Teágenes bien creo, que reconociera la Magestad de Astioristes [...]
>
> Oh how well the most beautiful Charicleia and most divine Argenis compare in the bulk of their trials, which is to say, they managed equally to withstand misfortunes, the one wandering through wastelands, through shipwrecks from Greece to Ethiopia, the other confined by the laws of decency fitting a Princess to the golden palaces of Sicily, since mischances frequent barren places as often as cities. Regarding the courtesy of Theagenes, well do I believe it would have been recognized by the Majesty of Astioristes [...] (5v)[10]

Pellicer goes on to claim that Barclay outdoes Heliodorus by elevating the social status of his protagonists, something that 'algunos modernos' ('some moderns' 5v) had thought fit to criticize. On the other hand, Nahum Tate, in his translation of Heliodorus, claims that while '[t]he Philosophy and Politicks deliver'd in the Romance of *Barclay* have render'd it worthy the perusal of the greatest Statesmen; yet, on the first view, we shall find the *Argenis* to be but a Copy of *Chariclea*' (sig. A3r).

Regardless of which work is favoured, the association of the two in the seventeenth century is clear. Barclay read Heliodorus, and his reliance on the Greek romance model has been firmly established.[11]

As I discussed briefly in chapter 1, Barclay uses the flexibility of Greek romance's chronotope as a platform for topicality.[12] The *Argenis*'s action opens when 'NONDUM Orbis adoraverat Romam, nondum Oceanus decesserat Tibri' ('The world as yet had not bowed to the Roman sceptre, nor the wide ocean stooped to the Tiber' *Argenis* 1, 1, 102; 103). Specifically, Barclay uses the flexibility of the Greek romance form to create a political romance that does not make one-to-one correspondences between fictional and real figures. Though Barclay hints at historical events, his chronology remains vague, and his places, though real places, are presented heterotopically. More important than the allegorical possibilities of individual countries – though this is a topic that could certainly stand a more systematic study – is the cosmopolitan world-view that the romance promotes. While Barclay supported his father's writings on absolute monarchy, even above Papal authority (a conciliarist move that understandably caused trouble for Barclay when he moved to Rome), in many respects the political theory elaborated in the numerous philosophical speeches in the *Argenis* resembles the theories of Hugo Grotius. Not only did Grotius apparently know Barclay personally, but he also read the *Argenis* while it was at the press and wrote commendatory lines that appeared in the first edition, printed by his and Barclay's mutual friend and publisher, Peiresc.[13] Barclay's promotion of *consortium* favoured the kind of sociability that appealed to Grotius and to other early defenders of international law and human rights.

The romance also contributes to the generic argument that preferred the Greek romance model to its chivalric cousin for moral and aesthetic reasons and, as I have suggested, for its capacity to represent cultural variety. The authorial figure Nicopompus's metafictional plans for his 'next' work of fiction (a text that sounds suspiciously like the *Argenis* itself) (*Argenis* 2, 14, 336; 337) resemble the plans of the Canon of Toledo in *Don Quijote*; both figures have planned to write books that adhere to the generic conventions of Greek romance.[14] The variety that so delights Barclay in his estimation of national characters in the *Icon animorum* plays a crucial role in this fiction's capacity to move the reader, reflecting the *varieta* that characterizes romance modes. Nicopompus will delight his readers with 'contemplatione diversa et veluti pictura locorum' ('divers contemplations and, as it were, with a map of places' *Argenis* 2, 14, 336; 337). The diversity of places included in the *Argenis* in fact extends all the way to Mauritania and Numidia. Moreover, the reception of Barclay's work by his contemporaries emphasizes the importance of this cultural variety to its success. The translator of the first English version that we have of the *Argenis*, Kingsmill Long, explains in his dedication that the *Argenis* 'is so full of wise and politique Discourses, and those so intermixed and seconded with pleasing accidents, so extolling Vertue and depressing Vice, that I have sometimes compared it to a greater Globe, wherein not onely the World, but even the businesse of it is represented' (*Argenis* 78). Here the moral ends of the *Icon* are expanded beyond the boundaries of Europe and are packaged in a humanist fiction that is self-conscious of its place in the reception of the Greek romance.

What interests me most about Barclay's romance is the way in which he adapts Heliodorus's ekphrastic characterization to reverse the direction of the *Aethiopica*'s cultural operation. Heliodorus's romance introduces Charicleia as Greek, but through a series of ekphrastic identifications, it turns out that, unbeknownst to her, Charicleia is a white Ethiopian who is, in the end, allowed to take her rightful place as an African princess. The *Aethiopica* essentially effects an acceptance of Europeans into African culture as she marries her Greek lover Theagenes. Barclay employs a Heliodoran emblematics of the self to draw Archombrotus, who is apparently Mauritanian, into European familial and political bonds – Archombrotus eventually discovers that he is half-Sicilian, and he marries a European woman. Barclay thus effects what Connors has called a 'reversal of Heliodorus' geopolitical structure' (263). In this sense, the *Argenis* resembles Cervantes's *Persiles*, though rather than performing the Heliodoran trick on a half-barbarian whose facility with verbal pictures is analogous to American pictographic practices (America does not seem to interest Barclay, perhaps for the reasons given in the *Icon animorum*), Barclay focuses his attention on Africa and on European 'hieroglyphic' traditions.[15] Barclay further elides cultural differences by making the Mauritanian court analogous to the court of Queen Elizabeth and to that of Queen Anne of Denmark, consort of King James I. This Heliodoran operation has both political and cultural significance.

The *Argenis* borrows heavily from its Greek romance predecessors for ekphrastic technique, and the aesthetic responses of characters to these verbal pictures disclose identity. From the time of its publication, the *Argenis* was spoken of in pictorial terms. Pellicer, for example, lauds the *Argenis* as 'aquella hermosa enigma, aquel simbolo animado' ('that beautiful enigma, that living image' 5v), and goes on to claim that countries' identities are allegorized 'con reboço deste Geoglifico' ('by the veil of this hieroglyphic' 5v), thereby likening the romance itself to hieroglyphics. The romance boasts numerous instances of ekphrasis, many of which function as proleptic similes, have sylleptic elements, and provide characters with a platform for expressing their ethos, all of which I have identified as ekphrastic techniques typically borrowed from Greek romance. These ekphrastic descriptions often activate interpretations based on a rich use of mythological material, mostly taken from Ovid and mostly set in Sicily and Africa.[16]

Ekphraseis of art objects that impel multiple interpretations by characters and readers are commonplace in Greek romance narratives, and Barclay includes numerous ekphraseis that invite interpretation and thematize love triangles. The fountain that depicts Galatea, Acis, and the Cyclops Polyphemus in Meleander's court, for example, invites several interpretations. The fountain, 'non plus aquis notabilis quam arte signorum, quae illic hospiti Coccalo aiebant Daedalum polivisse' ('not more notable for its water than for the imagery which Daedalus (they say) had carved for his guest Coccalus' 1, 10, 152, 154; 153, 155), is described in detail. The narrator pictures the waterworks,

> In medio Galatea tamquam in pelago lugebat recens extinctum Acim, qui iacebat in litore et, tamquam inciperet solvi in flumen, duos fontes ore solvebat et vulnere. In confinio aquae contumax Cyclopis imago simul alio saxo imminebat securae Galateae

> In the midst whereof, Galatea, as in the sea, bewailed her newly dead Acis, who lay on the shore, and as if he now began to be dissolved into a river, he sent forth two streams, one at his mouth, the other at his wound. In the brink of the water the furious image of the giant threatened secure Galatea with another stone (1, 10, 154; 155)

Verses uttered by Galatea and inscribed by Daedalus add a verbal complement to the ekphrasis, thereby emblematizing it. The multiple ways in which the triad of figures can be interpreted as a proleptic simile are in evidence in the poem's mythological allusions.

Typical of characters from Greek romance, Argenis relates the verbal picture to her own situation, speculating about the statues' possible substitutions as follows: 'Erat sibi Galatea; meliorem Acim flebat. Sed quis ille Polyphemus? Quamquam eo destinabat Lycogenem, tamen et culpae paternae invita meminerat' ('She seemed to herself Galatea and lamented a better Acis – but who should be the giant Polyphemus? Though she had pointed Lycogenes for the comparison, yet her father's fault comes into her mind against her will' 1, 10, 154; 155). At this point in the narrative, Argenis believes Poliarchus to be dead (he has, in fact, hidden in Timoclea's catacomb that has an underground spring), and she associates the Cyclops here both with the would-be usurper Lycogenes for the threat he poses to her kingdom of Sicily and with her father for the threat he has posed to her lover Poliarchus. For Argenis, then, the fountain is sylleptic. The myth of Galatea and Acis was most likely an invention of Ovid, and as is the case in Barclay's Sicilian setting in the *Argenis*, Ovid's myth was often interpreted to be a topical reference to Sicilian political strife.[17] But it also iterates the theme of ekphrastic triangles in the romance.[18] Barclay's particular affinity for sylleptic representations and the depiction of triadic figures in ekphrasis may come in part from Achilles Tatius's similar proclivity, especially in the diptych painting of Andromeda and Prometheus in Pelusium (Ach. Tat. 3, 6–8, 48–50), which depicts two sets of three figures that relate to the narrative in various ways,[19] and to the painting of Philomela (Ach. Tat. 5, 3–5, 78–80), which I have discussed at length in chapter 2. Furthermore, Heliodorus influences Barclay's ekphraseis, for example, in the circumstances surrounding a beautifully described ring given as reward for 'stolen goods.' The emerald ring that the Mauritanian Queen Hyanisbe offers to Poliarchus for returning her stolen treasure-chest (*Argenis* 2, 11, 324; 325) depicts the creation of Mount Atlas in Africa, and in Barclay's formulation, Mauritania specifically. The emerald ring is enamelled to depict Perseus aloft on Pegasus petrifying Atlas with Medusa's head, and this results in Atlas's metamorphosis into the mountain. Like the fountain of Galatea and Acis, it can be interpreted in multiple ways as the narrative progresses. Moreover, it resembles another African ring, the Ethiopian amethyst intricately carved with a pastoral scene that Calasiris offers to Nausicles for returning the kidnapped Charicleia to him (Hel. 5, 121–2). In this case, the circumstances of the exchange rather than the images carved on the rings are potentially akin. While Poliarchus only reluctantly accepts the ring from Hyanisbe's offer of many riches, Calasiris pretends to have conjured the amethyst out of thin air to safely satisfy Nausicles, who is much more sanguine about receiving a reward. This twist would give Barclay the chance to demonstrate the moral superiority of his characters over Heliodorus's. These verbal images and the interpretation that they invite should be familiar by now as typical ekphrastic conventions of the

Greek romance, but Barclay often imbeds these works with triangulations of African identity specifically.

Archombrotus and Emblems of Africa

The *Argenis* opens with an episode that represents in microcosm the arc of its plot: differences are overcome with a recognition of affinities that surpass cultural divides and are unveiled in emblematic terms. Like the *Aethiopica* and *Persiles* before it, Barclay's romance opens *in medias res* with a chaotic scene on a foreign beach. It does not, however, commence on the shores of Egypt or a barbarous septentrional (i.e., northern) isle as happens in the *Aethiopica* and *Persiles* respectively. Europe, Sicily in particular, is the foreign and apparently barbaric land.

Barclay immediately establishes the beauty and morality of this scene's leading man, who, much like Charicleia, is only later revealed to be an African. Archombrotus, a youth 'ingentis speciei' ('of remarkable feature [or beauty]' *Argenis* 1, 1, 102; 103), lands on Sicily's shores exhausted by his sea-voyage, only to be embroiled in tumultuous events. Timoclea, a beautiful Sicilian widow, comes crashing through the woods on horseback at top speed as follows:

> Silva erat in conspectu, raris quidem sed in ingens spatium effusis arboribus, subter quas tumuli, fruticum dumorumque caligine, velut ad insidias surrexerant. Hinc repente in campum erumpit femina optimi vultus, sed quae corruperat oculos fletu, sparso quoque in funebrem modum crine terribilis. Incitatus verberibus equus non sufficiebat in cursum effusae nec mitius quam in Phrygio aut Thebano furore ululanti.

> There was in sight a wood of thin but broad spreading trees, under whose shade certain dark thickets of shrubs and bushes arose as if on purpose to shelter treason, out of which suddenly rushed a woman of great beauty, but whose eyes stained with tears and her hair loose in the manner of a funeral made a sad and frightful spectacle. Though quickened with the whip, her horse equalled not her fearful haste, and she shrieked no less than the mad sacrificers of Bacchus in Thebes or Phrygia were wont to do. (1, 1, 102; 103)

This passage carries the romance reader from the beaches of Sicily to the fictional landscapes of Ariosto and Spenser. Timoclea resembles both Angelica in the opening of the *Orlando Furioso* and Florimell in book 3 of

The Faerie Queene, but the similarities end there. Archombrotus is immediately contrasted with the moral turpitude of Ariostan and Spenserian chivalric knights, who respond to these scenes of damsels in distress with lust, chasing these romance heroines in 'beauties chace.' Archombrotus, by contrast, responds both nobly and with prudence as follows:

> Concussere ilicò iuvenis mentem, praeter favorem in miseros pronum, etiam reverentia sexus gemendique atrocitas. Omen quoque in spectaculo captabat quod intranti Siciliam primum occurrerat
>
> The regard he had to women and the extremity of her moan made a deep impression in this young man, who was also by nature inclined to relieve the distressed, and he thought it ominous that this was the first spectacle that had greeted him since he landed in Sicily. (1, 1, 102; 103)

Unlike Ariosto's Rinaldo and Ferrau (*Orlando Furioso* 1, 10–81), or Spenser's Arthur and Guyon (*FQ* 3, 1, 19), Archombrotus responds nobly. He does not pursue the woman, but he also does not act impulsively or imprudently. In fact, his natural tendency to help the distressed does not prevent him from having the insight that this might be a bad omen.

Barclay further emphasizes Archombrotus's superlative qualities by equating him with Poliarchus, who we later learn is the Prince of Gaulia. Archombrotus quickly becomes fast friends with Poliarchus, the man set upon by thieves, whom Timoclea wishes him to aid. After dashing through the labyrinthine forest, Archombrotus and Timoclea arrive to find that Poliarchus has already vanquished his foes. The two men contemplate one another as follows:

> Tunc igitur alterius forma ad oculos alterius tota pervenit, et haesere mutua contemplatione perculsi, id quisque miratus in alio quo ipse vicissim mirantem rapiebat. Aetas, forma, habitus, et arcanus luminum vigor, pares anni, et quamvis in diversis frontibus una maiestas.
>
> Then each admires the other's feature, and seemed to stick in amazement, the one applauding those gifts in his friend, which his friend again thinks unmatchable in him: age, beauty, shape, piercing eyes, equal years, and though in several brows, the same seated majesty. (1, 1, 104, 106; 105, 107)

The mirroring and mutual admiration of Archombrotus and Poliarchus may illustrate homosocial desire,[20] and their subsequent rivalry over the love of Argenis can be read as mimetic rivalry or triangulated desire,[21] but these formulae for considering the pairing of these two characters does not account for Barclay's cultural twist: it turns out that Archombrotus is a Mauritanian. Barclay's likening of these two young men is thus potentially quite subversive. The equation of these two establishes early on the possibility for 'consortii' – the fellowship, conversation, or commerce – between people of different backgrounds, European and African. The relationship Archombrotus and Poliarchus have with Argenis, moreover, will in the end only cement their new connections.

Strikingly, the likeness between the two young men is elaborated in emblematic terms. Timoclea observes, 'Cum tanta specie monstrum erat fortitudinem convenisse' ('It was a wonder to see such valour coupled with such feature [or beauty]' *Argenis* 1, 1, 106; 105), and she decides to express her wonder with a work of visual art. She plans to make a monument to their meeting:

> Votum etiam fecit [...] se tabulam, in quam pictor vultum utriusque transtulisset, Erycinae Veneris templo daturam. Et quamquam varii casus distulere id votum, eo tandem se exsolvit his carminibus ad oram tabulae insertis.
>
> [...] she made a vow that she will dedicate to the Temple of Venus a tablet in which the painter shall draw both their portraits, and though divers accidents for a time deferred her promise, yet at length she performed it with these verses underwritten. (1, 1, 106; 105)

This emblematic rendition of the men's affinity becomes a benchmark for the kind of *consortium* expressed in the *Icon animorum* as a cultural ideal, and it is represented ekphrasticly. The ekphrasis of the monument, however, offers clues that this friendship will meet with obstacles. The narrator reveals that the emblematic monument is not constructed until after the narrative action of the romance is over, implying that its description may proleptically depict elements of the plot to come, which, in keeping with the ekphrastic tradition of Greek romance, it does.

The poem appended to the painting provides a verbal complement to the visual representation of Archombrotus and Poliarchus, essentially emblematizing the meeting, but it also provides a proleptic simile for the plot twist that, for a time, makes them enemies. The favourable comparison in lines 3–4 of the two with Leda's sons Castor and Pollux

– 'Non umquam sidere tanto / Oebalii micuere dei' ('nor with such fair light / Shine Leda's sons' 1, 1, 104; 106) – immediately anticipates Poliarchus's concealment in a tomb-like underground vault in the very next chapter, which he effects to escape King Meleander's mistaken accusation of treason (while Poliarchus is down, Archombrotus is up). Along these lines, Archombrotus and Poliarchus will, in fact, become brothers-in-law. But the poem also foreshadows the rivalry over the Princess Argenis that will split them until it is revealed that Argenis and Archombrotus are half-siblings. This antagonism is prefigured in lines 6–9 of the poem: 'Nec tu Lemniacis Mavors formosior armis / Fraena quatis, Paphiisve soles mitescere blandus / Cultibus, ab misero tantum metuende marito!' ('Not fairer is Mars, when clad in Lemnian arms, / He rides or smiles, pleased with fair Venus' charms, / Threatening to none, but her poor husband, harm!' 1, 1, 106; 107) Both young men are likened to Mars, and Mars is both lover and half-brother to Venus. The last line's exclamation again emphasizes the potential for rivalry, with its invocation of the strife between Vulcan and Mars over Venus.

It is not until the chapter following the ekphrasis of Timoclea's monument that Archombrotus reveals that he is an African, thereby unsettling the representation of his sameness with Poliarchus, but also disrupting stereotypes that both Poliarchus and Timoclea held about Africans. Only now do we get a taste of the kinds of preconceptions that might have otherwise influenced a European audience. When Timoclea asks him about himself,

> Ille se ab Africa patria sua venire respondit, nomen ac genus dissimulari eos velle, quibus in se arbitrium erat, dum rediret; Archombrotum iussisse appellari; neque se adversis actum ventis, sed in Siciliam cursum fuisse ut consortio fortium virorum frueretur, quos apud regem vivere fama vulgaverat. Nihil magis Poliarcho aut Timocleae mirum fuit quam quod ille ab Africa tanti candoris vultum afferret. Non reflexa tumuerant labra, non coacti in orbem oculi sub fronte recesserant. Ingentis quoque animi specimen erat, quod amore virtutis extra patriam trahebatur.

> He replied that his country was Africa, that his parents had enjoined him to conceal his name and pedigree, and to go by the name of Archombrotus until his return to Africa, and that he did not arrive in Sicily forced by a tempest but by his own intended course, so that he might enjoy the society of valiant men, whom fame had given out to live in this king's court. Nothing did seem to astonish Poliarchus and Timoclea more than that

> Africa should breed a youth of such rare beauty. He had no great pouting lips nor little eyes sunk into his head. Besides, his great desire to travel for improvement revealed in him a most noble disposition. (1, 2, 110; 111)

Archombrotus's ethnicity is shocking to Timoclea and Poliarchus for reasons that can be mapped on to the categories of local *spiritus* and wits and passions that Barclay considers in the *Icon animorum*. The fact that Archombrotus is African defies the Europeans' expectations both for physical and mental traits. From the romance's opening, Archombrotus has been described as a youth of *ingentis speciei*, remarkable good looks, and he has proven himself both valiant and interested in self-betterment. Though the term 'Moor' encompassed a wide range of ethnic designations in the period,[22] and though the figure of the white African was no stranger to European literature, Archombrotus's revelation defies Timoclea's and Poliarchus's expectations that all Africans are ugly, their standards of beauty clearly relying on European features as a benchmark.[23] Furthermore, his disposition – valiant and eager to learn – is shocking to his new friends and goes against many of the humoral assumptions that were prevalent in the period regarding the mental dispositions of Africans.[24] Archombrotus extends the model of passible, rooted cosmopolitanism that Barclay established for Europe in the *Icon* to Africa, and it would seem that the *Argenis* systematically explores the possibilities of Afro-European relations. The model of the Greek romance, particularly Heliodorus's *Aethiopica*, makes this kind of cultural exchange and acceptance possible. This opening episode thus promises the elisions of cultural differences that are realized in the romance's ending. Here in small we have a taste of the main tendencies of the plot, conflicts resolved with ekphrastic identification that also overcomes cultural differences.

The theme of cultural conversation between Africa and Europe continues when Archombrotus is mistaken for Poliarchus and brought to Meleander's court by a mob of peasants. Meleander suspects that the peasants' error results from their lack of education about foreign differences, and when Archombrotus proposes that he will dress in the Sicilian style in future, Meleander makes an argument for cultural relativism. The conversation follows:

> Tum rex: 'Immo expecta donec magis placeamus et consuetudo insolentiam nostri cultus apud te mitigarit. Nunc quidem tibi novi videmur. Places tibi plenus veteri consuetudine, necdum ex animo imagine populi tui deleta.

> Sed postquam impleverit mentem noster aspectus, miraberis te diversum et ferre non poteris. Equidem memini et cum iuvenis transirem in Africam, risisse me dispares a nobis amictus. Cumque deinde illos usu probassem redissemque in Siciliam, non minori aspernatum fastidio patrias vestes, donec has rursus mihi patientia vivendi conciliavit. Adeo nihil est iniustius quam damnare quae ipsi non facimus aut vidimus, si praesertim totae gentes in illa consenserint. Cum enim ipso tempore iis placemur, apparet non vitio suo, sed ignoratione nostra displicuisse primum visa. Et praeterea cogitandum est congruentes suis sedibus amictus atque mores singulas gentes habere, quod et tibi insinuabit genius regionis, si illum iustae morae experientia conceperis. Nihil te ergo praeter virtutem aut vitium magnopere moveat in tua gente vel extera. Velim tamen tuos ad mores atque usus, mi hospes, hic omnia tibi procedere.'
>
> 'Nay,' said the king, 'tarry till you like us better. Custom will lessen the strangeness of our attire. It may be now we seem strange to you. Your thoughts are yet filled with representation of your old society, and your country's fashion not yet wiped out of your mind. But when you are fully acquainted with our company, you'll wonder at the alteration and not endure it. I myself remember, when travelling as a young man in Africa, I laughed at their fashion, so much differing from ours, but when custom had made them familiar to me and I returned into Sicily, I did no less disdain the habit of my native soil until familiar sight of them had reconciled my liking again to them. So there is nothing more unjust than to condemn those things which ourselves do not or see not, especially when whole nations agree in it. For when only time makes them please us, it is apparent that when they at first displeased us, it was not their fault, but our ignorance. And it is to be thought that all countries have both manners and habits agreeing to their clime, which the genius of the country will infuse into you, if you have stayed long enough to conceive it. Let nothing therefore but virtue or vice greatly move you either in your own country or in a foreign. But I desire, kind stranger, that all things here may accord to your custom and liking.' (1, 16, 192; 193)

This exchange demonstrates the need to educate people about different national customs so that they can distinguish between foreigners, but it ultimately advocates cultural tolerance. Meleander's relation of travelling in Africa as a young man and the difficulty he experienced on his return to Sicily is a perfect description of culture shock, and his openmindedness and eagerness to make his African guest feel at home demonstrate the kind of ideals that the *Icon animorum* advocates. Meleander's view also aligns nicely with the view advocated in the *Icon* that people are passible: they are both susceptible to and capable of change. Ultimately, judgments ought to be made on the basis of virtuous or vile behaviour, and native customs should be viewed with patient tolerance. This emphasis on cultural tolerance between Africa and Europe persists, even when Archombrotus and Poliarchus become enemies, indicating that their differences will eventually be overcome.

The African Queen?

The chiastic cultural exchange in Timoclea's emblematic equation of Archombrotus and Poliarchus recurs writ large with the ekphrastic likening of Queen Hyanisbe, Lixa, and Mauritania respectively to Queen Elizabeth I, Greenwich, and London. Moreover, details of Barclay's representation of Africa correspond with the English court Barclay knew first-hand and with a queen with whom Barclay was doubtless acquainted, namely Queen Anne, who played at being an African on stage. Poliarchus lands in Mauritania to return to Queen Hyanisbe property that has been stolen by pirates. The ekphraseis of the city of Lixa, the queen's garden house, and an African religious image activate a number of cross-cultural references that break down stereotypes and cultural divides.

The depiction of Mauritania's capital city, Lixa, provides the first ekphrastic mediation of cultural differences in the encounter. Barclay's image of Lixa derives in part from Pliny's description of the ancient city of Lixus, but the attentive reader is quickly alerted to its similarities to London as well. As Connors has noted, the affinities between Barclay's description of Lixa in the *Argenis* and his depiction of the prospect from Greenwich Hill in the *Icon* are striking, and she cleverly refers to the African city as 'Lixa-on-Thames.'[25] I add that Barclay creates this cross-cultural commonplace by means of ekphrasis specifically, and that the amplification of his description of London into a picture of Africa links Africa not only with the Elizabethan and Jacobean courts, but with Europe more broadly. The great variety of this African city's description, in other words, makes it into a composite worthy of Barclay's cosmopolitan ideal.

Barclay's vivid representation of the port city of Lixa certainly borrows from Pliny, including references to Hercules, the garden of the Hesperides, and Mount Atlas; even more impressive, however, is the description's resemblance to the depiction of Greenwich Hill in the *Icon animorum*. The ekphraseis of London and Lixa have notable parallels. Poliarchus, delighted by 'pulcherrimo situ' ('the pleasantness of the situation' 2, 11, 312; 313), arrives at the African shores, and the narrator describes his entrance into the city and ascent to the queen's pleasure house on the top of a high hill in lengthy detail that mirrors Barclay's description of his ascent to the top of Greenwich hill and the view that he beholds. Both the ekphrasis of Greenwich and of Lixa comment on the fecundity of the rivers (*Icon* 2, 25; 38; *Argenis* 2, 11, 312; 313). Both cities boast busy maritime commerce, and they are both located upstream along the river with numerous buildings and churches, and with noblemen's houses along the river shores (*Icon* 2, 25–8; 38–41; *Argenis* 2, 11, 312, 314; 313, 315). Both ekphraseis describe the rough ascent over little hills to a planed hilltop which overlooks the city, river, meadows, and mountains, and the delightfulness of this prospect and its pleasing variety (*Icon* 2, 25; 37; *Argenis* 2, 11, 312, 314; 313, 315). Given these similarities, why might Barclay have drawn these two cities in such like ways? As Connors suggests, 'By having Poliarchus enjoy a view from the house of a queen very like Elizabeth, in a spot very like Greenwich, Barclay exposes Poliarchus to very much the same view that he presents as a metaphor for his political ideals' (268). Furthermore, the transposition of the view implies a transference of these political ideals (those of the *Icon*) to the *Argenis* and to Barclay's Africa specifically. In addition, the ekphrasis of Lixa, which is significantly longer and more detailed than the ekphrasis of Greenwich, functions as an amplification, both in the sense of the rhetorical exercise of *amplificatio* and in the sense of broadcasting Barclay's political ideals for Europe into a global context.

Other than Archombrotus, the most prominent African figure in the *Argenis* is Queen Hyanisbe of Mauritania, and as was noted in the keys that often accompanied the *Argenis*, she significantly resembles Queen Elizabeth I.[26] The London-like description of Lixa, along with details of Hyanisbe's government (in particular her tax policy), and the threat of Roderibans, whose Sardinian forces stand in for Spain, all serve to strengthen the connection. Both queens also are likened to Dido and Diana. Hyanisbe and Dido both have sisters named Anna, both are widows, and both rule a North African nation. Elizabeth was frequently likened to Dido in poetry and art, as is well known. A grove dedicated to Diana graces Hyanisbe's Greenwich-like garden and is inscribed with verses that laud the goddess and consecrate the grove to her, warning off potential interlopers (*Argenis* 2, 11, 314, 316; 315,

317). While this description of the grove likens Queen Hyanisbe (its owner) to Diana, it also calls to mind the Grove of Diana and its Latin verses erected at Nonsuch garden for Queen Elizabeth, who, again, was often likened to Diana or Cynthia.[27] But Elizabeth is not the only English queen being referred to here, and it is important to remember that after Elizabeth's death, James I granted Nonsuch to his consort, Queen Anne.

Beyond the transposition of Elizabeth's court to Africa, Barclay also alludes to a queen that he actually knew. Parallels between Queen Hyanisbe's dead sister, Anna, and Queen Anne make Mauritania stand for the Jacobean as well as the Elizabethan court.[28] Queen Anne often resided in the old Tudor Palace in Greenwich called the Palace of Placentia (sometimes written as the Palace of Pleasaunce), and she later commissioned Greenwich house (the queen's house) and gardens, which began to be built in 1614 when Barclay was still residing in England. I suggest that the house Barclay refers to might allude to this structure. The narrator describes the royal house on the Mauritanian hill as follows:

> In urbem ab litore euntibus dexter erat omnium qui sunt in Africa pulcherrimus collis et in eo Reginae suburbanum, quam dicebant Dominae villam. Illuc amabat Regina divertere curis fessa et ad negotiorum tumultum post alternam solitudinem reditura hilarior [...] Sub ipso montis iugo sublimis et sponte extensa planities erat in qua villam condiderant. Ad fores cum venisses, oblectabat oculos alia loci forma prospectusque in remota liberior. Quippe ante vestibulum patebat hominum curruumque area capax, paucis sed ingentibus distincta arboribus, ad quarum umbram sedilia et lapideas mensas milites custodesque extulerant. At ut editus locus erat, errores fluvii in valle monstrabat. Montes quoque ex adverso magnatum praediis distinctos. Visebatur a dextro latere pars potissima urbis, per suos colliculos et templorum fastigia elatae. Si oculos longius mitteres, mons Atlas, inculta hieme et sterilibus saxis, per multos vertices in nubibus fractus delectabat animum mutatione conspectus et propinquam felicitatem blandius commendabat asperitatis imagine. Domus pro Regina non ingens, sed debebat artifici quod venti, quicunque perflarent, admissi omnem aestum temperabant, et triclinia lumen accipere poterant non obnoxium radiis solis. Hortus deinde modicus et porrectus in longum Musis quidem erat dignus et omnibus diis quos cepit stirpium colendarum humanitas. A domo in illum porticus ducebat in qua solebat Regina convivari, aliquot signis et picturis exculta.

> On your right hand, as you pass from the shore to the city, was a hill, the pleasantest in all Africa, and on the same a fair country house, which they called the Queen's Manor. There, when she was oppressed with cares, she would usually sojourn, and then after some refreshment taken in turn with solitude, she would return more cheerfully to the trouble and broil of business [...] A little under the highest top was a high and even plain on which they had built the house. When you come to the gates, you have a different form of the place and a freer prospect to delight you. For before the outer gate was a spacious and fair piece of ground for men and coaches, wherein were growing in ranks not many trees, but huge, under whose shade the soldiers and warders had placed seats and marble tables. And as this place was very high, it showed the windings of the river underneath it and other hills over against it with divers noblemen's houses upon them. From the right side of the house might be seen the chief part of the city, mounted by little ascents, and the high structure of the churches. If you send your eye a little further, the mountain Atlas, with his winter's coat and barren rocks, broke among the clouds into many tops, and delights the mind with the change of view and more sweetly commends the nearby happiness through the imagination of that rough place. For a queen's court, the house itself was not great. But for one thing it was beholden to the workman: whatsoever wind blew cooled the summer's heat, and the fairest rooms took in full light, yet not subject to the sun's scorching beams. A small garden was there and stretched in length worthy to be a mansion for the Muses and all the gods that first took care of planting and sowing. Into the garden from the house stretched a gallery adorned with statues and pictures where the queen used to feast. (2, 11, 312; 313)

Like Queen Anne's house (which was later completed for Henrietta Maria), the queen's house in Mauritania is located just under the highest point of the hill, has an unobstructed view of the river, and is not large. It also has, like the Jacobean house, a gallery and well-planned garden, which is subsequently described in great detail and which contains the grove of Diana mentioned above. Designed by Inigo Jones, Queen Anne's was one of the first Palladian houses in England. There was a garden at Greenwich, moreover, designed by Salomon de Caus in 1612 that contained a new orchard, lodge, and grotto that doubtless would have been of interest to Barclay, who was apparently an avid gardener.[29] The Stuart house and what is left of the Tudor palace are now part of the Maritime Museum in Greenwich, and it is worth mentioning that these edifices and Greenwich Hill are to port as you travel up the Thames. Barclay's placement of his imagined buildings on the starboard side emphasize Lixa as an imagined, mirror image of the Greenwich described in the *Icon*.

Moreover, Anna of Mauritania, who dies before the narrative's opening, may shadow Queen Anne, who had died by the time Barclay wrote his romance,[30] and who played the role of an African in *The Masque of Blackness* by Ben Jonson and Inigo Jones in January of 1605.[31] Noticeably pregnant,[32] Queen Anne dressed in black face,[33] performing the role of one of the daughters of Niger, black Ethiopians who desire to be turned white. They travel through 'black Mauretania' (l. 173) on their way to England, where the 'blanching' will take place, though not onstage until the performance of the masque's sequel, *The Masque of Beauty*. While the masque doubtless refers to Heliodorus, and while it has often been an object of study for its troubling implications for early formulations of race,[34] Mary Floyd-Wilson, in her fascinating reading of the masque (111–31), reminds us that the unification of Scotland and England was an important subtext for its composition. Scots, who were believed to be as humorally extreme as Africans (though opposite in humours), in fact, sometimes traced their origins to Ethiopia, making the presentation of Queen Anne (of Scotland and England) in blackface as much about Scottish as African identity. A half-Scot himself, Barclay doubtless would have been sensitive to this valence of the masque and to the importance of unification, which he refers to in his *Icon*, explaining that after much conflict between the Scots and English, 'donec noxiosissimam aemulationem fata damnarunt, nunc utrisque imposito rege, cuius spiritu insula in unum imperium coaluit' ('the fates condemning at last this pernicious aemulation, conjoined them both under one King, by whose spirit, as it were, the whole Island is now united in one body' *Icon* 4; 99–100).[35] Barclay's 'aemulation' of English with African queens invites us to read the *Argenis* as an injunction to global political unification, just as Jonson's masque can be read as an invitation to unite Britain. Lixa's similarities to England are not its only connection to Europe and to the world more broadly.

Barclay expands his description of Lixa, drawing on architectural and horticultural models beyond that of Greenwich to mirror details of the gardens at the villa Madonna outside of Rome, which Barclay might have visited while living there. The description of the elephant fountain is particularly telling. The narrator describes how '[h]anc partem fons amoenus decorabat, e marmorei elephantis proboscide in tessellati operis alveum decurrens' ('[t]his side was beautified with a pleasant fountain running out of the trunk of a marble elephant into a channel of checker work' *Argenis* 2, 11, 314; 315). Here Barclay moves away from the English model to include details of his new life in Rome. The striking elephant fountain is still at the villa. In fact, it is evident that the ekphrasis of the garden goes beyond the boundaries of England and Italy for its inspiration, the narrator noting the great variety of animal and plant life, observing that '[c]ervi in eo et capreae et cetera animalia in Africam importata, quae ea pars terrarum gignere nescit' ('[h]ere were [stags], roebucks, and other beasts which that country never bred, that were brought out of foreign parts into Africa' 2, 11, 314; 315), and explaining:

> Longum esset singula memorare: ut natura inaequalitate locorum luserit, ut exiguo spatio retulerit omnes formas quibus totae regiones variantur, ut silvam ex aureis malis, rhododaphne, lauro, pinu, subere – paene totam non mutarit innoxia hiems [...]
>
> It were tedious to speak of all: how nature had made self-sport in the irregularity of places; how she represented in a little compass all the various shapes wherein whole regions differ one from another; how the harmless winter had not changed the grove, being almost all of it full of [golden apple] trees, with the rose-flower tree, the bay tree, the pine tree, the cork [...] (2, 11, 318; 319)

Barclay's image of Mauritania (which was actually under Spanish control after 1610) becomes a *pictura locorum*. Not only can aspects of England and Italy be found in this African *locus amoenus*, but elements of the whole world.

After mirroring Africa and Europe, Barclay, just as in Archombrotus's exchange with Meleander, presents a scene of cultural relativism. On his second, accidental arrival at Lixa, Poliarchus (a Druid) puts religious differences aside to thank the African gods for his safe arrival on the shores of Mauritania as follows:

> Concitata iuveni erat ex maritimo periculo pietas ut nec invitus ad Numinis Afri limen accederet. Vidit ergo et amoris sui vota illi Caelesti commendavit, quam seu Venerem seu Iunonem existimes, virginis specie factam leo vehebat oculis in altum erectis, pectore quoque et primis pedibus in sublime ita versis, ut in caelum eniti videretur. Caelestem Venerem, Parcarum natu maximam, primi Assyrii coluêre. Hinc non longe ad Tyrios potuit commeare religio et ab iis inter Carthaginis auspicia Africae tradi.

> Tunc quidem in honore praecipuo Mauris erat, et sub signo istos versus marmore inciderant, quibus non modo illa dea sed et Africa celebrabatur.

> The young prince's religion was moved by his own late danger at sea, so much so that willingly he approached to the temple of the Africans, viewed it, and offered his vows to their deity. The goddess was made in the shape of a virgin, whether it were Venus or Juno, and borne upon a lion, its face lifted upwards, its body also and its fore feet so erected as if she were going up into heaven. The Assyrians first worshipped the heavenly Venus, the eldest of the Destinies, and from them not long after she was honoured among the Tyrians, and by them delivered among the religious rites of Carthage to Africa. Now she was chiefly honoured by the Mauritanians, and under her image they cut these verses in marble, in which not only that goddess, but Africa itself is dignified. (4, 17, 728; 729)

The religious image lauds the Libyan goddess, who is probably a representation of Astarte, Selene, or the Phoenician version of Venus, the identification being left open. As is Barclay's usual style, the image is emblematized with verses (4, 17, 730; 731). The poem first enjoins the goddess to occupy the temple, 'Magis hic tua limina serva' ('Dwell in this temple here' l. 2), and promises that if she does so, Africa will not be outdone by Europe, which, after all, even got its name from the story of Europa, a Tyrian maid (ll. 4–5), nor will it be surpassed by Asia (ll. 7–8). The poem then lauds Africa with a list of gods and marvels that have their origins there. This tableau is not unlike the opening scene of Tatius's *Leucippe and Clitophon*. Like Tatius's framing narrator, Poliarchus gives thanks to what is probably a Phoenician goddess after surviving a storm at sea. The religious image functions as a votive offering to the goddess, and it is described in an ekphrasis and alludes to Europa.

The image of the goddess and its accompanying poem in the *Argenis*, moreover, fit the European conception of African hieroglyphics. Deriving from a Neoplatonic understanding of enigmatic hieroglyphics, Europeans believed hieroglyphics to be a universal visual language that held deep spiritual mysteries and truths.[36] This understanding of hieroglyphics was, of course, mistaken, but it was nonetheless a rich tradition of visual interpretation. Descriptions of the gods and their attributes, like Barclay's ekphrasis of the African goddess, were in the humanist tradition thought to be hieroglyphic. They were translated into medieval ekphrastic traditions – the *Liber ymaginum deorum*, probably by Alexander Neckam, for example – humanist traditions that based their understanding of hieroglyphics on Horapollo's *Hieroglyphica*, and into poetic traditions as well, as in Petrarch's ekphraseis of pagan gods in the Mauritanian palace of book 3 of his *Africa* (46–50). By worshipping this image, Poliarchus engages not only in the ekphrastic tradition of Greek romance, but in an ecumenical cosmopolitanism, putting aside religious differences to worship an African idol that is not at all shy about promoting African religion and the continent itself. While it is true that Barclay is resorting to a mythical past to accomplish this ecumenical vision, in which there are no explicitly Christian figures, he is not reticent about making topical references in the *Argenis* to the religious strife of his day. While Poliarchus and the Gauls are Druids and Meleander is a pagan, the Hyperapherians are coded as unruly Protestants.

The reconciliation between Poliarchus and Archombrotus occurs in the fifth and final book of the romance, when the two rivals arrive on the Sicilian shore, approach Meleander's palace in a pageant-like procession, and finally learn that Archombrotus is, in fact, the son of Meleander and Anna of Mauritania, and thus half-brother to the Princess Argenis. The description of the two young men and the reaction of the crowd once again liken the two young princes as did Timoclea's promised emblematic monument in the beginning of book 1.

> Aderant a Meleandro equi, in quos ambo ascenderunt regio cultu eximii. Poliarchus gentile sagulum multo colore variatum braccasque gestabat propemodum sub gemmis latentes. Aureus torquis cervicem laevumque humerum cingens eburneam gladii vaginam fibulis gemmeis tenebat. Lacertos aliqua parte nudos colebant armillae recocto auro fulgentes. Verticem propexa et rutila caesarie vel sine alio cultu placiturum insuper regia fascia ex murice auroque revinxerat. Super haec eminebat oris decor et amoenae gratiae genius, cuius virtute omnes ipsius motus, omnes nutus placebant. Ergo populus in illum intueri, plaudere multi, et qui eum in privato habitu vidisse meminerant se ipsos accusare, quod iam tum non deprehendissent indolem illam nisi regibus a diis non tribui. Cum vero et ipse Archombrotus evasit in equum, vix forma deterior aut fortunam minori spiritu implens, amictuque insignis quem Mauri regium habebant, incerta ac prope divisa aliquandiu studia fuêre, moxque votis meliori praesagio confusis, utrique mirabili consensu applausum est.

> Meleander had sent two excellent horses with princely furniture upon which they mounted. Poliarchus had on a cassock in his native fashion of divers colours and wore a mantle almost hid with jewels. A golden chain

> encircling his neck and left arm held his sword in an ivory scabbard with jewelled bosses. Upon his bare arms he had bracelets of refined gold. His head, that with his long and bright combed locks without any other decking showed well enough, he had bound about with a garland of gold-wrought purple. Above all this, the comeliness of his countenance and his brave and sweet grace and behaviour made every motion, every gesture of his pleasing. The people therefore all fixed their eyes upon him. Many applauded him and those who remembered they had seen him in a private habit now blamed themselves that they had not then apprehended that the gods bestow no such rare endowments upon any but kings. But when Archombrotus also mounted, being of a presence little inferior to the other and bearing his state with equal courage, attired in the usual habit of the kings of Mauritania, the people's affections were for a good while wavering and almost divided. But afterwards, their wishes growing equal in sign of good luck, they gave them a general and unanimous applause. (5, 17, 924; 925)

The equation of the two young princes and their subsequent reconciliation is a metaphor for political and cultural conversation between Europe, Africa, and beyond. The two heroes of the story, European and African, while they maintain their native garb and appreciation of their national *spiritus*, are applauded equally by the crowd of spectators, and their reconciliation forges marital and political unions: Poliarchus marries Argenis, Archombrotus marries Poliarchus's sister, and Gaul, Sicily, and Mauritania are politically allied.

Barclay's romance overcomes cultural preconceptions and divides with the help of ekphrastic conventions borrowed from the Greek romance, and it ends with romance wish-fulfilment. The text opens with an example, in microcosm, of how emblematic representation expresses the kind of conversation across cultural divides that Barclay felt was necessary to achieve political and religious accord. Africans are drawn (figuratively and literally) through the European fascination with African hieroglyphics into fictive visions of global unity within what in Barclay's day was a faltering Holy Roman Empire. Descriptions of ornamentation, statues, gardens, altars, and finally pageants help to deconstruct differences in the text, perhaps reflecting the capacity of ekphrasis itself to bridge divides between the verbal and the visual. Barclay's romance ultimately unites Africans and Europeans in familiar and political alliances, and it does so in part through the emblematics of the self.

6 'We are all picturd in that Piece': Lovers, Persians, Tartars, and the 'Tottering' Romance Globe in Lady Mary Wroth's *Urania*

'What accident,' said Celina, 'hath brought you hither?'
'Sadnesse and mischance,' said the other.
'What procured them?' said the first.
'Love,' cryd the second, 'the Lord of hearts, and of yours too
I hope, and so should seeme by your lookes.'
'Mine eies and lookes are but true to my heart,' said Celina.
'If they tell you so, they are but the glasses which I see my
selfe in,' said the other drawne to misery.
'We are all picturd in that piece,' said she, 'a large cloth, and
full of much worke.'

(I, 4, 650)

In her *Countess of Montgomery's Urania,* Lady Mary Wroth weaves a 'cloth of love' that depicts a gallery of shadowed but familiar faces and a far-reaching map of places.[1] Wroth was a remarkable person with both poetic and political talents. Highly educated, she was the first English woman to publish a Petrarchan sonnet sequence, which was appended to her *Urania*. The *Urania* was, in turn, the first published original romance by an English woman (volume I of the *Urania* appearing in 1621). Her pastoral tragicomedy, *Love's Victory*, may have been the first such play to be written by an English woman. Furthermore, her interest in and knowledge of international affairs is well documented, her travel and family connections providing her with a wealth of information.[2] It is no surprise, then, that the Greek romance with its strong female characters and emphasis on foreign cultures offered Wroth an appealing template for her romance. Her uncle Philip Sidney's *Arcadia* was heavily influenced by the genre, as I have shown, and the popularity of the

Greek romance in English literature was well established with so many popular romances that one scholar calls the trend the Elizabethan 'Heliodoran vogue' (Mentz, *Romance* 15). Like Barclay's *Argenis*, which was published in the same year as the first volume of Wroth's romance, the *Urania* employs ekphrastic conventions from the Greek romance, and its characters' interactions with verbal images reveal identity in the emblematics of the self.

Ekphrastic formulations of gender, religious, and foreign identities are all in evidence in the *Urania*, but Wroth's romance does not end with the same domestic, ecumenical, and political unions exemplified here in works by Cervantes and Barclay, and her work disturbs many of the conventions that had been typical of Renaissance romances in the Greek style. Wroth pictures her characters in a rich embroidery of enchantments, masques, and paintings, but disjunctions between word and image – the degradation of ekphrasis – emblematize the failure of love to govern the domestic and international strife that plagues the *Urania*. Wroth systematically undoes the promised unions of her romance – marital and political – with a series of ekphraseis that eventually subvert the links between image and text evident in Wroth's Greek romance models.

The first volume of the *Urania* (1621) promises the unification of Europe through marital and military alliances. Wroth's characters express identity by negotiating a series of intricately wrought enchantments that emphasize female constancy in private relationships and female sovereignty in public spheres. Wroth's women express themselves by decoding the highly ekphrastic enchantments that they face, and each enchantment offers to assimilate foreigners into European social and political alliances. Departing from the Greek romance model, however, the trials of the lover/protagonists Pamphilia and Amphilanthus become increasingly hard for the characters to bear, and the ekphrastic episodes that mark these trials become more difficult for characters to interpret. Eventually, Pamphilia's 'heroic constancy' (*Gender* 73), the term Lamb uses to describe the valour of Sidneian heroines, does not prevail, as her promised marriage to Amphilanthus is precluded by their marriages to other characters.

Nevertheless, the second volume turns farther east to attempt the assimilation of foreigners into Wroth's romance globe. Persians and Tartars are the pieces necessary to complete Wroth's woven cloth of love in this volume; but again, the denial of this romance ending contravenes the *modus operandi* of imitations of Greek romance such as those by Cervantes and Barclay. Despite the adeptness with which Persian and Tartarian characters create visual images that admirably express their identities and desires, Wroth's European characters refuse to engage these images with their own interpretations. Wroth's cloth of love frays as does the potential for the 'Knott Never to Bee Untide' (Wroth II, 1, 35) in private and public life. The *Urania* thus focuses on the power of enchantments and their ekphrastic interpretation to figure forth the faults of love and to subvert peaceful unions on the *Urania*'s romance globe.

Urania imitates ancient Greek romance, including its geographical range, lack of historical specificity, and ekphrastic characterization. The numerous episodes of kidnapping by pirates and separation of lovers reflect similar episodes in Heliodorus's *Aethiopica*.[3] Tatius's *Leucippe and Clitophon* may have inspired the numerous false deaths and enchantments in the *Urania*.[4] Furthermore, Wroth names Longus's *Daphnis and Chloe* in the Newberry manuscript.[5] Her borrowings from Greek romance, however, are difficult to pinpoint, because they are mediated through the substantial previous borrowings of authors by whom Wroth was also influenced.[6] Yet Wroth makes alterations to the shape of the genre, subverting its most prevalent feature, the marriage of its lover/protagonists.

Unravelling Enchantments

The *Urania*'s first volume offers the possibility of what we might call a Holy Romance Empire through the union of Amphilanthus, 'Light of the West,' and Pamphilia, 'Star of the East.' Their relationship is drawn out through three enchantments: the Throne of Love on Cyprus, the Theatre of the World in the Gulf of Lepanto, and the Hell of Deceit in Pamphilia's Kingdom. Wroth uses the wide geographical range and historical instability of the Greek romance model to illuminate a fictional romance globe with links to the politics of her time.

The geographical scope of volume I encompasses most of Europe and the Mediterranean. Though Wroth uses pre-Islamic place names, all of the locations that she mentions, unless noted as magical, correspond to real places. Josephine Roberts points out that almost all of the place names in the first volume of the *Urania* can be found on Mercator's 1611 maps of Asia and Greece and suggests that Wroth also might have been familiar with Ortelius's *Theatre of the Whole World* and George Sandys's *A Relation of a Journey*.[7] In the second half of the *Urania*, Wroth's text goes even further afield, ranging eastward to Tartaria, Persia, and

Babylon. Wroth's interest in these locations may reflect anxieties over the threatening power of the Ottoman Empire, but her place names, as in the first half of the *Urania*, maintain pre-Islamic nomenclature.[8]

Furthermore, Wroth uses the lack of historical specificity of the Greek model for topicality. There is rarely a one-to-one correspondence between Wroth's characters and her contemporaries, and Wroth veils her social references by creating multiple characters that reflect different aspects of people she knew. Despite Wroth's cloaking of her social and political allusions, the publication of the first volume of the *Urania* offended Lord Edward Denny, who famously upbraided Wroth in his 'To Pamphilia from the father-in-law of Seralius.'[9] Though Wroth defended herself poetically, she sought to recall the published volumes of the *Urania*, going so far as to deny having known of their publication.

Desire for political union in the *Urania* mirrors similar hopes for the unification of Europe under the Holy Roman Empire in Wroth's time.[10] As Roberts asserts, 'At the heart of the *Urania* lies one of the most powerful political fantasies of sixteenth and seventeenth-century Europe – the revival of the Holy Roman Empire in the West' ('Critical Introduction' xxxix). Wroth first crowns Amphilanthus King of the Romans (I, 1, 45) and, subsequently, Holy Roman Emperor (I, 3, 463). She crowns Pamphilia Queen of the realm of Pamphilia (I, 1, 168), located in Asia Minor where her family controls large territories.

Wroth frames this potential union in pageant-like enchantments that use the global iconography typical of early modern projections of political goals. This iconography often ornamented public spectacles, paintings, and processions, where European royal families employed visual images in their efforts to consolidate power. For example, Carlos V, King of Spain and Holy Roman Emperor, used paintings and processions extensively to portray himself as a specifically Roman emperor. Queen Elizabeth I also made elaborate use of visual spectacle in securing her kingdom, as did the French monarchs of the Valois court and the Medici of Florence.[11] James I learned from his predecessors, putting on the most extravagant spectacles that England had ever seen. As Roberts observes of the emblematic pageant that marked James's triumphal entry into London in 1604, 'The royal spectacle celebrated James's act of bringing all Britain under one rule, as a prelude to the renewal of empire' ('Critical Introduction' xxxix).[12] The prevalence of such visual spectacles and the iconography of global Empire provide a context for Wroth's ekphrastic enchantments and their link to the utopian desire for the unification of the Western world in the first volume of the *Urania*.

The three major enchantments of the first volume function like graphic puzzles, borrowing from well-established ekphrastic techniques to reveal aspects of the characters' identities and to present the potential for love to create lasting unions in the text. The enchantments become increasingly resistant to interpretation as the narrative progresses, but the first enchantment, the Throne of Love, presents the most complete emblematic expression of identity and union in the romance. Wroth crafts a verbal picture that requires a local ekphrastic interpreter to be understood, demands an equal allotment of trials to the male and female protagonists to be solved, and results in the assimilation of foreigners into European society, all of which, as I have argued, are typical conventions of Renaissance imitations of the Greek romance. The enchantment involves most of the characters that have been introduced into the plot, and its effects last for almost all of book 1.

The search for lost identity, especially the identity of female characters, is a prevalent theme of the *Urania*. The work opens with the beautiful shepherdess, Urania, lamenting her lost identity. Wroth builds on the work of her uncle, Philip Sidney, in lifting this character from the opening of the *New Arcadia*, where the shepherds Strephon and Claius lament the departure of their beloved Urania (1, 1, 1–3), who only ever makes an appearance in the *Arcadia* in an ekphrasis: Sidney's Urania is presented in a portrait.

From Wroth's *Urania*'s first episode, identity is related to ekphrasis through the intertextual allusion to Sidney's work. In Sidney's *New Arcadia*, Urania's portrait is one of a group for which Phalantus of Corinth jousts, acquiring these prizes on behalf of his lady, Artesia (1, 16, 160). Sidney's ekphrasis of the portrait follows:

> It was of a young maid which sat pulling out a thorn out of a Lamb's foot, with her look so attentive uppon it, as if that little foot could have been the circle of her thoughts; her apparel so poor as it had nothing but the inside to adorn it; a sheep-hook lying by her with a bottle upon it. But with all that povertie, beauty played the prince and commanded as many hearts as the greatest Queen there did. Her beauty and her estate made her quickly to be known to be the fair shepeardesse Urania, whom a rich knight called Lacemon, farre in love with her, had unluckely defended. (NA 1, 16, 160–1)

Wroth provides a text and story for Sidney's incomplete picture of the foundling shepherdess, whom Wroth envisions as the Princess of Naples, sister to Amphilanthus. Along with her adoption of the Sidneian character Urania, Wroth imitates the *New Arcadia*'s highly ekphrastic jousting-for-portraits episode with her own jousting episode in which the Knight Polarchos of Cyprus fights for ladies' portraits to honour his own ungrateful lover, the Princess of Rhodes (Wroth I, 2, 237–40). Verbal images in Sidney's romance thus generate images in Wroth's own highly ekphrastic romance.[13]

Wroth marks her Sidneian literary pedigree, printing her romance with the authority of her family's poetic reputation emblazoned on the title page. Like her uncle, she borrows from Greek romance to subject her protagonists to trials that test their bonds to one another and their abilities to interpret verbal images; unlike Sidney, however, she increasingly loosens her bonds of love and makes her verbal images difficult to decode. These ekphraseis, nonetheless, drive the *Urania*'s action.

The Throne of Love

The first enchantment, the Throne of Love, occurs on Cyprus. A boatload of lovers, including Urania and her first love, Parselius, are shipwrecked there in a storm; however, Wroth crafts a more magical world than that of the typical Greek romance, resorting to chivalric marvels to ensure that her characters will stay on the island. Like the boat that pulled into the harbour before them, our characters' boat bursts into flames as they land: '[T]hey landed in the Island, which no sooner was done, but their former wonder was encreased, by the sudden falling a fire of their own Ship' (I, 1, 47). The loss of their ship is still more frightening in light of the reputation of the island's inhabitants: '[T]his not onely amazed them, but much troubled them, considering the barbarousnes of the people who there inhabited' (I, 1, 46). Since they have no means of escape, the ship's loss 'brought new sorrow to them, considering they were in a strange Country, among barbarous people, depriv'd of all hope to get thence any more, but there to continue at the mercy of unchristened creatures' (I, 1, 49). Cyprus, mythical birthplace of Venus, was under Ottoman control while Wroth wrote, making the unruly 'barbarous' and 'unchristened creatures' of the text stand in for 'Turks' (or Muslims), who were also reputed to be venal and lascivious.

The travellers next encounter an architectural spectacle, which is described in detail. Since the ekphrasis's details are significant to the decoding of the enchantment and for later intratextual allusions, I cite the majority of the passage. The narrator depicts the scene:

> Thus, on they went (but as in a Labyrinth without a thrid) till they came within sight of a rare and admirable Pallace. It was scituated on a Hill, but that Hill formed, as if the world would needs raise one place of purpose to build Loves throne upon [...] This sumptuous House was square, set all upon Pillars of blacke Marble, the ground paved with the same. Every one of those pillars, presenting the lively Image (as perfectly as carving could demonstrate) of brave, and mighty men, and sweet and delicate Ladies, such as had been conquer'd by loves power: but placed there, as still to mainetaine, and uphold the honour, and House of Love [...] The upper story had the Gods most fairely and richly appearing in their thrones: their proportions such as their powers, and quallities are described. As Mars in Armes, weapons of Warre about him, Trophies of his Victories, and many demonstrations of his Warre-like God-head. Apollo with Musicke, Mercurie, Saturne, and the rest in their kind.
>
> At the foote of this Hill ranne a pleasant and sweetly passing river, over which was a Bridge, on which were three Towres: Upon the first was the Image of Cupid, curiously carv'd with his Bow bent, and Quiver at his backe, but with his right hand pointing to the next Towre; on which was a statue of white Marble, representing Venus, but so richly adorn'd, as it might for rarenesse, and exquisitenesse have beene taken for the Goddesse her selfe, and have causd as strange an affection as the Image did to her maker, when he fell in love with his owne worke. Shee was crownd with Mirtle, and Pansies, in her left hand holding a flaming Heart, her right, directing to the third Towre, before which, in all dainty riches, and rich delicacy, was the figure of Constancy, holding in her hand the Keyes of the Pallace: which shewed, that place was not to be open to all, but to few possessed with that vertue. (I, 1, 47–8)

The description of architecture was part of the ekphrastic tradition, as is evident from Pliny's *Historia naturalis*.[14] Along with being pictured in words, this architectural spectacle is depicted in the lower half of Simon Van de Passe's frontispiece for the *Urania*, reproduced in figure 6.1.[15] The illustration of the view would have amplified its vividness and underscored the importance of its ekphrastic description. Wroth easily could have given Van de Passe guidance in the crafting of this frontispiece. Roberts notes that Mary Sidney's secretary, Hugh Sanford, for example, gave directions to the engraver of the title page for her 1593 edition of the *New Arcadia*, as did Sir John Harrington for his translation of the *Orlando Furioso*. Even if Wroth did not have a hand

6.1. Simon Van de Passe, engraved frontispiece to Lady Mary Wroth's *Countess of Montgomery's Urania*, 1621. By Permission of the Folger Shakespeare Library, Washington, DC.

in the composition of the frontispiece, its content reflects close familiarity with the text.

The presentation of the palace begs ekphrastic interpretation from women in the text partly because of its female authorship and similarities to other female authorial constructions. Wroth's description of the palace resembles architectural projects authored by women who were her contemporaries. For instance, Shannon Miller argues that the palace in the Throne of Love episode, with its Palladian style and towers, reflects similar buildings executed by Lady Mary (Sidney) Herbert (Mary Wroth's aunt), and Elizabeth Hardwick, Countess of Shrewsbury. Bess of Hardwick built Hardwick Hall to her specifications beginning in 1590. Miller explains that 'the house loudly declares itself Elizabeth Shrewsbury's through her initials,' which were repeated on the crests of towers such that 'certain views of the house then triple the view of Bess's initials' (139). She then goes on to compare Bess's architectural project with Wroth's explorations of female identity as follows: 'The *Urania's* architectural structures, both visual and thematic, serve Wroth as a strategy for negotiating female identity. Much like Bess of Hardwick's inscription of her initials on the crested towers of Hardwick Hall, Wroth's text employs such structures to provide an avenue for an expression of the female self' (142). Though Miller's insights here seem to promise an analysis of how female characters interpret the structures that Wroth builds in the text, her reading instead seeks internalized female subjectivity through female characters' negotiations of caves and closets, spaces that have little to do with the large-scale enchantments that Wroth crafts. Readings of interior spaces by critics like Bernadette Andrea indicate that Wroth was beginning to elaborate the kind of internalized and psychological self that critics have come to expect from modern novels.[16] In searching for an internalized, psychological female self, however, both Andrea and Miller overlook the potential for architectural ekphrasis to disclose identity. Furthermore, the fact that the enchanter in this adventure turns out to be female (i.e., Venus) underscores Wroth's self-consciousness about her own female authorship of the architectural ekphrasis and enchantment.

As we have seen in previous chapters, romance characters can express identity through ekphrastic creation and interpretation. In the enchantment of the Throne of Love, the characters are at first unable to interpret the spectacular scene: 'Comming towards it, they imagined it some Magicall work, for so daintily it appear'd in curiositie, as it seem'd as if it hung in the ayre' (I, 1, 47). Further on, the narrator explains that '[t]hey all beheld this place with great wonder, Parselius resolving it was some Enchauntment; wherefore was the nicer how they proceeded in the entring of it' (I, 1, 50). Though Parselius's view is voiced by the narrator, all of the characters remain silent. Despite the fact that the characters perceive the scene as having special or hidden meanings, they do not know how to interpret it.

In keeping with the Second Sophistic's ekphrastic tradition, however, the images are interpreted for the travellers by an old man.

> there came an aged Man, with so good a countenance and grave aspect, as it strucke reverence into them, to be shewed to him, by them. He saluted them thus: Faire company, your beholding this place with so much curiosity, and besides your habits makes me know you are strangers, therefore fit to let you understand the truth of this brave Building, which is dedicated to Love. Venus (whose Priest I am) thinking her self in these latter times, not so much, or much lesse honour'd then in ages past, hath built this, calling it the throne of Love. Here is She dayly serv'd, by my selfe, and others of my profession, and heere is the triall of false or faithfull Lovers. (Wroth I, 1, 50)

The role of ekphrastic interpreter is filled here by the old man, a Cypriot priest of Venus. As Bartsch argues, citing examples from Lucian, Cebes, and other ekphrasists from antiquity, the wise old man is a standard feature of ekphrastic narratives that have a hidden meaning. The typical ekphrastic narrator first presents the ekphrasis and then either expresses confusion or gives the characters a chance to indicate their bewilderment (Wroth's characters view the scene as 'magical'). Bartsch avers that in cases like these, an interpretation of the ekphrasis does not take place 'until the inevitable introduction of the learned interpreter,' who is 'Often a wise and elderly figure, or a character with privileged knowledge (such as a native of the region [...])' (26). Wroth fulfils ekphrastic expectations with the introduction of a learned interpreter, and she also begins to assimilate foreigners into European and, in this case, Christian society through ekphrastic interpretation. The old man is, after all, precisely one of the 'barbarous' people whom the travellers feared, but he is immediately 'reverenced' by them when he gives his ekphrastic interpretation. Moreover, the old man welcomes Wroth's characters, even though they are obviously foreigners. Thus, the old man emphasizes that the travellers are now the ones who are strangers and subverts their expectations of barbarism with his ekphrastic hospitality.

The old man explains the rules of the enchantment, delineating the trials of each of the three towers that lead to the palace. He describes the enchantment as follows:

> Those that are false, may enter this Towre, which is Cupids Towre, or the Towre of Desire: but therein once inclosed, they endure torments fit for such a fault. Into the second any Lover may enter, which is the Towre of Love: but there they suffer unexpressable tortures, in severall kindes as their affections are most incident to; as Jealosie, Despaire, Feare, Hope, Longings, and such like. The third which is guarded by Constancy, can bee entred by none, till the valiantest Knight, with the loyallest Lady come together, and open that gate, when all these Charmes shal have conclusion. Till then, all that venture into these Towres, remaine prisoners; this is the truth. Now if your hearts will serve you adventure it. (I, 1, 48–9)

The stranded characters prudently decline the old man's invitation, but unwisely decide to picnic on the river's bank, forgetting a cardinal rule of visiting any magical locale: never drink the water. Having learned the perils of the place, they are, nonetheless, impassioned by the river water 'whereof they had but drunke, when in them seuerall Passions did instantly aboun' (Wroth I, 1, 51).

Fitting what David Konstan terms the sexual symmetry of Greek romance, the enchantment of the Throne of Love is an ekphrastic puzzle that can only be solved by a man and woman together. The decoding of the enchantment occurs at the end of book 1, when Pamphilia and Amphilanthus are political equals, having both been recently crowned as rulers of their own kingdoms. Both characters have a part to play in solving the enchantment, and both arrive dressed according to their state, a visual expression of their passions. Pamphilia's appearance is described in the following prosopographia:

> Pamphilia being thus apparreld in a Gowne of light Tawny or Murrey, embrodered with the richest, and perfectest Pearle for round-nesse and whitenes, the work contrived into knots and Garlands; on her head she wore a crowne of Diamonds, without foiles, to shew her clearenesse, such as needed no foile to set forth the true brightnesse of it: (I, 1, 169)

The description of Pamphilia's garments emblematizes her identity. Clothing, especially the choice of colour and ornament, was one way in which wealthy men and women could convey their status and state of mind in the early modern period. These garments function symbolically as would a personal *impresa* or heraldry. Pamphilia's colours include murrey, a deep purple mulberry that signifies constancy.[17] The ornaments she chooses include pearl, which expresses pureness or virginity, and diamonds, which signify steadfastness and which, needing no metal backing or foil to increase their lustre, indicate that she too needs no foil or counterpart to offset her perfections.[18]

Not only does Pamphilia display her identity in her sartorial choices, but she also shows that she is a good interpreter of the visual signs that other characters exhibit. Amphilanthus's garments demonstrate that he has not been as constant as Pamphilia, and she chides him by commenting on his clothes. She asks him, 'But what colour shall wee have next: the last I saw was Crimson, now Watchet and White; do you adde to your inconstancy, as fast as to your colours?' (I, 1, 165). Accordingly, Amphilanthus's clothing is described as follows: 'He was in Ashcolour, witnessing his repentance, yet was his cloake, and the rest of his suite so sumptuously embroidred with gold, as spake for him, that his repentance was most glorious' (Wroth I, 1, 169). His livery, as the narrator explains, may purport to convey repentance, but the 'glorious' aspect of this repentance will later signify that it is not lasting, for Amphilanthus proves to be gloriously unfaithful to Pamphilia.

The lovers' navigation of the enchantment underscores Pamphilia's constancy and Amphilanthus's desirability. It is Amphilanthus who braves Cupid's tower, that of desire (I, 1, 169). The two together brave the tower of Venus, that of love (I, 1, 169). Finally, only Pamphilia braves the tower of constancy (I, 1, 169). Amphilanthus questions Pamphilia as they arrive at Venus's second tower: '"What say you to this, brave Queene?" said hee. "Have you so much love, as can warrant you to adventure for this?"' (I, 1, 169). Pamphilia replies: '"I have," answerd shee, "as much as will bring me to the next Tower, where I must (I believe) first adventure for that"' (I, 1, 169). This exchange reminds the reader that, at this point in the narrative, Amphilanthus's unfaithfulness is somewhat understandable given Pamphilia's unwillingness to admit her love in the past. Amphilanthus's addressing Pamphilia as 'brave Queen,' the only occasion in the text that he mentions her royal status, emphasizes that at this moment, the two are political equals. The ethos of the statue of Constancy is channelled into Pamphilia's being, as the work of visual art, spirit-like, dissolves and enters her body through her breast: '[They] passed to the last Tower, where Constancy stood holding the keyes, which Pamphilia tooke; at which instant

Constancy vanished, as metamorphosing her self into her breast' (I, 1, 169). The ekphrastic figure is literally personified and embodies Pamphilia's character in a strange physical and figurative melding. Finally, the enchantment draws to a close, Pamphilia and Amphilanthus freeing the imprisoned knights and ladies from their bonds.

Pamphilia and Amphilanthus's performance also inspires the religious conversion of the Cypriots. Ekphrastic display thus facilitates the inclusion of foreigners as follows:

> The King of Ciprus, who out of love to the Christian Faith, which before he contemned, seeing such excellent, and happy Princes professors of it, desired to receive it, which Amphilanthus infinitly rejoycing at, and all the rest, Christned him with his wife, excellently faire daughter, and Polarchos his valiant Sonne, and so became the whole Island Christians. (I, 1, 170)

The Cypriots, who are at first considered to be 'barbarous,' become 'christened creatures' for the love the Cypriot king feels for the travellers once they have solved the enchantment. In other words, he is passible to the spectacle. Ekphrastic interpretation of the enchantment results in religious unification – an example of the wish-fulfilment that typifies Greek romance narratives.

Wroth's first ekphrastic spectacle also conforms to Greek romance norms in its presentation of proleptic similes. The resolution of the enchantment through love and the subsequent religious conversion is prefigured in the most detailed of the narrator's descriptions, that of the statue of Venus, maker of the enchantment. This ekphrasis will also have a bearing on later enchantments, specifically as a commentary on the impossibility of global unification in the enchantment I call the Theatre of the World. Venus is 'crownd with Mirtle, and Pansies, in her left hand holding a flaming Heart' (I, 1, 48). The flaming heart was a popular Christian symbol, and when accompanied by clasped hands forms the favourite emblem of the Familist spiritualist sect of the sixteenth and early seventeenth centuries.[19] Hence, this depiction of the flaming heart along with the detail that in the resolution of the enchantment Pamphilia's 'left Glove was off, holding the King by the hand who held most hearts' (I, 1, 169) would have been an emblem of love, union, and toleration that anticipates the Cypriots' conversion. Yet, this emblem of love does not hold. The statues of Cupid and Mars receive almost as much ekphrastic detail as does the statue of Venus in the description of the Throne of Love, foreshadowing the roles that desire and militarism still have to play in the romance.

The Throne of Love enchantment represents Wroth's iteration of an ekphrastic theme prevalent in Renaissance imitations of the Greek romance. She uses traditional ekphrastic techniques – the insertion of a wise old interpreter, multivalent imagery, proleptic similes – for the presentation and interpretation of the enchantment. The graphic puzzle demands an equal proportioning of trials to the male and female protagonists and allows them to express identity through an emblematics of the self. The resolution of the enchantment finally assimilates foreigners into European religious and political alliances. Thus, the navigation of the Throne of Love does result in unification – an example of Greek romance wish-fulfilment – but Wroth quickly subverts the model that she instantiates.

The Theatre of the World

The second major enchantment of the *Urania*, which dominates the narrative of the third book, takes place in a large enchanted theatre on a mysterious 'rockie island' (Wroth I, 3, 399) in the Gulf of Lepanto. In this enchantment, which I refer to as the Theatre of the World, Wroth begins to unravel the bonds between her lover/protagonists and starts to deny the creation of a Holy Romance Empire. The Theatre of the World episode subverts the emblem of love that is elaborated in the Throne of Love to show that humanist and neo-Stoic ideas of cosmopolitanism do not hold sway in the fictional world of the *Urania*. This destabilization of the unions in the text results in both a nostalgia for Elizabethan modes of romance and an increasingly problematic relation between the visual and the verbal.

In this adventure, yet another shipwreck leads many of the main characters to fall into an enchantment. The setting on an unnamed island in the Gulf of Lepanto, through its evocation of the eponymous battle of 1571,[20] builds expectations for the coming conflict between East and West. After their wreck, Pamphilia and Urania encounter an intricately described architectural view. Pamphilia first happens upon the scene, followed by Urania, who exclaims:

> 'I feare this storme, and adventure,' said Urania, 'ever since I was carried to Ciprus; if it be an inchantment, woe be to us, who may be bewitched to the misery of never seeing our desires fulfil'd, once was I made wretched by such a mischeife.' (I, 3, 372).

Urania immediately compares the view to the one in Cyprus, setting up for the reader similar expectations of an ekphrasis and subsequent interpretation by a wise man or native inhabitant. No such figure appears, and the ladies send their servants to investigate. They find 'a round building like a Theater, carved curiously, and in mighty pillars; light they might in many places discerne betweene the pillars of the upper row, but what was within, they could not discover, nor find the gate to enter it' (I, 3, 372–3). This structure is depicted on a hilltop in the upper half of the *Urania*'s frontispiece (figure 6.1), again emphasizing the importance of the ekphrasis. As in the Throne of Love episode, the characters again have difficulty deciphering the meaning of the ekphrastic spectacle.

In the absence of an authoritative interpreter, Pamphilia attempts to decode the graphic puzzle on her own. The mysterious building resembles a puzzle box, and it mirrors the perspectival trick of Bess of Hardwick's house. The narrator describes the building further:

> they found in one of the pillars, a letter ingraven, and on an other, another letter. They understood not the meaning, while Pamphilia (more desirous of knowledge then the rest) went as far behind that pillar as she could, and there perceived a space, as if halfe of the pillar, and then a plaine place, and so halfe of the other behind it had left a passage through them. She came backe and finding her imagination likely, she look'd upon the middle plaine which made the space, while the foure pillars making a square, and therein found a key-hole. She looked for the key, while the other three did likewise busie them selves in such search, having found in every plaine such a place, Pamphilia at last found the key, at the foote of one of the pillars. (I, 3, 373)

The specific letters on each of the pillars, reminiscent of the 'ES' initials on the towers of Hardwick Hall, are not revealed, and the arrangement of these pillars is difficult to parse. Nonetheless, Pamphilia's opening of the theatre resembles her navigation of the three towers of the enchantment in Cyprus, which culminated in her acquisition of the keys to the palace in the tower of Constancy. Finding the keys in this enchantment, however, does not mark a resolution. Instead, unlocking the theatre results in deeper enchantment.

Moreover, Pamphilia's evident curiosity in entering the theatre, rather than being praised as an adventurous heroine's worthy action, is depicted as a vice. When she opens the building, 'instantly appeard as magnificent a Theater, as Art could frame' (Wroth I, 3, 373). The theatre is sumptuously described with marble thrones, rich carpets, and beautiful embroidery. Pamphilia next enters the theatre as follows:

> Needs this richnes must be neerer beheld, and (like women) must see novelties; nay even Pamphilia was inticed to vanity in this kind. In they goe, and venture to ascend the Throne, when instantly the sweetest musicke, and most inchanting harmony of voyces, so overruld their senses, as they thought no more of any thing, but went up, and sate downe in the chayers. The gate was instantly lock'd againe, and so was all thought in them shut up for their comming forth thence, till the man most loving, and most beloved, used his force, who should release them, but himselfe be inclosed till by the freeing of the sweetest and loveliest creature, that poore habits had disguised greatnesse in, he should be redeem'd, and then should all bee finished. (I, 3, 373)

Like the episode of the Throne of Love, this enchantment's masque-like tableau requires the participation of a man, 'most loving, and most beloved,' and a woman, 'the sweetest and loveliest creature, that poor habits had disguised greatnesse in,' to be resolved. However, the criticism of Pamphilia's Pandora-like curiosity sets up negative expectations for the enchantment's outcome, and the male and female participation in this enchantment illustrates the folly of both sexes.

While women's curiosity is criticized, since even Pamphilia is 'inticed to vanity in this kind' (I, 3, 373), Wroth doles out an equal portion of blame to men's folly. The characters, after having been enchanted, are described:

> To say these brave princes were in paine, I should say amisse, for all the comfort their owne hearts could imagine to them selves, they felt there, seeing before them, (as they thought) their loves smiling, and joying in them; thus flattering love deceiv'd the true, and brought contrary effects to the most good. (I, 3, 373)

Here, flattering love holds the characters enthralled, content to play their part in the enchanted theatre. Wroth may be influenced by Erasmus, who constructs his version of a *theatrum mundi* in his *Encomium Moriae* (*In Praise of Folly*), where Folly explains:

> If anyone tries to take the masks off the actors when they're playing a scene on the stage and show their true, natural faces to the audience, he'll certainly spoil the whole play and deserve to be stoned and thrown out of the theatre for a maniac [...] To destroy the illusion is to ruin the whole play, for it's really the illusion and make-up which hold the audience's eye.

> Now, what else is the whole life of man but a sort of play? Actors come on wearing their different masks and all play their parts until the producer orders them off the stage [...] (44)

Along with love, Erasmus argues that war is also folly, a sentiment that Wroth seconds. Wroth compares the folly of flattering love to the empty victory that the princes achieve in winning back the kingdom of Albania only to find out that while they are distracted by military glory their ladies have been enchanted in the Theatre of the World. The false experience of love in Wroth's theatre is compared to the fruitlessness of sending news of the Albanian victory to Morea, Pamphilia's parents' kingdom (and here a possible pun on *moria*, folly).

> [T]his those brave Princes felt, when at the concluding of the last battel, just as they had taken possession of the greater townes of that Kingdome, and setled all things in quiet [...] resolving thence to send newes to Morea, and every one to their loves, of their brave and happy successe, there arrived a messenger with the heavy tidings of the losse of the whole worlds beauty. (I, 3, 373–4)

Wroth's treatment of her misguided characters suggests she is less sanguine about folly than Erasmus. Whereas Erasmus argues that the illusions folly creates should not be unmasked – for they are the glue that holds society together – Wroth systematically disenchants her theatre through the undoing of social bonds, proving to be precisely the kind of 'maniac' that the character of Folly disparages (Erasmus 44).

Complementing the intertextual play between Wroth's Theatre of the World and Erasmus's *theatrum mundi*, I believe that Wroth's choice of a theatre as an organizing motif in this enchantment refers to a highly ekphrastic work, Abraham Ortelius's *Theatrum Orbis Terrarum*, or *Theatre of the Whole World*, which was the first atlas-style collection of maps made in Europe and which contained maps of different parts of the known world with corresponding ekphrastic texts on the verso of each map describing the places and their inhabitants. The best-selling *Theatrum* would have been available to Wroth in a number of editions, including a 1606 English translation.[21]

Held motionless in the enchanted theatre, the international group of characters become representations of the world, a depiction of foreign peoples that represents the possibility of cosmopolitan global union. The narrator describes the number and variety of peoples, 'all joyed in others loves, and a fine sight it was to see them in their various habits, yet all to one purpose, imitating the world' (I, 3, 421). The description of three female characters dressed as foreigners from the various corners of the globe highlights the link to Ortelius's work, which Wroth's characters enact with their 'various habbits.'

Wroth's enchantment comes to resemble the title page of Ortelius's *Theatrum* (figure 6.2) as women disguised in foreign garb join the enchanted crowd. These women mirror Ortelius's female allegorical representations of continents festooning the Doric columns that bear the title of the work. Europe, pictured in Imperial purple with orb and sceptre, crowns the image. Asia is represented by a woman in silk depicted on the left with incense burning. Africa stands with sun and balsam branch on the right, and America, with her bow and arrows, rests naked on the ground grasping a severed head in her hand. Wroth's enchanted theatre features an analogue of Ortelius's America in Musalina, who is disguised 'like an Amason' (I, 3, 422).[22] Africa is represented by 'Lucenia like an Aegyptian' (I, 3, 422), and Asia is represented by the Queen of Bulgaria, who dresses as 'a Persian' (Wroth I, 3, 441).

In referring to Ortelius, Wroth emblematizes both political and spiritual wish-fulfilment. Early modern neo-Stoic articulations of Christian cosmopolitanism offered a humanist counterdiscourse to territorial acquisition through conquest and were promoted by Ortelius in his *Theatrum* and the *Parergon* that he appended to it. Dennis Cosgrove explains:

> [T]he image of the globe acted more subtly than merely as an icon of universal power. The contemplative tradition – dating back to the Athenian Stoics, revived by Cicero and Seneca, and inflected by late Roman neo-Platonism and Patristic spiritualism – figured the globe also as a moral space, offering the soul the opportunity of transcendence against the grandeur of cosmic creation [...] This tradition dominates the conceptual development of the *theatrum mundi*. While working with the rhetoric of global empire, cosmographers and geographers – among them Ortelius – drew upon the alternative figure of global space, especially in the light of Europe's other dominant sixteenth-century experience, that of religious division. In doing so, some of them developed a more liberal and tolerant approach to global knowledge itself than appears in Camões's and even Ercilla's imperial panegyrics. (862)

Whereas early modern epics (Cosgrove's examples being Camões's *Os Lusíadas* and Ercilla's *Araucana*) figure the globe as an emblem of

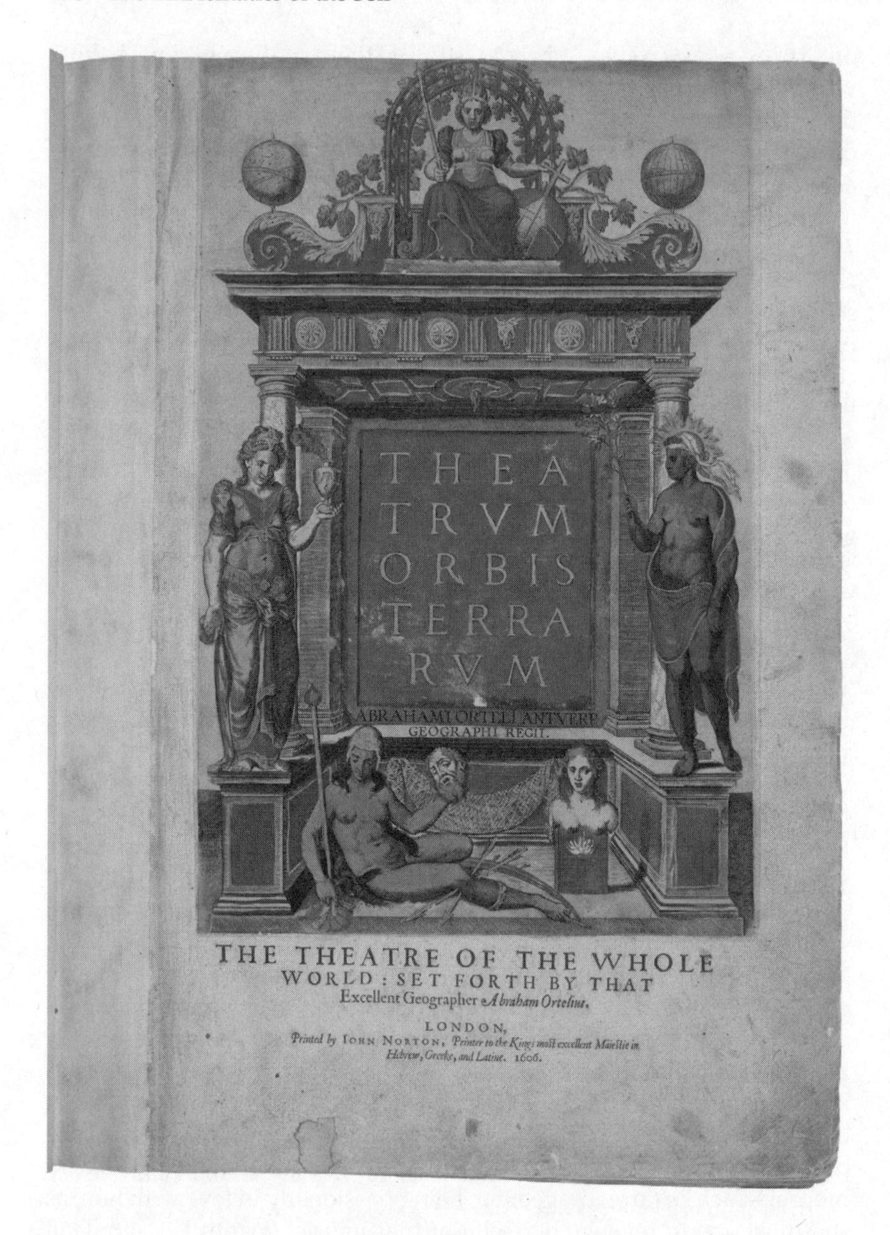

6.2. Abraham Ortelius, engraved title page to *Teatrum orbis terrarum*, 1606 [1608?]. By Permission of the Folger Shakespeare Library, Washington, DC.

universal power, Cosgrove avers that philosophers and geographers like Ortelius adopt the stoical world-view to create an alternative vision of global union. Wroth's reference to Ortelius may also hark back to the flaming heart and clasped hands of the Throne of Love as a Familist emblem of love. Ortelius himself was a known Familist, and his frontispiece and other prefatory material reflect the neo-Stoic and Christian cosmopolitan values that Familist and similar spiritualist sects espoused.[23] Romance could, with its discourse of love, be the poetic version of this cosmopolitan world-view.

Yet Wroth alludes to these cosmopolitan dreams only to dash them with their own iconography. As the Queen of Bulgaria's servant explains, the theatre now bears an inscription directing how to solve the enchantment, and many women try to disguise themselves to complete the female half of the trial: 'many are gone thither, and some put on disguises of purpose, but that will not serve, surely Fate hath no deceit' (Wroth I, 3, 400). Despite the ingenuity of these costumes, the comment of the servant, along with the emphasis on the falseness of the disguises, demonstrates the futility of this vision of unification.

When Amphilanthus arrives on the rocky island, his actions preclude the re-creation of the Familist love emblem and prevent his union with Pamphilia. Enchanted, 'the star of the East' awaits his arrival 'leaning her cheeke on her hand, her eyes lifted upwards as asking helpe' (Wroth I, 3, 421). Instead of joining Pamphilia and taking her hand, as he did in the Throne of Love enchantment, Amphilanthus gets caught holding Musalina's Amazon hand. His indiscretion refers to the possible Familist illusion, but only to deny its applicability to Wroth's romance globe. Moreover, the three women representing America, Africa, and Asia all have flirtations with Amphilanthus, implying that his inconstancy is of global proportions.

Wroth's invocation of a global geography to highlight the inconstancy of Amphilanthus may reflect European women's fears regarding the seductive threat of foreign women in the Renaissance. Along these lines, Kim Hall suggests that the vision Urania's maid experiences after drinking the water at the Throne of Love illustrates the perceived sexual threat of foreign women. Enchanted by the water, the maid 'beheld as she beleev'd Allimarlus in the second Towre, kissing and embracing a Blackmoore; which so farre inraged her, being passionatly in love with him, as she must goe to revenge her selfe of that injurie' (Wroth I, 1, 49). Hall suggests that 'Allimarlus's embrace of the black woman represents female fears of the foreign difference that heroes – and travelers

– encounter on these romantic adventures' (*Things of Darkness* 189). The fact that the women who figure America, Asia, and Africa all play a part in Amphilanthus's betrayals may indicate that Wroth others foreign women, but Hall's view that Wroth does so specifically to negotiate a better subject position for her female protagonists and, by extension, for herself as a woman writer in a misogynist society is not borne out in this case. Pamphilia is not elevated by these foreign influences, not even through their criticism, and is not even able to resolve the enchantment.

In the Theatre of the World, characters manage to decode the graphic puzzle that the enchanter presents, but at the cost of Amphilanthus's betrayal of Pamphilia. His disloyalty makes their union and the unification of the Western world that it allegorically represents more remote. Lamenting her hoped-for bond with Amphilanthus, Pamphilia is described as follows: 'her continuall passions, which not utter'd did weare her spirits and waste them, as rich imbroyderies will spoyle one another, if laid without papers betweene them, fretting each other, as her thoughts and imaginations did her rich and incomparable minde' (Wroth I, 3, 499). Pamphilia's anguish frays the cloth of love woven in Wroth's romance.

Wroth's disavowal of her global imagery most likely had topical significance. James I refused to support the Elector Palatine Frederic V of Bohemia and Frederic's wife Elizabeth (James's own daughter) to avoid involvement in the Thirty Years' War. James also attempted a dynastic union with Spain through the failed Spanish marriage, but these peacekeeping policies did not prevent Europe from descending into terrible religious conflict. Wroth's Theatre of the World highlights unfulfilled aspects of the emblem of love that the Throne of Love first proposes, and that, perhaps, reflected hopes for similar political unions in her own time.

With female characters representing Asia, Africa, and America, who represents Europe? Pamphilia, an Asian Queen, cannot be the crowning glory of this Theatre of the World. Amphilanthus, though his political position as Holy Roman Emperor might seem to make him a potential candidate, cannot solve this part of the enchantment because he is a man. To traverse this aporia the narrative turns back to Arcadia, where Urania, both the character and the text, have their inception. Urania's search for identity, which opens Wroth's romance's action, ends in the resolution of the Theatre of the World as does the mystery of a new character, the Arcadian shepherdess Veralinda, who echoes Urania's story and who solves the enchantment.

Hence, Wroth finds her missing character and Ortelian representation of Europe in Arcadia. This discovery is marked ekphrastically, when Amphilanthus's brother Leonius comes upon a fountain in Arcadia:

> hee discerned a Fountaine made in the fashion of an Emperiall Crowne with a Globe on the toppe, out of which like a full shower of raine the water came so plentifully, and showringly, as it resembled such plenty, so finely was it counterfeited [...]. (Wroth I, 3, 424)

Leonius has followed a beautiful maid (later revealed to be Veralinda), who is dressed like a shepherdess, to this fountain. The girl's shepherdish attire and her close call with a bear that attempts to maul her remind the reader of Wroth's character Urania, but also of the sequestered princesses of Sidney's *Arcadia*.[24] The fountain, with its globe and imperial crown – what one scholar has recently called an 'Arcadian theme park' (Alexander, *Writing* 299) – signals that Veralinda will be the one to resolve the enchantment of the Theatre of the World.

After Leonius cross-dresses to woo Veralinda Sidneian-style, the foundling shepherdess's father reveals that she is not his daughter and explains that the enchantment of the Theatre of the World must be resolved for her to learn about her past. Veralinda and her trusty companion, Leonia (Leonius cross-dressed, of course), adventure the enchantment. The theatre opens to Veralinda immediately, and the disenchantment takes place as follows:

> Apollo appear'd, commanding Veralinda to touch them with a rod he threw her down; she did so when they all awaked, and held each one his lover by the hand, then stood they up, and as amazed gazed on the Shepherdesse, and Nimph. Amphilanthus at his waking tooke Musalinas hand [...] When this was done, and all the couples stood round as the roome was, suddenly the Chaires were vanished, and a Pillar of Gold stood in their stead, on which hung a Booke, every one there strove to take that down, but none could gaine it; Pamphilia and Urania came, they both resolved to try, but the first place was given by their consents unto Urania, who tooke it downe, wherewith the inchantment partly ended as the Musique and charme, but the house remayning and the Pillar of Gold, as memory of the bravest inchantment that inclosed the number of the worthiest the world did ever know. (I, 3, 455)

This enchantment is resolved in part with the help of Apollo, implying a move away from Love as a possible solution to the characters' trials and towards the poetic production and rule of reason that Apollo represents. The entire stories of both Urania and Veralinda appear in the magic book. Veralinda is revealed to be Princess of Frigia, kidnapped from her kingdom in much the same way as Urania was kidnapped from Naples. Thus, the resolution of the Theatre of the World is literally a romance within the romance – the prize at the enchantment's resolution is a book that tells both Urania's and Veralinda's romance stories. The found romance functions as the text to accompany the highly wrought image of the enchantment, yet the book does not explain the enchantment's images, the text is not provided by an ekphrastic interpreter (the entire enchantment is orchestrated by a mysterious enchanter),[25] it cannot mend the rift between Pamphilia and Amphilanthus, and it does not resolve the growing international religious and military conflicts of the narrative. From here on out, amorous and civil bonds deteriorate. This tension between the fictional romance world and Wroth's own world is emphasized, moreover, by her growing insistence on the unfulfilled emblem of love that she first draws in the Throne of Love episode.

The Hell of Deceit

The final enchantment of the *Urania*'s first volume further destabilizes both the bonds between Pamphilia and Amphilanthus and the readability of visual images. The episode is referred to as the Hell of Deceit. Once Pamphilia and Amphilanthus are reconciled after his hand-holding affair with Musalina, they set off together to enjoy some hunting in Pamphilia's kingdom. To any reader of romance, the potential dangers of this sport would be obvious, but Pamphilia and Amphilanthus happily hunt boar together until Amphilanthus disappears. Upon looking for him, the distraught Pamphilia finds only a hellish spectacle played out inside a great stone:

> Pamphilia adventured, and pulling hard at a ring of iron which appeared, opend the great stone, when a doore shewed entrance, but within she might see a place like a Hell of flames, and fire, and as if many walking and throwing pieces of men and women up and downe the flames, partly burnt, and they still stirring the fire, and more brought in, and the longer she looked, the more she discernd, yet all as in the hell of deceit, at last she saw Musalina sitting in a Chaire of Gold, a Crowne on her head, and Lucenia holding a sword, which Musalina tooke in her hand, and before

> them Amphilanthus was standing, with his heart ript open, and Pamphilia written in it, Musalina ready with the point of the sword to conclude all, by razing that name out, and so his heart as the wound to perish. (I, 4, 583)

Pamphilia charges forward to the rescue, only to be thrust out again by a phantasmal force. When she regains consciousness, the stone no longer opens to the spectacle and instead bears the following inscription: 'Faithfull lovers keepe from hence / None but false ones here can enter: / This conclusion hath from whence / Falsehood flowes: and such may venter' (Wroth I, 4, 584). Helen Hackett notes that this scene inverts the episode of Busirane's tapestries in Spenser's *Faerie Queene*, and Wroth's perversion of Spenser's model demonstrates how far her romance globe has swerved from its Elizabethan predecessors.[26] The severed body parts roast in the fire, suggesting cannibalism, and the flames that surround the scene function to invoke the flaming heart emblem of the Throne of Love. This picture appears with two texts – Pamphilia's name, which will be obliterated by Musalina's sword, and the 'faithful lovers keep from hence' that denies Pamphilia's entrance – subverting the expectations for a verbal interpretation of the visual scene.

Amphilanthus also endures the Hell of Deceit, but his enchantment is far from equal to Pamphilia's trials, and he does not remain chaste. While he hunts, Musalina binds Amphilanthus with a spell. He first loses his horse, which a boar gores. He kills the boar, and then is set upon by a group of enchanted soldiers. He kills one of these soldiers, who then is falsely revealed to be Pamphilia, and Amphilanthus is then dragged into a stone where he witnesses a scene similar to the spectacle that Pamphilia viewed:

> [A] Ring of iron hee then saw, which pulling hard, opened the stone; there did hee perceive perfectly within it Pamphilia dead, lying within an arch, her breast open and in it his name made, in little flames burning like pretty lamps which made the letters, as if set round with diamonds, and so cleare it was, as hee distinctly saw the letters ingraven at the bottome in Characters of bloud; he ran to take her up, and try how to uncharme her, but he was instantly throwne out of the Cave in a trance, and being come againe to himselfe [...] he saw these words onely written in place of the entrance. This no wonder's of much waight, Tis the hell of deepe deceit. (I, 4, 655–6)

Again, characters and reader are offered no interpretation of this scene, and the two texts that accompany it only show its inscrutability: indeed a 'hell of deepe deceit.' Both Pamphilia and Amphilanthus encounter a terrifying image with unhelpful texts, and both are literally shut out of further opportunities to interpret or engage the horrible spectacle that they encounter. Here the flaming heart of the Throne of Love enchantment is made ghoulishly real by two ripped-open chests with wounded hearts framed in flame. These flaming hearts, however, are emblems of deceit and death, not love and union. The two iron rings may foreshadow the marriages that Wroth plans for Pamphilia and Amphilanthus in the second half of the *Urania*.[27]

Musalina and Lucenia, the costumed America and Africa respectively, are revealed to be the enchanters behind this episode, not Venus or some other beneficent sorcerer: 'Musalina having by divellish Art beene the cause of all this' (Wroth I, 4, 656). While Amphilanthus reads the inscription on the rock, he is distracted by yet another spell: 'he was called to for helpe by Musalina, her hee saw, she must be followed, Pamphilia is forgotten, and now may lie and burne in the Cave, Lucenia must bee rescued also' (Wroth I, 4, 656). Before Amphilanthus can even begin to interpret the spectacle and text that have appeared before him, he is pulled into another chase, this time after phantoms of Musalina and Lucenia, that eventually leads him to find the real women, who await his arrival in Tenedos. The only fruits of this enchantment, other than yet another sybaritic sojourn for Amphilanthus, are pain, separation, and a representation of wasted life. After Amphilanthus's disappearance, knights spread out across the globe looking for him, and the cloth of love unravels.

Though Wroth does reconcile these lovers one last time at the end of the *Urania*, they are not married by the volume's end, which terminates, as does Sidney's revision of his *New Arcadia*, in mid-sentence. '[A]s in a Labyrinth without a thrid' (Wroth, I, 1, 47), characters in the first half of the *Urania* become increasingly lost in the intricate cloth of love that Wroth weaves. The bonds between characters are unravelled as are the ekphrastic conventions that usually guide the interpretation of romance spectacles. The self-expression that ekphrastic interpretation affords and its assistance in the assimilation of foreigners in the fabric of European society are also diminished, such that, by the end of the narrative, the emblematics of the self is denied, perhaps reflecting Wroth's own personal and political frustrations. Thus, Wroth pictures her characters' disappointment through disruptive ekphrastic enchantments, and her use and perversion of previous romance models marks nostalgia for the amorous and civil bonds necessary for a proper romance ending, an ending that the *Urania* will not have.

Picturing Persia and Masquing Blackness

> [A]nd a fine sight it was to see them in their various habits, yet all to one purpose, imitating the world, which for all the changes and varieties she hath, must have but one conclusion, and one end. (Wroth I, 3, 421)

Whereas the first half of the *Urania* focuses on Europe and the Mediterranean for its action, in the second half Wroth widens her geography to include Persia, Tartaria, and Babylon – all territories with some degree of independence from the Ottoman Empire and alleged potential for conversion to Christianity in Wroth's time. Religious difference is heightened in the second half of the *Urania*, although early modern formulations of the tension between Christians and 'Turks' are never described precisely as such. As Gossett and Mueller claim:

> [T]he double standard typical of strong ideological bias is operative everywhere in the passages opposing Christians and Muslims in Part Two of the *Urania*. Christianity is exalted as the repository of all the values of civility, cultivation, and chivalry [...] But the Christians of Part Two are indistinguishable from the Muslims in their recourse to verbal abuse, torture, and mutilation [...] All in all, the broadest shift in conception distinguishing Part Two from Part One of the *Urania*, is the pervasive atmosphere of diminished expectations regarding the continued ascendancy of the Western cultural ideals identified with the romance genre. (xxxiv)

The two main impediments to the 'continued ascendancy of the Western ideals' associated with romance in the second half of the *Urania* are the undermining of the *de praesenti* marriage that Pamphilia and Amphilanthus enact in book 1 of the second volume (II, 1, 35) and the failed assimilation of foreigners, including Persians and Tartars, into long-term familial and political alliances with Europeans.

Predicated on the reconciliation between Pamphilia and Amphilanthus that takes place at the end of the first half of the romance, the couple perform a ceremony that by the legal standards of Wroth's day would have been binding. In a possible gesture to Wroth's own failed union with William Herbert, this 'Knott Never to Bee Untide' (Wroth II, 1, 35) is cut.[28] Amphilanthus ends up married to a Slavonian princess (Wroth II, 1, 133–4) and Pamphilia to Rodomandro, King of Tartaria (Wroth II, 2, 274).

In the second half of the romance, the presentation of foreigners defies European expectations of uncivil behaviour and entertains the possibility of their inclusion into Christian European society through marriage and political alliance. Though the action is not governed by a series of enchantments as it was in the first half of the romance, Wroth again uses ekphraseis to propose the assimilation of these foreigners. This is most pronounced in her treatment of Lindafillia, the rightful Sophy of Persia, and Rodomandro, the King of Tartaria and husband of Pamphilia.

During Wroth's time, Persia was considered a likely leverage point for destabilizing the Ottoman Empire. As Andrea observes, 'Western Christians and Persian Shi'as sought bi-lateral alliances throughout the early modern period against their common enemy, the Ottoman Sunnis' ('Lady Sherley' 279). The Shi'a branch of Islam, though not well understood by the English, was thought to be less threatening and more amenable to Christianity partly because of English travel accounts that painted the Shi'a as potential allies. Wroth could have easily been familiar with examples of such accounts of Persia through her family's connections with the Sherley brothers, whose travels to Persia were notorious, and with Thomas Herbert, who was her kinsman.[29] Moreover, Wroth could have seen plays that related journeys and embassies to and from Persia at the turn of the seventeenth century. Finally, as Andrea suggests, the appearance in London of Lady Teresa Sampsonia Sherley, a Christian Circassian from Shah 'Abbas I's court, with her husband Sir Robert Sherley in 1611 may have inspired Wroth's character Lindafillia, the 'rightful Sophia' of Persia.[30]

The Sherleys' 1611 visit also inspired a vogue for Persian costume and portraiture that may be reflected in Wroth's critical depiction of the Queen of Bulgaria's Persian disguise in the Theatre of the World.[31] Flattering the queen, Amphilanthus commends her ...

> for her choice of habit, becomming her so well, as it was a great pitty, he said, she was not sole Lady of those parts, that dressing so well befitting her; she tooke it like her owne conceit, and so as shee lovd him better for commending her, then for his owne worth, prising her selfe above any worldly treasure. (I, 3, 342)

The eventual appearance of Lindafillia, the rightful Sophy of Persia, corrects this false representation of Persia pictured by the Bulgarian Queen and may gesture to English hopes for political alliances with the Persians. Lindafillia, the daughter to a deposed and murdered Sultan or 'Sophy of Persia,' is held prisoner by her usurping uncle, who also threatens to take Pamphilia's kingdom and her person by force. The potential for Lindafillia to be restored implies the possible Christianization of Persia: Lindafillia, like Teresa Sherley, is a Christian. Lady Sherley was also often depicted as a close relation, often a niece, of the Persian Sultan, though the truth of these accounts is doubtful.

Wroth depicts her Persian princess in ekphraseis, including a detailed blazon and a description of Lindafillia's library and painting gallery. Rosindy, the youngest of Pamphilia's three brothers, frees the Sophy from her initial imprisonment and is the first to meet Lindafillia. The narrator describes her as follows:

> She satt in a throne of pure Golde, yett was her shining farr purer. Her Clothe of state over her hed of noe other substance butt that purest mettle, imbellished with the purest pearle the Orient cowld afforde, interlaced with innestimable diamounds and blushing Rubies [...] A Crowne upon her head off the most matchles stones, and for Pearle as matchles, yett farr short of that which they incompassed, surrounding the Globe of all wisdoome and perfect perfectnes [...] Her apparell of the Asian fashion: for couler, as much as cowld for the infinite rich imbroidery of Juells and pearle bee discride, one may say itt was of the sweetest Pinck couler, ore Virgine blush. The lower part of her robe was cutt in gores, and som thing thinn above, setting forthe the true proportion of her best-proportioned body, longe bote sleeves to the ground [...] Butt what was rarest and richest was the wearing sleeve, beeing cutt beetweene the borders, discoverd a cuttwourke smock. Butt thorough that – O what? The milky way was durt to that! The snowe on the Mountaine topes, the black sea to itt! What was itt, then? The perfect figure of the most immaculate soule, shining in her skinn. Skinn? O such a skinn as would make thousand Jasons madd on travaile butt to see, though nott to touch soe pretious a fleece! Such, O such was and is her skinn, the perfectest of mortall creatures. (II, 1, 168)

The blazon begins with Lindafillia sitting under a rich Cloth of State. Only female rulers sit under cloths of state in the *Urania*, including Pamphilia and Dalinia, but this is the most elaborate description of such a cloth.[32] Lindafillia's crown is associated with the globe, harking back to the Theatre of the World and hinting at possible global alliances. The description of Lindafillia's clothing reflects similar depictions of Persian garb that could be found in costume books of Wroth's time.[33] Finally, Lindafillia's physical description contrasts the paleness

Fig. 6.3. Marcus Gheeraerts the Younger, *An Unknown Lady in Fancy Dress*, also known as *The Persian Lady*, c. 1600, oil on panel, 216.5 x 135.3 cm. The Royal Collection © 2010 Her Majesty Queen Elizabeth II, Hampton Court Palace, Middlesex, UK.

of her skin with dark golden undertones that echo descriptions of Lady Sherley and may reflect portraits of ladies in Persian dress that Wroth could have seen. Marcus Gheeraerts the younger's 'portrait of an unknown lady' (figure 6.3), in which a beautiful brunette appears in Persian garb, similarly features an abundance of gold and pearls. It depicts the lady as being extremely pale. Furthermore, not only was the costume in this painting apparently based on one of the costume book illustrations of Persian garb mentioned above, but some art historians speculate that the portrait is of the Countess of Essex, who was first the widow of Wroth's uncle, Philip Sidney. [34]

Despite the sumptuous description of Lindafillia's charms that could, in and of itself, constitute an enchantment, Rosindy is dull to Persian visual display. The narrator explains, 'All this did nott amase the matchles Rosindy,' conceding that 'yett did hee some admiration beehold her' (II, 1, 168). Rosindy's lack of interest in visual images is further displayed in his reluctance to look upon the gallery that Lindafillia houses in her library. Lindafillia explains that she has been assisted by 'a mighty scoller, and soe great an one as is counted a magisian,' who reads her astrological chart and predicts that she will be aided by members of the Morean court, whose 'names hee sett downe all, and gave mee ther pictures with ther names writen on them [...] and the Very day of ther arivalls heere.' She then triumphantly proclaims:

> This is the day for the dauntles Rosindy, secound son to the Morean King, and by his wyfe King of Macedon, to come hether, and this makes us knowe you are hee. Therfor, I beeseech you, pardon the boldnes hath binn committed towards you, soe great and mighty a King, and consider if I have nott most just cause to demaund ayde of all Christian princes (I beeing a Christian my self) to assist mee and deliver mee out of the hands of such wickednes and treacherie. (II, 1, 170)

The astrologer's proleptic pictures with explanatory texts seem worthy of Greek romance. The predictions have, moreover, proven true thus far, for Rosindy has come on his appointed day.

Keeping in mind that Lindafillia's restoration would entail the Christianization of Persia, one might think that Rosindy would be as responsive as possible to her plight. Lindafillia shows Rosindy her 'most rich and sumptious galery,' which along with her paintings contains her library:

> the most sumptious in the world for a woeman to have, and the rarest, since non butt the rarest of bookes were permitted to bee ther [...] she beeing exactly and parfectly learned in all siences, and learning well beestowed on her, who honored learning for the truth of learnings sake, perfect knowledg. The bookes held him a little longer then she would have had them; therfor she called him to see the pictures [...] (II, 1, 171)

Again, Rosindy is oblivious to the visual spectacle that the princess displays, this time to the point that she must nudge him along in his perusal of the gallery. Despite the fact that Lindafillia '[delivers] him the magicians directions to peruse,' no description of the proleptic paintings follows. Wroth interrupts the text at this point, the narrator interjecting 'Wher can wee better leave him then thus delighted, thus honored, and contented, while wee goe to som others requiring need and help divers ways?' (II, 1, 171). Thus, though the Sophy proves to be highly skilled at the manipulation of visual images and is herself associated closely with works of visual art, her European counterpart does not respond to these stimuli with an ekphrastic contribution.

Though the exchange between the West and the Persian Empire in the *Urania* seems promising, with a reciprocal trade of ambassadors that resembles the hoped-for exchanges of Wroth's own time, Wroth's Persian narrative, like the Anglo-Persian relations of the late sixteenth and early seventeenth centuries, does not achieve lasting political alliances.[35] Before the *Urania* comes to its abrupt ending, Lindafillia has once again been enchanted with no resolution (II, 2, 354). Wroth's Persian storyline does hold out hope as part of a greater wish-fulfilment of romance, offering Lindafillia as a possible Christian link to the Persian world. Yet this world empire is not possible in Wroth's romance globe, a fact that Wroth highlights through the diminishing impact of the iconography of empire and proleptic pictures that Lindafillia displays to an unmoved European spectator.

The other major narrative that fictionalizes the possible inclusion of Eastern foreigners into the second half of the *Urania* is the story of Rodomandro, the King, or Great Cham, of Tartaria. Rodomandro, who is the fictional ruler of what was under Genghis Khan or his descendant Tamerlane one of the largest kingdoms in the world, offers Pamphilia a marriage that would be territorially comparable to the powerful alliance with Amphilanthus, Holy Roman Emperor. Yet Wroth's account of Rodomandro is most appealing for its subversion of negative stereotypes, both of blackness and of the alleged barbarity of the Tartars. As Sheila

Cavanagh observes, 'This union between Pamphilia and Rodomandro offers an especially intriguing portrait of intercultural relations' ('Prisoners' 97). Wroth depicts Rodomandro as civil and as a worthy husband for Pamphilia, and, given the mixed impressions of Tartaria that would have been available to Wroth, her positive depiction of the Cham leans towards the idealized world that romance can promise. Early modern and ancient travel accounts and histories of Tartaria and the Tartars ranged broadly from descriptions of Mongol nomads who drank the blood of their horses to the rulers of beautiful and civilized kingdoms.[36] The nomadic identity of the Tartars supports Wroth's representation of Rodomandro having wandered so far from home, but it also holds out an open identity that Wroth chooses to mark as civil and Christian rather than bloodthirsty and pagan, or, as was most likely the case of real Tartars, Muslim.[37]

Wroth, moreover, represents the possible acceptance of Rodomandro first through bodily description and later through ekphrastic display in the form of a spectacular masque. Rodomandro's introduction occurs while Pamphilia and Amphilanthus are out hunting. Given their past experiences, hunting seems like a risky pastime. This time, however, it is not Amphilanthus who disappears, but rather their quarry, a black stag,

> being for couler and greatnes strange, the stag beeing cole blacke, hornes and all, and as big as t[wo] ordinary ones were, onely one white spott on the left side in shape of an arrowe. This beast they went forthe to slay and sawe him and pursued him hottly and fiercly, yett cowld nott kill him, for when they had him (as they thought) att ther bay, as att their dogs, the Queene shuting att him, hee vanisht. (II, 1, 43)

This chase may allude back to the Hell of Deceit. On the one hand, the vanishing of the stag refers to the disappearance of their longed-for union, providing no real closure to the previous hunt, but it also proves to be a presentiment of Rodomandro's role in Pamphilia's story.

While Pamphilia and Amphilanthus are hunting, the Prince of Tartaria has come to Pamphilia's court. He is introduced in a blazon that emphasizes his civility, which is contrasted to and brought out by his blackness. He is described as:

> A brave and Comly Gentleman, shaped of body soe curiously as noe art cowld counterfeit soe rare a proportion, of an excellent stature neither to high nor of the meanest stature, his hands soe white as wowld have beecome a great Lady, his face of curious and exact features, butt for the couler

> of itt, itt plainely shewed the sunn had either liked itt to much, and soe had too hard kissed itt, ore in fury of his delicasy, had made his beames to strongly to burne him, yett cowld not take away the perfect sweetnes of his lovelines. His diamound eyes (though attired in black) did soe sparcle gainst his rays as made them in ther owne hardnes knowe strength against his beames, and power to resist his strongest burning heat; and soe certainly had the conquest, for though black yett hee had the true parfection of lovlines, and in lovelines the purest beauty. For what is fairnes with out feature, even as a picture is with out the life peece itt self? (II, 1, 42)

Likened to a beautiful work of art, Rodomandro's character is built on contrasts. Just as his beauty shines more brightly against his blackness, his nobility is marked by self-effacement, reflected in the black stag's vanishing and in Rodomandro's eventual disappearance from the narrative. When Pamphilia and Amphilanthus return from their hunt, 'they found this brave Tartarian, black as the stag and as humble, giving such testimony of that as rather hee wowld seeme to vanish to[o] th[a]n to show the least disrespect to any of that Court' (II, 1, 43). Clearly Wroth associates blackness with ugliness here, adhering to the prejudice of the time, but his blackness does not preclude Rodomandro's success at court. Kim Hall suggests that Rodomandro's blackness is made palatable by his amenability to whiteness in the whiteness of his hands, which are like the white arrow on the black stag.[38] Yet Wroth seems genuinely to accept this character, blackness and all, a tolerance that was not readily apparent in her description of characters with black skin in the first half of the *Urania*. Just as Lindafillia functions as a corrective image of Persia to the Queen of Bulgaria's display, Rodomandro provides a more tolerant and approving depiction of people with dark skin.

Wroth's participation in Jonson's *Masque of Blackness* may have made her sensitive to tropes of blackness, and the courtliness of Rodomandro indicates a willingness, similar to that of Barclay, to include foreigners.[39] Rodomandro expresses his courtliness with a masque of his own invention, in which:

> him self beeing one of the twelve maskers, and four and twenty torchbearers hee had all aparelled like horse men in counterfett armes, bases and boots with great longe spurrs, faire plumes of feathers; visards they had non, the most of them having faces grimm and hard enough to bee counted visards [...] Their aparell after the Tartarian fashion was all alike: their uper

> parts of a rich, white clothe of gold made in fashion of an armoure and trimd with Gold as if the Joints of the armour; ther baces of Carnation velvett laced all over with Gold; their boots white leather laced att the tops as the baces were; and spurrs of pure golde (II, 1, 46)

Unlike Wroth's performance in *The Masque of Blackness*, Rodomandro and his men need no 'visards' or paint. By confidently displaying the splendour of Tartarian garb, Rodomandro demonstrates his skilful manipulation of the highly visual medium in a way that suggests he may be making a subtle play for Pamphilia's affection. After this opening, the masque proceeds with the introduction of the allegorical figures of Honour and Cupid. The masque first pictures the victory of Honour over Cupid in Honour's holding rule over the group of travelling Tartars and later over the group of 'Kings and Princes' that observe the masque. The masque seems to refer to the enchantment of the Throne of Love in the first half of the *Urania* and displays Rodomandro's skill at crafting spectacles that incorporate the visual and the verbal to elaborate a view of honourable, rather than lustful love.

The audience has an opportunity to react and show their appreciation for Rodomandro's skill after the last dance, but although they give '[m]any and great thanks [...] to this brave Tartarian, whos witt and pleasant feator did give much pleasure and admiration to the beeholders' (II, 1, 49), no characters venture an interpretation of its meaning or comment on the Tartar's possible familiarity with the enchantments that have proven that Amphilanthus has been ruled by Cupid and not Honour. As in the episode of Lindafillia's painting gallery, to highlight the lack of interpretation, Wroth enacts an Ariostan narratival jump to another thread of her narrative: 'Butt heere wee have longe stayd; therfor wee must a while leave this Court in all hapines and content, and a little accompany some of the other knights, among which number Dolorindus must bee the first' (II, 1, 49). Active interpretation of the masque is thus stifled much as it is for Lindafillia's Persian pictures.

Rodomandro also resembles Shakespeare's Othello in certain respects, but rather than being ominous, these traits emphasize Rodomandro's suitability as a husband for Pamphilia. Rodomandro echoes Othello by claiming to be no orator in his suit to Pamphilia: 'the Tartarians are noe Orators, butt plaine blunt men. Our harts are rich in truthe and loyalltie. Prowde indeed wee ar, butt onely of Ladys favours, knowing our sunn-burnt faces can butt rarely attaine to faire ladys likings' (II, 2, 271). Commenting on his own blackness, Rodomandro again uses self-effacement to win favour and prove his civility, but like Othello, he nonetheless hopes to win his lady's love.[40] Just as Rodomandro's physical description oscillates between blackness and beauty, his speeches illustrate his merits indirectly. When Pamphilia gently rebuffs him, explaining that all she desires is solitude – 'a booke and solitarines beeing the companions I desire in thes my unfortunate days' (II, 2, 271) – Rodomandro makes the following emblematic proposal:

> Love your booke, butt love mee soe farr as that I may hold itt to you that, while you peruse that, I may Joye in beeholding you; and som times gaine a looke from you, if butt to chide mee for soe carelessly parforming my office, when love will by chance make my hand shake, purposely to obtaine a sweet looke. (II, 2, 272)

He eventually does win Pamphilia: she marries him, but only after Amphilanthus's marriage to the Princess of Slavonia. Ironically, in offering himself as the picture for her text, Rodomandro proposes an emblem of love that cannot be fulfilled, as it is revealed later in the book that Rodomandro and the son that he has with Pamphilia will both die before their time.

Rodomandro's last appearance in the romance ends with another vanishing act. Years after two of her three brothers and her mother die, Pamphilia's father, the King of Morea, travels to Tartaria to see Pamphilia and finds her alone as follows:

> When hee arived in Tartaria, hee found a great change: the King dead, his deerest Pamphilia a widow, yett the mother of a brave boy, who soone after his arivall to that Court also died. (II, 2, 406)

Despite Rodomandro's and his son's deaths – events which prevent lasting union between Pamphilia's and Rodomandro's families and lands – Rodomandro is afforded one last opportunity to speak before the end of the manuscript. His reappearance shortly after the revelation of his death has been viewed as a bizarre mistake on the part of the author. It seems to me rather that the reappearance of Rodomandro takes place chronologically before (though it is placed in the manuscript after) Pamphilia's father's journey to Tartaria where he finds her a widow. Her father's visit takes place many years after the death of Pamphilia's brother Parselius – at least three years elapse while Pamphilia's mother mourns the death of her son and then finally dies herself (Wroth II, 2, 406). By contrast, the 'reappearance' of Rodomandro occurs right after Parselius's funeral. Wroth might have made the chronology clearer with the use of a more specific transition between the two episodes or she simply could have inserted Rodomandro's last episode into the manuscript before Pamphilia's father's travels. Though she did neither, the funeral's timing is significant.

Directly after Parselius's funeral, Pamphilia, Rodomandro, and Amphilanthus travel east. In their voyage from Constantinople to Asia, a storm blows them to Cyprus, where the first enchantment of the *Urania* is revisited. Rodomandro reveals that he knows of the Throne of Love after all, implying that the masque he performed was specifically designed to gain her affection:

> The Tartarian cried,
> 'O!' sayd hee, 'how fittly hath love now showed him self to see, since hee hath guided us to his Royallest seat (butt in our owne harts, wher hee hath his greatest honor).' Looking most amourously on the Queene Pamphilia, who with a respective kinde of loving, reseaved his words and sweetly demaunded of him what was the reason of that his speech.
> 'Why, sweet hart,' sayd h[ee], 'knowe you nott this Country?'
> 'Noe, indeed, my lord,' sayd she.
> Amphilanthus smiling sayd, 'He[ere] bee noe more inchauntments now to try your goodnes by, for this is Ciprus.'
> 'In trothe, my lord,' sayd she, 'I knew itt nott. Itt was soe longe since I was heere, and surely wee may now bee secure from all charming businesses.'
> 'I were a most fitt fellowe,' sayd the Chamm, 'to finish them.' (II, 2, 407)

The banter between these three indicates not only that Rodomandro has won Pamphilia's affection, but also that Amphilanthus is content to let Rodomandro show his fitness as an honourable mate for her. Yet Rodomandro vanishes from the narrative mysteriously at this point, fulfilling the prolepsis of the chase of the black stag. Even if Rodomandro's gesture to the enchantment of the Throne of Love makes it seem that Pamphilia will find happiness, it does not take away from the childless widowhood that is promised by the relation of her father's travel to Tartaria. The Cham is not the piece that completes the cloth of Pamphilia's love story, and the narrative breaks off without a reunion with Amphilanthus.

In conclusion, Wroth distorts the ekphrastic and emblematic expressions of identity that empower marginalized and foreign identities in her Greek romance antecedents. She pictures her characters' anguish and disappointment through spectacles and enchantments that are increasingly hostile to interpretation. The internalized self that many scholars seek to discover through investigations of interior spaces in the *Urania*, such as closets and caves, most often leads to the discovery of sonnets or books. It is appropriate that Wroth, who sought to make herself known through the publication of the first half of the *Urania*, would begin to elaborate a female writing subject in her text; yet books and sonnets in the *Urania* are often responses to characters' inability to understand the world that surrounds them. As Hackett notes:

> While Wroth's depiction of Pamphilia explores ideas of selfhood and the literary expression of subjectivity which look forward to novelistic models of psychology and to romantic ideas of the self realized in solitude, at the same time she makes extremely fruitful use in episodes [...] of non-naturalistic and symbolic methods of representing interior states. These at once look back to Medieval and Spenserian techniques of allegory, and forward to later non-naturalistic conventions such as the gothic. (174)

Wroth's evocation of romance models for the construction of her enchantments – ancient Greek romance, Iberian romance, Sidneian and Spenserian romance – all indicate a wish to continue in the rich ekphrastic tradition of the emblematics of the self; however, her narrative marks her nostalgia for forms that could no longer forge the bonds required for a proper romance ending. Ekphrastic characterization is increasingly thwarted in the text as were the romantic and civic bonds in Wroth's life and times.

Wroth's disruption of connections between the visual and the verbal in the first half of her romance becomes more pronounced in the second half, as do the disjunctions in the world that she depicts. Through enchantments that invoke highly ekphrastic allegorical modes of visual literacy, Wroth subverts expectations for the readability of such visual spectacles and correspondingly undoes the romantic and political ties between her characters by staging global unions that prove to be folly. In the second half of the *Urania*, even sonnets no longer serve for the characters to express identity. Antissia, for example, finds that writing poetry, and the life that she led while doing so, were nothing but a folly, and the frequency of poems composed by the main characters drops dramatically. What Wroth does do in the second half of the *Urania* is to turn to the East for the possibility of new bonds of love and new political alliances that might mend her romance world, and the pictures of Persia and masques of blackness that she presents do provide evidence that Wroth's romance, if finished, might have presented a theatre of the world where Persians and Tartars could join the West in a peaceful completion of Wroth's cloth of love. Yet, as the manuscript stands, we are left with, as Amphilanthus puts it, a 'tottering, decieptfull world' (II, 2, 377), in which pictures cannot illuminate Wroth's romance globe.

Conclusions

When Homer forged an ekphrastic world on the disk of Achilles' shield (*Iliad* 18, 483–7), he ensured that this fictional world would endure. It is Homer's all-knowing vision of the world, as his authority was figured and passed down to the Renaissance, that assures this wholeness. The description of Achilles' shield is a part of this inheritance, and Homer's verbal representation outlives many visual representations from antiquity, an argument that was often invoked by writers in the paragone of the sister arts. Only Homer *sees* this shield through his narratorial voice, and his legendary blindness serves to emphasize that his project is supremely ekphrastic, an act of ekphrastic hope that recreates a world by bringing it before the mind's eye of the reader. Achilles' shield, in light of its reverenced place in literary history, is the benchmark for ekphrasis in Western literature.

Yet Homer did not let his heroes comment on what the shield meant to them: Menelaus and Helen did not question the endurance of the bridal pact, Odysseus did not ask whether the story that Hephestos wrought was true, Achilles did not even have the chance to express ignorance at the images as did Aeneas when presented with his own *mise-en-abyme* in Virgil's epic. The Homeric shield is the narrator's vision alone, but Homer's is not one man's legacy.

This ekphrastic epic discourse was quick to be questioned, broken down, reshuffled. From the opening of the *Aethiopica*, Heliodorus achieves what we now call a cinematic effect by introducing his characters in the midst of a battlefield through the eyes of a series of marauders. Achilles Tatius's protagonists give varying interpretations of the multivalent artworks that they encounter. The presence of multiple characters from places all over the Levant makes a univocal articulation of these narratives' highly visual worlds impossible. Romance presents ekphrasis as a polyglot creation; it even questions the univocality of Homer's shield. Heliodorus crafts an alternative birth story for Homer. Calasiris claims that though '[Homer] is at home everywhere [...] it is certain that [he] was an Egyptian and that his city was Thebes of the Hundred Gates' (3, 79). When Knemon asks why Homer's origin had been concealed, Calasiris explains 'Possibly because he was ashamed of being an exile [...] his "father" banished him because the blemish on his body proved him illegitimate. Or possibly he purposely kept his true origin secret so that he could claim every country as his fatherland' (3, 79). The ancient Greek romance delightedly recasts Homer and the epic tradition he represents to the margins, banished to a cosmopolitan life of exile and mysterious parentage.

The reception of Greek romances in the Renaissance echoes Heliodorus's metamorphoses of Homer. One early modern editor of the *Aethiopica* remarks that the *Aethiopica* 'hath (as is well knowne) travailed thorow all Countreys, and speaketh many Languages [...] It could no sooner arrive in any strange place, but as soone it found friendly entertainment, and as bénigne Patrons, as the matchlesse worth of so inimitable a piece might justly deserve' (Barret A2–3). The *Aethiopica* thus travels through the European Republic of Letters like a cosmopolitan wanderer. The Greek romance's reception in the Renaissance appreciates and reinforces its cultural diversity and its use of ekphrasis to figure this diversity forth. Renaissance romancers build on the works of the Second Sophistic to represent the vast geographies of the sixteenth and seventeenth centuries; they populate their romance globes widely to give a polyvalent image of the multicultural world in which they lived. Reinoso's images, dreamed and embroidered, give a female voice to religious exile, and Sidney's 'speaking pictures' are shifting emblems of gender passibility amplified by the Countess of Pembroke's edits and additions. Cervantes pictures a romance that embraces Native Americans through transatlantic reflections and refractions of pictographic language. Barclay's chiastic ekphraseis draw Afro-European emblems of fellowship and love. Wroth embroiders a romance tapestry that promises to unite East and West through enchantments, pictures of Persia, and Tartarian masques, but instead distorts previous visions of romance.

The word 'globe,' which comes from the Latin *globus*, meaning a crowd of people as well as a sphere, does not enter into English use as a representation of the world until after the discovery of the Americas. The Renaissance romancer is well positioned to imagine this early modern world, interlacing the partial views presented by crowds of characters in multi-volume works that remind the reader that romance is never done illuminating its globes. Jameson remarks, 'romance is precisely that form in which the worldness of world reveals or manifests itself' (*The Political Unconscious* 112), and in its ekphrastic articulations of self in the world romance expresses utopian desires through the coordination of literary heterotopias.

The multiplicity of characters and points of view in the heteroglossia of romance narrative appeals to today's readers and critics, and numerous recent studies have focused on Greek romances and the history of their reception. Tracing its influence beyond the early modern period demands a flexible understanding of romance that balances what Jameson identifies as the semantic and syntactic poles of a 'dialectic use of genre' (*The Political Unconscious* 103–50).[1] Barbara Fuchs's recent definition of the romance genre as a strategy is most helpful here, both in looking back at the romance's uncertain fit in neoclassical genre systems and in examining its tenacity in the modern novel. Romance, itself a mixed mode, also has a tendency to contaminate other kinds of texts, and I propose that we can trace it not only in the romance's 'concatenation of both narratological elements and literary topoi' (Fuchs, *Romance* 9), but also in its insistence on crafting identity through the emblematics of the self.

The romance's ability to render forth the 'worldness of world' entails the representation of social realities that sometimes make the coordination of heterotopian views precisely utopian. While authors like Cervantes, Barclay, and, for the most part, Sidney craft romances that use the emblematics of the self to articulate favourable representations of gender, ethnic, and religious identities, Reinoso and Wroth here bracket romance's capacity to lament social obstacles. Reinoso's romance does not result in a happy ending for its protagonist Isea, a reflection of the realities of exile that occludes the wish-fulfilment embodied by Clareo and Florisea's marriage. Isea emblematizes her loneliness and sense of rootlessness with the ekphrastic conventions that were available to Reinoso in his Greek romance model. Reinoso thus makes use of the emblematics of the self in his fictional romance to illustrate what was for him a pressing social reality. Furthermore, when Wroth tries to illuminate a politically unified romance globe through her highly ekphrastic enchantments, she manages to articulate the pieces of her cloth of love, bringing together a community of leaders, but these leaders cut the knots that would bind them. The union of marriage between Pamphilia and Amphilanthus, and by extension, the union of Eastern and Western peoples, is impossible in the *Urania*. The romance's multiplicity becomes its own enemy when the love interests become multiple, and its marvellous renditions of foreigners preclude lasting alliances when the characters themselves become enchanted and vanish. What should be a reflective mirror-text becomes a self-conscious distortion and perversion of earlier ekphrastic romance modes, perhaps reflecting Wroth's own failures in love and fall in social status.

Looking beyond the Renaissance, the literary assimilation of marginalized groups and foreigners into the fabric of European society through ekphrasis is often denied in romance texts of the late seventeenth and early eighteenth centuries. The resistance to the romance's convention of wish-fulfilment in this regard, I suggest, occurs in part because of writers' awareness of the violence perpetrated against real foreigners and marginalized groups through colonial actions taken in Africa and in the New World in particular. Aphra Behn (1640–89), for example, uses romance strategies to play on this impediment in her *Oroonoko* (1688). By Behn's lifetime, the violence of the African slave trade makes the alliance of African peoples with Europeans, a romance proposition that Barclay's *Argenis* achieved in 1621, impossible even in fiction.

The visual mark of black skin in *Oroonoko* becomes a leverage point for ekphrastic renderings that deny hope. Behn uses the discourse of romance to set up a love story between the African Prince Oroonoko and his beloved Princess Imoinda in the first half of the work, replete with highly visual descriptions and works of art in the text, but this romance vision is denied through their loss of identity as they are captured and enslaved by nefarious slave traders. It is precisely their skin colour that makes this possible despite their noble status. The denial of romance elements in *Oroonoko* not only reflects the beginnings of modern racism but also expresses anxieties about assaults on sovereignty: a king had been killed in Britain, after all. Oroonoko's skin colour, moreover, would have damned his royal offspring to slavery, as Oroonoko concludes to rationalize his killing of the consenting and pregnant Imoinda. Ekphrastic passages in the work render forth Oroonoko's beauty but dwell on his and Imoinda's blackness, denying their assimilation. Behn negotiates her own position as a female author in relation to this failed romance pair by emphasizing her narrator's social superiority to the royal slaves and simultaneously denying the narrator the ability to intercede on their behalf because of limitations to her own social power, namely her status as a woman.

We might also consider how the nineteenth-century novel (a genre that owes much to its romance ancestors) can employ romance strategies to illustrate how capitalist and racial discourse denied a voice to marginalized peoples. Herman Melville's *Moby-Dick or the Whale* (1851), for instance, tells much about the developments of the emblematics of the self in romance strategy. *Moby-Dick* is in many respects about the impossibility of ekphrasis. The indescribable painting in the Spouter Inn begins this discourse of ekphrastic fear, and the narrator's self-consciously compulsive attempts to describe whales prove to be, like descriptions of the sublime itself, pointedly impossible. An emblematics of the self for marginalized or foreign peoples in *Moby-Dick* is precluded by the way in which capitalism and racial discourse block what in a sixteenth- or early seventeenth-century context would have provided marginalized characters a means of expressing identity through ekphrastic discourse. When Melville sets up a Homeric description of the Ecuadorian doubloon in chapter 99, the characters' subsequent attempts at ekphrastic interpretation of the object highlight this ekphrastic dilemma. Far from having Antonio the Barbarian's ekphrastic fluency in the *Persiles,* Melville's barbarians, including Native Americans, Africans, Persians, and other 'savages,' are depicted as visual signs themselves and are incapable of translating images into words. Queequeg, for example, would only seem to recognize without comment the doubloon's reproduction in one of his many tattoos. Even the Nantucketers' descriptions are one-sided, and when the Manx sailor tries to view the other side of this heraldic doubloon, this too is denied. The doubloon is, in terms of its narratival function, a one-sided coin, like the coin in 'El Zahir' that drives Borges's characters insane.[2] If Melville's doubloon tells a world in its making like Achilles' shield, it is a world in which marginalized and foreign groups are excluded and denied agency. The impossibility of describing the world makes for unreasonable negotiations of that world. Though Ishmael goes to sea precisely to heal his sense of alienation, he ends up alone in the ocean, buoyed by his lover's coffin – the ultimate denial of a romance ending.

To take another leap forward, postmodern formulations of romance also use the emblematics of the self as a romance strategy. Thomas Pynchon's *The Crying of Lot 49* is, in many respects, a romance in reverse: the narrative opens in a marriage, and ends with a lady errant. Rather than constituting her identity, the emblematics of the self reveals Oedipa Mass's sense of profound alienation, and, not unlike Pamphilia in Wroth's *Urania,* her attempts to interpret the ekphrastic enigmas that abound in Pynchon's work only illustrate her increasing isolation. One by one, her ties to other people and even to reality are undone. The ekphrastic deconstruction of Oedipa's identity commences with her viewing of a Remedios Varo painting, called *Bordando el Manto del Mundo Terrestre.* The painting is real and part of a Varo triptych; as Stefan Mattessich has observed, Oedipa's viewing of the painting not only makes her question her relationship with Pierce Inverarity but causes her to have a sort of ontological crisis, questioning her very way of being in the world. As the narrative progresses, Oedipa's interpretation of visual signs crafted much like Renaissance emblems and *imprese* in the form of muted post horns, inamorati anonymous insignias, and deviant stamp collections impels the action of the story and makes Oedipa into an ambivalent exile, whose separation from society is figured alternately as mental illness or supreme independence. Pynchon uses the romance conventions of ekphrasis and ekphrastic interpretation precisely to create a romance dystopia that comments on a panoply of marginalized identities, what Pynchon incorporates into his W.A.S.T.E. society.

Postcolonial literature also deploys the emblematics of the self as a romance strategy to depict subaltern identities. This can be traced in the reception of the Greek romance genre, in the uses of ekphrasis in postcolonial literature, and in the applicability of passible identity to postcolonial discourse. In her discussion of the *Aethiopica* as the first 'passing' novel, Judith Perkins notes that Heliodorus's romance 'explicitly locates its narrative focus on identity and authenticity, on place and displacement in a wider cultural dialogue,' and suggests that it thus conforms well to 'contemporary criticism's post-colonial paradigm' (197n1). Using the American generic tradition of novels that trace how black characters 'pass' as white and drawing on Bhabha's concept of cultural 'fixity' or stereotype (Bhabha 66), Perkins claims that the Aethiopica 'manifests some of the same concerns as these contemporary "passing" novels [...] through its characterization of Charikleia, it destabilizes the reader's sense of the "fixity" of cultural otherness, the primary element in establishing any cultural hierarchy' (199). In turn, W.J.T. Mitchell has investigated ekphrasis's particular abilities to destabilize formulations of Otherness, for instance in its deployment in slave narratives, where it instantiates a spatial memory of self that, rather than reinforcing the discourse of 'speaking self' and 'silent, depicted Other,' can 'talk back' to subjection through reflexive, autobiographical self-portraiture.[3] Mary Lou Emery similarly explores the use of ekphrasis in postcolonial literature by authors like Jean Rhys, Jamaica Kincaid, and Michelle Cliff as a mode of countercolonial discourse; but, in juxtaposing this mode of postcolonial ekphrasis with what she sees as the dominant tradition of colonial ekphrasis, her reading could be enhanced by considering what these women ekphrasists so aptly accomplish in the intertextual and historical context represented by the pre-modern and early modern texts that have been the focus of this study. Passibility, as I have articulated it in the emblematics of the self, fits particularly well with the non-essentialist flexible models of subaltern identity that postcolonial literary critics theorize and trace in literature today. The Greek romance and the ekphrasis that it so often deploys in the depiction of character grew up, so to speak, under the Roman Empire, yet at its margins. Their early modern imitators, as I have demonstrated, are attracted to this genre for its cultural diversity and ability to speak for a variety of peoples in a rapidly widening world. The authors of Greek romance (ancient and early modern) were able to articulate a cosmopolitan understanding of identity in part because this was the identity that they most likely lived. It is not surprising then that Greek romances like the *Aethiopica* have, as Iyengar suggests, 'obsessed scholars and critics in three historical periods: the English Renaissance, the Harlem Renaissance, and our own era' (19).

Here I suggest that considering Greek romance, ekphrasis, and identity together can make for fruitful readings beyond the early modern period in fiction concerned with the representation of subaltern identity. I do not pretend that this brief sketch of these few examples constitutes a history or even a trajectory of ekphrastic characterization in prose narrative; rather, I offer this sketch of how ekphrasis continues to illuminate romance globes because I believe that attending to this romance strategy offers readers a new approach to an old understanding of identity that elegantly combines aesthetics and ethics, rhetorical form, and cultural meaning to craft passible renditions of personhood. The emblematics of the self does not require characters to speak from a position of power; in fact it often provides a platform for questioning hegemonic discourse. Romance characters continue to picture forth their trials and loves in verbal pictures. We need only listen.

Notes

Introduction

1 See Goldhill, 'What Is Ekphrasis For?' in which he considers psychological effects of ancient ekphrasis and its role in creating verisimilitude.

2 My understanding of this term is indebted to Reiss, esp. *Mirages* 98–119. 'Passible' comes from the Late Latin *passibilis*, e. adj., which is derived from *patior*, *passus*, v. 'to suffer.' According to the *OED*, its definitions include: 1. Capable of suffering or feeling; susceptible to sensation or emotion; and 2. Liable to undergo change or decay.

3 While identity and subjectivity are often used interchangeably or conceived of as interdependent – e.g., postcolonial and queer theorists often focus on the intertwining of these concepts – they have distinct philosophical genealogies. One way of making a useful, though *per force* reductive, distinction between the two is to observe that though both describe the constitution of the self, identity is established through the recognition of sameness and subjectivity through the recognition of difference (from an object). Two things that are qualitatively identical are two things that are more or less the same. Personal identity, which is social, refers to one's sense of self and the persistence of that self. The term has been used in the twentieth century in identity politics to mobilize oppressed social groups and by cultural studies scholars like Stuart Hall and Paul Gilroy in relation to class. Identity has been criticized for being essentialist, though essentialism is not necessarily a part of personal identity in its philosophical history. I use it here in its personal, qualitative sense as a way to indicate more or less sameness with a group or collectivity. Subjectivity is a more reflexive articulation of the self, consciousness, or self-knowledge in relation to an object. It is most often used to speak of the position of a person as a

thinking, individual agent. Subjectivity is used both by psychoanalytic and Marxist thinkers and by poststructuralist theorists from Lacan and Žižek to Derrida and Foucault. Finally, I use individual agency here to mean the capacity to make choices independent of social circumstances or structures.

4 I cite book, line, and page numbers from the Fagles translation. The passage describing the forging of Achilles' arms in book 18 describes the metal relief work on the hero's shield, which also represents Greek cosmos and *paideia*.

5 I cite book, section, and page numbers from Whitmarsh's translation of Tatius.

6 *Europa* (c. 1560–2) was one of a series of six mythological paintings that Titian was commissioned to paint for King Philip II of Spain. Titian's voluptuous female figure, her physical position in relation to the bull, the image of Eros, and Titian's acquaintance with the Italian translator of Tatius's work indicate, as Rosand has argued, that Titian had the ekphrasis in mind.

7 See Newcomb's study of Greene as popular author, esp. 21–76.

8 In the *Morando*, Greene also takes material from Primaudaye's *Academie*, trans. Thomas Bowes, 1586. But unlike Primaudaye, Greene sides with women in his *querelle des femmes*. Greene's alterations of Tatius's ekphrasis indicate his intended direction: Jove, using 'sinister means,' becomes not only a bull but a 'prowling pirate' (5), and Europa is depicted in less sensuous and more chaste terms.

9 Greene also makes use of Tatius's romance as a model in *The Carde of Fancie*.

10 The ekphraseis that interest me here are not imitations of extant works of art, but rather imitate ancient ekphraseis and their rhetorical techniques, as is illustrated by this example from Greene. To borrow a term from Hollander, the ekphraseis under examination here are thus 'notional' (209).

11 For Bakhtin's definition of hybridity and polyglossia, see *Dialogic Imagination*, esp. 14, 16. As I discuss in greater detail in chapter 1, he argues that the adventure-time chronotope of Greek romance prohibits character development whenever it appears in romance: see esp. 87–95. Scholars who have argued effectively against his judgment of romance characterization include Doody 135, and Konstan 44–6.

12 See esp. 43–55. Unlike Bakhtin, Steiner does not condemn what she deems to be static characterization *per se*, but her criteria for romance identity are based on modern subjectivity and individual agency.

13 Since the publication of *Renaissance Self-Fashioning*, it is important to recognize that New Historicists including Greenblatt have certainly

concentrated their study on marginal or foreign groups, but problematic definitions of personhood based on independent, individual agency persist.

14 I omit a litany of past scholarly disparagements of English prose romances here, in part because the tendency to trot out this history perpetuates what is no longer a pervasive view. Though it was true in many cases that these romances were only read insofar as they constituted a history of prose – something to be studied as a backdrop to drama or to the development of the novel – these texts have been taken seriously for over thirty years now, thanks in part to the work of scholars like Paul Salzman among many others. Today they are recognized for their structural and cultural richness in scholarship that considers their readership (Newcomb), place in the early modern marketplace (Mentz, *Romance for Sale*), and roots in ancient precedents (Plazenet, and Doody). It should also be noted that Hispanists have always given pride of place to their rich early modern prose traditions.

15 In 'Creative Writers and Daydreaming,' Freud argues that fantasy is the basis of all stories, and he suggests that creative writers' talent lies in the 'secret' of their '*Ars poetica*,' their ability to craft their fantasies into palatable forms that result in a 'liberation of tensions in our minds' and enable us 'to enjoy our own daydreams without self-reproach or shame' (514). Though Freud opens his essay by likening curiosity about the source material of stories to a similar question put to the most famous of Renaissance romancers, Ariosto (509), and though he uses 'the less pretentious authors of novels, romances, and short stories' (509) for his examples, it was Northrop Frye who first described 'wish-fulfillment' as an essential aspect of the romance genre, writing '[t]he romance is the nearest of all literary forms to the wish-fulfillment dream' (*Anatomy* 186).

16 See Fuchs, *Romance* 4–9.

1. The Romance Globe: Why the Renaissance Repainted Greek Romance

1 For readers unfamiliar with the genre, ancient Greek romances are long prose narratives that tend to include these elements: a pair of loyal lovers portrayed as equals – usually high-born, though often unaware of their status – who come from the Levant; their meeting and falling in love; a long, unforeseen separation in which they undergo trials of strength and chastity. These trials include shipwrecks, kidnapping and/or enslavement at the hands of pirates and/or thieves, falling victim to witches' spells, extensive travel around the Mediterranean and beyond, disguises and transvestism, prophetic dreams, significant spectacles, extensive ekphraseis,

descriptions of foreign peoples and lands, the deciphering of tokens of recognition, the lovers' eventual reunion (often under life-threatening circumstances). The trials are followed by their marriage. These narratives have complex structures that interpolate many tales which nonetheless tie back to the main story.

2 The five complete, surviving Greek romances are Chariton's *Chaereas and Callirhoe*, Xenophon's *Ephesiaca*, Longus's *Daphnis and Chloe*, Achilles Tatius's *Leucippe and Clitophon*, and Heliodorus's *Aethiopica*. Other Greek prose narratives, fragmented and whole, are often considered a part of the genre, as are Latin novels such as Petronius's *Satyricon* and Apuleius's *Metamorphosis* or *The Golden Ass*. Out of the Greek romances, works by Longus, Tatius, and Heliodorus exerted the most influence on Renaissance romance, though Longus's influence was more confined to pastoral modes. See Perry 96–148 and Hagg 5–80 for summaries and studies of the so-called big five Greek romances. See Holzberg and also Goldhill, 'Genre,' for the genre's nature and scope.

3 For the philological approach, see Rohde.

4 For more on the Greek romance's renaissance, see Hagg 192–228.

5 For stylistic and content variation between the Greek and chivalric models, see Wilson, *Allegories* 11–20. She draws her summary of the traits of chivalric romance from Eisenberg 55–74.

6 The *Alexander Romance* and *Apollonius of Tyre* held particular sway through the Middle Ages. For the influence of the Greek romance on medieval Byzantine and European romance, see Beaton.

7 See Cooper for the history of chivalric romance in medieval and early modern England. A bibliography for studies of chivalric romance on the continent and in the Americas is too large to summarize here, but see Robinson 1–26 for recent approaches. While both Cooper's and Robinson's work make important contributions to romance studies, their focus on chivalric romance makes their insights less applicable for my purposes here.

8 On chastity in Greek romance, see Egger, and on Renaissance responses to this chastity, see Greenhalgh.

9 For more on Amyot's aesthetic criteria, see Camerlingo 46.

10 As Forcione notes, *Cervantes, Aristotle* 55, Amyot's aesthetics are based on Horace and Strabo.

11 In 'Genre of Genre' 25n37, Selden lists early modern evaluations of the Greek romance as epic.

12 For more on Scaliger's take on Heliodorus, see Forcione, *Cervantes, Aristotle* 64–6.

13 Among sixteenth-century critics, El Pinciano is most interested in the *Aethiopica*, perhaps because of Spain's rich history of producing prose narratives, the legitimacy of which was less contested there than, for example, in Italy or England.

14 The letter is from Ferrara, 20 May 1575. See Tasso, *Le lettere* 78. It is also cited in Forcione, *Cervantes, Aristotle* notes 41, 66.

15 French and English chivalric romance traditions are invested in assertions of cultural dominance in their portrayal of a group of national heroes who display a direct inheritance (*translatio*) of the learning and knowledge (*studii*) and political authority (*imperii*) of Rome. The Carolingian and Arthurian legends compete for cultural ascendancy. See Cooper 45–77, and see Camerlingo 63–4 for more on nationalism in chivalric genres.

16 See Romm for the influence of travel writing on Greek romance.

17 For Ficino's commentary on icastic and fantastic art in Neoplatonism, see Allen 117–205.

18 For Persinna's conception of Charicleia as it relates to early modern formulations of race, see Iyengar 19–43.

19 Fuchs identifies romance elements of Tasso's epic as 'romance strategy,' *Romance* 72–5, a term she coins to describe the infiltration of romance into other genres. For Tasso's incorporation of Charicleia's story into *Gerusalemme Liberata*, see W. Stephens.

20 Prose fiction and travel accounts were often closely and sometimes anxiously entwined in England, which could not connect travel accounts directly with a narrative of vigorous national territorial expansion in the sixteenth and early seventeenth centuries, as could, for instance, Spain. For the relationship of early Elizabethan prose fiction to ethnography, see Relihan 1–26, and for anxieties about the potential for continental prose to impose foreign influences on England, see Maslen 1–20. As Greek romance (which is a subset of prose) tends to promote cosmopolitan rather than nationalist agendas, I would argue that it also circumvents much of this anxiety.

21 Leonard, in *Books of the Brave*, explains how chivalric romance both helped Spain to construct and was, in part, constructed by the discourse of conquest in the Americas. Encounters with the New World thus became a place for working out new frontiers between the icastic and fantastic, both in life and in fiction.

22 I agree on this point with Kim, who, while he acknowledges stylistic affinities between historical prose and the Greek novels, believes that these works do not pretend to be historical and asserts that 'none of the extant novels could be mistaken for a history' (146).

23 Sidney's critics continue the tradition of reading his romance as a political text. See McCoy, Worden, Lockey, and Stillman for varied political interpretations of the *Arcadia*s from stridently Protestant to cosmopolitan and ecumenical.

24 See Rendall xv for the key.

25 I cite book, chapter, and page numbers from the Riley and Huber edition of the *Argenis* with facing-page translation.

26 Cultural analysis in classics scholarship has been aided by scholars like F. Zeitlin, Perkins, Goldhill, and Morales, who have built theoretically rich readings of Otherness and gender in the ancient Greek romances.

27 See Aristot. *Rhet*. 2: 12–2, 17, on describing character type, and on the rhetorical function of vivid description in the urbane style, see 3: 10–3, 11. There are many accounts of the history of ekphrasis in rhetoric. I bring up these examples simply to show the connection between ekphrasis and ethos in the Western rhetorical and literary imagination.

28 For Cicero's estimations of vivid writing, both in creating commonplaces and in illustrating character type through ethnic stereotype, see Vasaly.

29 See Quintilian, *Institutio* 6.2:29–34.

30 For early modern reception and translations, see Sider. For Cebes in education, see Ruiz Gito and Tucker 109–51.

31 Translations of the *progymnasmata* were used in sixteenth-century European education, but early modern scholars also made new pedagogical use of ekphrasis. See 'De copia' 11.5, where Erasmus reviews what he calls hypotyposes and explains Cicero's and Quintilian's views on vivid description. Erasmus also writes examples of how to interpret visual images allegorically in several of his *Colloquies*, which Bagley, 'Some Pedagogical Uses' 45–50, argues provided didactic models for verbal interpretation of the visual. For the revival of rhetoric in the Renaissance, see Kennedy, *Classical Rhetoric* 226–58.

32 The bibliography on emblem studies is substantial, but see Bath on emblematics, Russell on emblems, and Caldwell on *imprese* for excellent starting points.

33 For the influence of emblems on Renaissance literature see Praz, Freeman, and Daly.

34 See Bagley, 'Some Pedagogical Uses.'

35 Focalization, which Bal defines as 'the relation between the vision, the agent which sees, and that which is seen' (*Narratology* 142), is a useful word for what other narratologists simply refer to as point of view, because it distinguishes between that which sees and that which speaks about what it sees.

36 Bal defines the focalizer as follows: 'The subject of focalization, the focalizer, is the point from which the elements are viewed' (*Narratology* 146). A character focalizer is simply a focalizer that is a character in the text. Bal goes on to elaborate what she calls a 'visual narratology,' especially in her later study, '*Rembrandt*,' which provides an excellent model for analysing complex or multiple interpretations of an extant visual object. But I do not use the complete vocabulary of narratology in this project, for this would entail the need to choose between many such vocabularies, and as Bal herself expresses, such vocabularies can be 'cumbersome.' However, this brief examination of how the concept of focalization works in the case of multiple focalizers is helpful in showing how characterization and ekphrastic interpretation are linked.

37 For Peirce's triadic thought, see Reiss, *Uncertainty* 19–55.

38 Aptly, Benjamin's Angel of History is developed out of his ekphrasis of Paul Klee's *Angelus novus* in 'Theses on the Philosophy of History' – 'Where we perceive a chain of events, [the angel] sees one single catastrophe which keeps piling wreckage upon wreckage and hurls it in front of his feet' (257).

2. *Converso Convertida*: *Leucippe and Clitophon* and *Clareo y Florisea*

1 For the early transmission of the *Leucippe*, see Plepelits 391–4. For its Renaissance reception see Reeve.

2 The *Amorosi ragionamenti*, an incomplete translation by Dolce, was the basis for Reinoso's work. Though he coyly claims otherwise in the epistle, it has been convincingly argued by Zimic, 'Alonso Núñez de Reinoso,' Teijeiro, *La novela*, and González that Reinoso knew the full version of *Leucippe* before publishing *Clareo y Florisea*.

3 For more on the Mendoza copy of the *Leucippe*, which was lost in a fire in 1617, see Vilborg lxxv.

4 See Rosand.

5 For more on Juán Micas and the Nasci family of Jews who fled from Spain to Portugal to Italy and, finally, to Constantinople, see Salomón.

6 For observations on *Clareo y Florisea*'s circulation, in its Portuguese translation, its interest to *converso* circles, and its status as a *converso* work, see Galperín 317–26.

7 Morales suggests that '[i]nterest in the history of sexuality, perhaps more than any other factor, has defined the genre of the ancient novel as we now know it' ('The History of Sexuality' 39). Along with Foucault, *The*

Care of the Self, see Konstan; Goldhill, *Foucault's Virginity;* and Morales, *Vision and Narrative*.

8 Poor authorship is not an acceptable answer given the respect that critics have at this point for Tatius's writerly skills, and there is no evidence to show that lacunae are to blame. Winkler suggests that the *Leucippe*'s open-endedness reflects Plato's framing narration of the *Symposium* (284n72). Most stresses the generic conventions of first-person narratives as necessarily being framed as tales of woe. My proposal that Tatius's tale is actually told from Melite's perspective, as we will see, supports Most's attribution of first-person generic conventions to Tatius's work. Finally, 'strategic open-endedness' (Whitmarsh and Bartsch 243) would seem to be the most widely accepted view: see Fusillo, and see Morales, *Vision and Narrative* 143–51. If the narrator must be Clitophon, this last explanation would be the least convoluted, but it also reflects a possible projection of postmodern aesthetics onto an ancient text that I believe stresses polyvalence to delight rather than to frustrate the reader.

9 I cite book, section, and page numbers from Whitmarsh's translation of Tatius.

10 Though Melite's exact age is not given, Satyrus calls her 'extremely rich, and young' (Ach. Tat. 5, 11, 84), and we can be certain that she is not old enough to be bearded. There has been a misconception on the part of Tatius scholars that Melite is the 'older woman'; but though she is probably older than Leucippe, she is still young.

11 Clitophon's description of his dream of being bodily fused with and then severed from his half-sister Calligone (Ach. Tat. 1, 3, 6) – much like Aristophanes' androgyne in Plato's *Symposium* – and the ekphrasis of the diptych painting of Thesius and Andromeda paired with Hercules and Prometheus in Pelusium (Ach. Tat. 3, 6–8, 48–50) exemplify the text's ekphrastic obsession with gender ambiguity. Though Brethes does not claim that the narrator of the *Leucippe* is Melite, his argument that Clitophon's masculinity is suspect supports the view that the person who speaks as Clitophon is actually a woman.

12 Reinoso acknowledges Ovid's *Tristia* as one of his authorities in the epistle to Mendoza (238). Though several critics investigate Reinoso's sources, Deyermond and Galperín are particularly interested in precedents for female first-person narration. Galperín's analysis is the most thorough, especially in terms of her contextualization of Reinoso's work in Iberia.

13 See Bataillon 72–4 for how this passage encodes *converso* identity.

14 While I agree with Fuchs's misgivings about Rose's tendency to draw 'one to one' correspondences between the life of Reinoso and his work, I also

concur with her view that Rose's 'careful contextualization of the heroine's laments and the theme of adverse fortune with respect to contemporary *converso* experience is highly persuasive' (*Passing* 101).

15 Morales reads this comment about female predilections for myth 'not only as an ironic reflection on the misogynist tale he is about to tell Leucippe, but also as a self-conscious nod to some of Achilles' readers' 'Introduction' xii), some of whom she argues were likely to be women. This irony reaches its full potential for delectation, however, if we assume that Melite utters it.

16 Summing up these two interpretations of the scene, Bartsch explains, 'the depiction of a man wronging his wife with another woman is proleptic of Clitophon wronging Leucippe with Melite, and then of Thersander wronging Melite with Leucippe' (69).

17 The description of dreams was an accepted topic for ekphrasis in the Second Sophistic, and the subject of this ekphrasis, coupled with the tradition of oneirography, emphasizes the allegorical and prophetic aspects of Clareo's dream. For more on oneirography and ekphrasis, see Bartsch 80–109.

18 All the characters that Isea depicts in her embroidery either are mentioned or are narrators in Ovid's *Heroides*, further emphasizing the embroidery as a self-conscious act of female narration. For the *Heroides* in Spanish medieval and early modern sources and the text's possible influence on Reinoso, see Galperín 30–84.

19 For more on the widowed turtle-dove trope, see Bataillon 144–66. The trope can be traced back to biblical sources, patristic writings, and medieval bestiaries.

20 The turtle-dove was recommended as a sacrificial animal for burnt or sin offerings in Jewish ceremonies; see Gen. 15:9; Lev. 1:14, 5:7, 12:6, 12:8, 14:22, etc. It also carried an amorous connotation, Song of Solomon 2:12, 2:14, etc. Its voice is likened to the lamentation of the Jews in Isaiah 38:14, 59:11. It is correspondingly discussed in the Midrash Rabba. For more on the turtle-dove as a symbol of sacrifice and lamentation in both Christian and Jewish culture and its representation in sixteenth-century Spanish poetry, see Calvert.

21 The Henares flows by Guadalajara, Reinoso's home town.

22 See Zimic, '*Leucipe y Clitofonte*' for this hypothesis.

3. Amazon Eyes and Shifting Emblems in Sidney's Greek *Arcadia*

1 For Mary Sidney Herbert's literary centrality, especially in the innovation of religious lyric, see Coles. For her biography, see Hannay, *Philip's Phoenix*.

2 Sidney probably composed most of the original, now called *Old Arcadia*, at his sister's estate at Wilton c. 1577–80. As he explains in the dedication: 'Your dear self can best witness the manner; being done in loose sheets of paper, most of it in your presence, the rest by sheets sent unto you as fast as they were done' (*OA* 3). This first version, which remained in manuscript, was not rediscovered until 1907. Sidney revised the first three books of the text before he died, and his friend Fulke Greville published this incomplete revision in 1590. Sidney's sister later published her own edition, adding on the fourth and fifth books of the *Old Arcadia* to the initial three revised books in 1593. This was the version that was predominant for hundreds of years. For the publishing history of the *Arcadia*s and differences between the versions, see Zandvoort, and see Skretkowicz, 'Building Sidney's Reputation.' I cite the Duncan-Jones edition of the *OA*, and I cite book and page numbers from the 1593 *New Arcadia* (*NA*) edited by Evans with Greville's (1590) chapter numbers for the reader's convenience. The Skretkowicz edition of the *NA* is currently out of print and hard to come by, and a complete works of Sidney has not been issued since Feuilerat's 1912, which is out of print and incomplete.
3 For the strong female influence in Sidney's upbringing, see Duncan-Jones, *Sir Philip Sidney* 1–21.
4 For Pamela's resemblance to Elizabeth I, see Biester. She prays while imprisoned by Cecropia (*NA* 3, 6, 463–4). John Milton famously inveighs against Charles's alleged appropriation of Sidney because the speech is 'stol'n word for word from the mouth of a Heathen fiction praying to a heathen God' (362). Though the *Arcadia* is 'full of worthy witt,' it is 'among religious thoughts, and duties not worthy to be nam'd' (362), and Charles I's plagiarism of the passage is to Milton another instance of his poor stewardship of the nation. Though Royalists identified with the *Arcadia*, Sidney's politically complex romance was open to Republican readings as well, as Smith has argued (234–9).
5 Most of the numerous studies of Sidney's representation of gender focus on the *Old Arcadia*. In *Gender and Authorship*, Lamb investigates gender in the *New Arcadia* from the vantage point of neostoicism; in *Masculinity and Emotion*, Vaught considers it in terms of the passions; and in 'The Thigh and the Sword,' Mentz investigates androgyny through performative display.
6 On Sidney's travels, see Stewart, and see Buxton.
7 Citations from *Defence of Poesy* come from Duncan-Jones, ed., *Sir Philip Sidney: Major Works*.
8 Underdowne's translation of the *Aethiopica* was available to Sidney, as Hagg has argued (197–201).

9 See ch. 2 for Tatius's reception.

10 In the *New Arcadia*, Leucippe is the beloved of Pamphilus, the son of Kalander is named Clitophon, and Clinias is an actor turned undercover agent for Cecropia.

11 Sidney's borrowings from a series of Spanish romances such as Jorge de Montemayor's *Diana* (many of which in turn imitated the Greek romance) complicate the question of sources. For a thorough recent estimation of the influence of Spanish romance on Sidney, see Crowley. See also Oliveira e Silva, who argues that Sidney had a command of Spanish. For more on Sidney's Spanish connections see my 'Sidney's,' and see Lockey esp. 19–29.

12 Studies that acknowledge Heliodorus's influence on Sidney are numerous, but see esp. Plazenet, and see Mentz, *Romance for Sale* 47–104.

13 The entertainment can be found in Duncan-Jones, ed., *Major Works* 5–13. For various political readings, see Hager 41–62, and Berry.

14 For entertainments and masques as multimedia endeavours, see Orgel, 'Poetics of Spectacle.'

15 For the *imprese* in the triumph, see Duncan-Jones, 'Sidney's Personal Imprese,' and for heraldic devices and emblems in the *Arcadia* see Scanlon, and Skretkowicz, 'Devices and Their Narrative Function' and 'Sir Philip Sidney and the Elizabethan Literary Device.'

16 Fraunce dedicated a manuscript treatise on *imprese* to Sidney, Bodleian Library MS Rawl. D. 345, a printed treatise to Sidney's brother Robert, *Insignia*, and a manuscript version of the same again to Robert, *Symbolicae*. Samuel Daniel, also a member of Sidney's circle, translated Giovio's treatise on *imprese*, *The Worthy Tract*. See Buxton 148–51, on Fraunce, Sidney, and their influence on emblems, devices, and *imprese* in England. See Alexander, *Writing* 154–8, for Robert Sidney's emblematic skills.

17 See Fraunce, *Symbolicae* 46–51.

18 Sidney sat for Veronese among others, but he also considered Tintoretto. On his acquaintance with Hilliard and interest in the visual arts, see Hulse 115–56. For his familiarity with the work of Federico Zuccaro and Giovanni Paolo Lomazzo, see Camerlingo 162. Though his extant letters from the continent do not describe artwork, Sidney doubtless was exposed to masterpieces of Renaissance art. See Duncan-Jones, 'Sidney and Titian' 1–12.

19 A brief outline of character relationships in the *New Arcadia* may be helpful to the reader. King Basilius of Arcadia misinterprets a prophecy that he receives from the oracle at Delphi and removes his family, Queen Gynecia, Princess Pamela (future ruler of Arcadia), and Princess Philoclea, from his court to the pastoral 'desart' of Arcadia. The cousins and best friends

Prince Musidorus of Thessalia and Prince Pyrocles of Macedon discover the sequestered Arcadian princesses and disguise themselves to gain their love. Musidorus becomes Dorus the shepherd for Pamela's sake, and Pyrocles becomes Zelmane the Amazon for Philoclea's sake. Both King Basilius and Queen Gynecia fall for Pyrocles while he is disguised as Zelmane, complicating his efforts to seduce Philoclea. Some of the other obstacles to the princes' love include Pamela's clownish guardians, a peasant rebellion, and the would-be usurper and sister-in-law of Basilius (Cecropia).

20 What Foucault views as a 'new erotics' of Greek romance might be an essential aspect of romance ethos from its nascence in the *Odyssey*, where Odysseus and Penelope are continually presented as equals, to the exclusion of other, unequal mates. Konstan, Goldhill, and Morales have questioned and elaborated the applicability of Foucault's 'new erotics' to ancient narrative.

21 Like Morales, I do not take a psychoanalytical approach to formulations of the gaze. Morales explains that she 'employ[s] the term "gaze" more loosely than psychoanalytic critics do, partly because they have a tendency to make rigid distinctions between glance and gaze which are not only employed in ways often contradictory to common usage, which can be confusing, but are also hard to map onto ancient descriptions of viewing without distorting or suppressing the rich Greek vocabulary of sight' (*Vision and Narrative* 40). I agree, given that, like ancient models, early modern formulations of optics differ significantly from modern ones, and given my consideration of passibility rather than psychoanalytic models of subjectivity.

22 Morales draws on Peter de Bolla, who defines 'metaphorics of the gaze' as 'the collection of figurative expressions [...] of specific forms of visual experience' (Bolla 283, ct Morales, *Vision and Narrative* 32).

23 The character that Sidney calls Clitophon in the *New Arcadia* is Kalander's son, so, if the reader will forgive the infelicity of the following explanation, Tatius's Clitophon's father's garden thus resembles Sidney's Clitophon's father's garden.

24 These images have been interpreted both as sculpted and/or painted. For an argument in favour of these being paintings and for an analysis of Virgilian ekphraseis, see Mitsi 70.

25 Clitophon's first sighting of Leucippe (who has also been exiled from her father's court to seek allegedly safer harbours) is also figured in painterly terms, as Clitophon compares her to a 'picture I had once seen of Selene on a bull' (1, 4, 2–3). The comparison links the girl directly to the opening ekphrasis of Tatius's romance.

26 In Ovid's *Metamorphoses*, 3.318–38, Tiresias is turned back into a man after another encounter with mating serpents.

27 Hercules was sold to Omphale, queen of Lydia, as a slave for three years as a punishment for murdering Iphitus. She made him her lover, and he cross-dressed and did women's tasks like working the loom and distaff while she donned his lion's skin and club. See Apollod. 2.6.3; Diod. 4.31; Ov. *Fast*. 2.305; Eur. *Her*. 9.53. Hercules also cross-dresses with Iole, but only after he has killed her father and raped her. One aspect of the Hercules / Iole story that is important for Sidney's ekphrastic play is that Pan too tried to rape Iole, but finds himself, rather inconveniently, slipping into bed with a cross-dressed Hercules instead. Sidney used the story in 'The Lady of May': 'When wanton Pan, deceived with lion's skin / Came to the bed, where wound for kiss he got' (*Major Works* 12).

28 For the curious perspective, a term which refers to numerous manipulations of Albertian perspective including anamorphosis in works of art, see Gilman.

29 Examples of queer readings of *Arcadia* that focus on instances of homoerotic tension between men and between women respectively include Grossberg and Crawford.

30 For more on Pyrocles' clothing as a reflection of both gender and genre ambiguity in the *Arcadia*, see Mentz, 'The Thigh and the Sword.'

31 For emblematic depictions of the cross-dressed Hercules, see Bagley, 'Hercules.'

32 The reader will remember that the first physical description of Pyrocles in the *New Arcadia* depicts him astride the mast of a sinking ship where 'he held a sword aloft with his fair arm, which often he waved about his crown as though he would threaten the world in that extremity' (*NA* 1, 1, 67). See Skretkowicz, 'Hercules in Sidney and Spenser' for more on Sidney's use of the Hercules myth.

33 Hermes was the god of exchange, profit, and communication; hence, Zeus commanded him to find a buyer for Heracles. See Apollod. 2.6.3.

34 Ov. *Fast* 2.303–58.

35 For more on Philoclea's homoerotic desire, see Levin.

36 For more on how the Arcadia measures up to Renaissance pedagogical models, see Dolven, who reads the romance as a series of failed 'scenes of instruction.'

37 I cannot find a precedent for this version of Cupid's birth, and as the narrator claims that Dicus 'had given Cupid a quite new form' it must suffice to assume that the emblem is Sidney's invention.

38 See my 'Sidney's,' for the relationship between Fernando de Rojas's *Celestina* and Sidney's *New Arcadia*. Though Sidney might have read Rojas's work in Spanish, there were numerous translations available.

39 See Hannay, *Philip's Phoenix* 130–1.

40 Mary Sidney Herbert was intimately involved in promoting her brother's fiction by editing with Hugh Sanford the 1593 and 1598 editions of the *Arcadia*. What is less clear (and less important for my claims here) is the extent to which she revised Sidney's revision. The question is not whether she was capable of doing so, as recent studies demonstrate her superior abilities as a writer. For a conservative estimation of how much she altered the *New Arcadia* in putting it into print, see Hannay, *Philip's Phoenix* 70–8.

4. Painting Counterfeit Canvases: Cervantes's *Persiles*

1 The *Persiles*'s inclusion is not complete; the exclusion of some Jewish, *morisco*, and *converso* characters is clear, as is noted by both Fuchs and Childers. But the work is inclusive overall.

2 On opening *in medias res* and verisimilitude, see Forcione, *Cervantes, Aristotle*. For contrasting views of the pilgrimage, see Deffis de Calvo, Lozano, and Childers. For a catalogue of twentieth-century critical estimations of the *Persiles*, see González 228–32.

3 Fuchs notes that the Byzantine model 'suggests that the *Persiles*'s [cultural] daring is at least partially connected to the specific possibilities of the genre and to its riskier transformations' (*Passing* 99). While she traces this influence through Reinoso's imitation of Tatius, contrasting his narrative's goals with those of the *Persiles*, her consideration of the genre's cultural influence on the *Persiles* specifically is brief, and she does not consider Heliodoran ekphrasis.

4 More problematic is Sacchetti's claim that the Greek model typically exhibits 'flat characterization,' 'moral polarization of good and evil,' and 'unfailing happy ending[s]' (40), faulty assumptions about the genre that she uses as a springboard to analyse what she sees as the more 'novelistic' attributes of the *Persiles*.

5 Childers and I have come independently and by different means to similar conclusions about the cultural possibilities that the *Persiles* represents. His reading, while it does not focus on ekphrasis or the influence of Greek romance, makes a theoretically and historically informed contribution to our understanding of the romance's representation of subaltern groups.

6 Forcione notes how ekphrasis 'becomes an integrated, meaningful element in the author's examination of the aesthetic problems of verisimilitude

and unity' (*Cervantes, Aristotle* 238n62), and Deffis de Calvo asks 'si las novelas mismas no pueden considerarse como amplificaciones de ciertos emblemas' ('if the novels themselves couldn't be considered to be amplifications of certain emblems' 14). Though critics have found ekphrasis in the *Persiles* intriguing, Graf is the only other scholar I know of who has considered the impact of Heliodoran ekphrasis on the *Persiles*, though his thesis focuses on how ekphrasis forges a feminist precursor to the modern novel rather than reflecting on early modern identity *per se*.

7 I cite the Mena translation of Heliodorus here, because it was the one Cervantes most likely knew. See Lopez Estrada on Castillian translations of the *Aethiopica*. In *An Ethiopian Romance*, Hadas renders the Greek original as follows: 'The characters were Ethiopic, not, however, of the demotic variety but the royal script, which is like the Egyptian writing called hieratic' (93–4). This confirms Mena in his translation of the script as being hieroglyphic or pictographic.

8 See Wilson, 'Cervantes and the New World' and Fernández, 'The Bonds of Patrimony,' for bibliographies and synopses of transatlantic approaches to Cervantes's work and life that focus on the *Quijote* and *Novelas Ejemplares* respectively. See Reiss, *Against Autonomy* 360–404, Correa-Díaz, and Childers for some ramifications of Cervantes's American interests in Latin American politics, art, and identity.

9 For an inventory of European exposure to and recording of Mexican paintings, see Boon.

10 I believe, as do Forcione and Wilson, that the *Persiles*'s *bárbaros* have a polyvalent function. The story of the young Antonio's evolving relationship with paintings in the narrative draws on both Heliodorus's ancient model of ekphrastic assimilation and the reception of Native Americans and their artwork in Europe. Though my analysis of the *bárbaros* is analogical rather than allegorical, the *Persiles* is often read allegorically, and allegorical readings of its paintings such as the unauthorized painting of Auristela are certainly valid. Forcione considers the role of allegory in the *Persiles* in *Cervantes's Christian Romance* 51–64, and Wilson incorporates the theories of Paul de Man and Freud in her definition of allegorical modes in *Allegories* 45–77.

11 See Mariscal on Antonio's 'barbarian' family as a representation of *mestizaje* in Spanish social schema based on purity of blood and standards of masculinity.

12 Though it is not called American, most Cervantistas agree that the description of the island with its use of American vocabulary and apparel, and with its social habits such as cannibalism, is highly inflected as

American. Wilson notes its American linguistic and cultural markers along with references to colonial texts that describe the New World, concluding that the island is a hybrid representation of American and European imperial desires. See *Cervantes, the Novel* 150. I add that the objection that the island cannot be American owing to its inhabitants being called *bárbaros* rather than *Indios* and to its being septentrional or northern can be surmounted by similarities between Cervantes's *bárbaros setentrionales* and the American 'bárbaros septentrionales' as they are described by colonial explorers and authors such as Valadés in his *Rhetorica Christiana*.

13 These figures may also be found in Gruzinski, *Conquest*, plates 1 and 2.

14 For other accounts of *lienzos*, see Díaz 336, and Durán, esp. 513–15.

15 Cervantes joined a Franciscan lay order in late life. He thus might have learned of iconic proselytizing techniques and Christian rhetorical texts like that of Valadés.

16 For the hybridization of Christian images in Mexican painting see Gruzinski, *Mestizo Mind* 107–20.

17 Spanish artists strove to elevate painting to a liberal art, partly to avoid taxation, as E. Bergmann 17–57, and Baxandall 1–29, have noted. Painters focused on 'the divine origins of painting and the religious importance of the visual arts' (E. Bergmann 24–5), espousing Neoplatonic formulations of art-making that gained currency in the last third of the sixteenth century. On the theocentric theory of art, see Curtius 546. On the Counter-Reformation Spanish Church's use of 'jeroglíficos y pinturas' ('hieroglyphs and paintings' 120) to stave off heterodox views, and how this influenced the *Persiles*, see Castillo and Spadaccini. On how Counter-Reformation doctrine was taught iconically, see Maravall 497–520.

18 Citations of the *Persiles* are from the Romero Muñoz edition and the translations are from Weller and Colahan. I also include book and chapter numbers for the reader.

19 In accordance with the art of memory, Della Porta defines the painting of mnemonic canvases by 'making a summary of the principal narrative sequences and freezing them in a series of paintings positioned in the places of memory' (ct. Bolzoni 215–16). For more on the history of the art of memory in the Renaissance, see Bolzoni, and for a discussion of memory in the works of Cervantes see Egido.

20 As Egido avers, not only the characters but also the reader frequently needs 'ayuda-memorias que no le impidan perder el hilo narrative' ('memory aids to keep them from losing the narrative thread' 288), the complexity of which she attributes to the narrative's Greek romance model.

21 See Boon and Cummins for evidential *lienzos* in colonial courts, where *lienzos* and their ekphraseis were at first accepted as evidence and contract. Also see Zeitlin and Thomas, who emphasize the adaptability of Native Americans and their iconic languages to the New World court system.

22 The canvas also omits Transila, the Amazon-like translator, whose story dominates several chapters. Antonio's sensitivity to the absence of female representation is interesting in light of theories of the androgyne, where an androgynous state is also a metaphorical goal of lovers. See El Saffar, 'Fiction and the Androgyne in the Works of Cervantes' and Wilson, *Allegories* 78–105.

23 See Forcione, *Cervantes, Aristotle,* for Cervantes's use of Renaissance literary theory in the *Persiles*, and see Riley for Cervantes's engagement with formulations of the early novel.

24 For the *paragone*, or contest between writing and the visual arts, see Barkan, *Unearthing* 1–63, and Hagstrum.

25 Wilson argues for the parodic interpretation of the barbarous isle in *Cervantes, the Novel* 180.

26 Wilson suggests the *auto* was written by Luis Hurtado de Toledo (1523–90), and Micael de Carvajal, 'a writer who had been to the Indies' (*Cervantes, the Novel* 22).

27 As I have argued elsewhere (Bearden, 'Sidney's'), the English viewed Spaniards as both glorious conquerors and imperial overreachers. For more on the connections between Spain and England in the early modern period, see Fuchs and Lockey, eds., *Anglo-Spanish Relations.* For more on the black legend, see Greer et al., eds., *Rereading the Black Legend*.

28 Even the Ottoman navy was quite diverse. For example, Barbarossa Hayreddin Pasha, Fleet Admiral under Suleyman the Magnificent, was a Muslim of mixed Greek and Turkish descent born on the Greek island of Lesbos. For more on the ethnic and religious diversity of corsair crews and cultural elisions between 'Turks' and Native Americans, see Matar.

29 The translation of 'falsos' as 'counterfeit' is appropriate considering the concentration on economic exchange and duplication of false images in the tale. The false captives, like two coins, are barely distinguishable, as are the mayors who confront them.

30 For an informative analysis of this concept see Brito Díaz.

31 See Haedo 246–54 for descriptions of captivity and renegade practices in Algiers, and see Garcés for the correspondences between the counterfeits' tale and Cervantes's real captivity.

32 See Gaylord 141 on the presentation of *requerimientos* as a trope for vexed speech acts in *DQ*.

33 See Gruzinski, *Conquest*.

34 For a Mexican pictographic version of the conquest, see Muñoz Camargo's *Historia de Tlaxcala* (c. 1585) with the *Tlaxcala Codex* (probably a copy of the *Lienzo de Tlaxcala* c. 1550). Also of interest is Guamán Pomaa's pictographic manuscript addressed to Phillip III and composed in Cuzco (1613).

5. *Pictura Locorum*: Barclay's *Argenis*

1 I cite chapter numbers and pages from the 1614 Latin edition of the *Icon* published in London and page numbers from the 1631 edition of the May translation. Though I have consulted copies in the Folger Shakespeare Library, these editions are available on EEBO, and there is also an excellent online Latin edition made available by Cultural Heritage Language Technologies in partnership with the Perseus project at: http://www.chlt.org/sandbox/colloquia/IconAnimorum/page.2.php

2 For Barclay's life and travels, see Fleming, 'Introduction' ix–xiii, and 'John Barclay: Neo-Latinist at the Jacobean Court.' For a list of his works, see Riley and Huber 81.

3 Dedicated to a thirteen-year-old Louis XIII, the *Icon* was appended to Barclay's picaresque *Satyricon* as its 'forth Part.' For the influence of the *Icon*, see Fumaroli, 'A Scottish Voltaire.' Barclay's *Satyricon* and his *Argenis* received over fifty editions and *Argenis* was translated into all major European languages in its first hundred years. For a list of editions and translations of the *Satyricon*, see Barclay, *Euphormionis* 355–8, and for the *Argenis*, see Riley and Huber 51–8.

4 Tacitus, particularly his *Agricola* and *Germania* [*De origine et situ Germanorum*], probably influenced Barclay's *Icon*, given the popularity of Lipsius's edition of Tacitus at the English court (a particular favourite with the Sidneys), and given Barclay's fluency in silver-age Latin. For Barclay's style, see IJsewijn, and see Riley and Huber 39–43.

5 Often referred to as 'climate theory,' the belief that a person's humours were balanced according to where they were born, what Mary Floyd-Wilson usefully terms geohumoralism, was commonplace in the Renaissance. Geohumoralism combines ancient and early modern beliefs about how local climates imbued their inhabitants with both physical and mental traits. It varied in terms of its projected effects and in terms of how malleable these effects were seen to be. For more on geohumoralism, see Floyd-Wilson 23–47.

6 The word *consortium*, ii, n. can also be translated as fellowship or society (*Lewis & Short* II), or the sharing of property, or community of goods (*Lewis*

& Short I). Though Barclay's *Icon* is part of the 'character of nations' tradition, it is cosmopolitan and, more than national divides, it describes characteristics of different peoples.

7 This citation appears in the introductory index of the Latin and in the argument of the second chapter in the English.

8 The cons of these countries, according to Barclay, run along the following lines: Persia is separated by 'superstitious impiety' and distance; India by distance (only the Portuguese have a foothold); China wants nothing to do with Europe; Europe wants nothing to do with the Tartars; and America, insofar as it is civilized at all, is completely controlled by the Spaniards (*Icon* 10, 61–4).

9 I cite book, chapter, and page numbers from the Riley and Huber edition of the *Argenis* with facing-page translation.

10 This is from the 'Oracion' that prefaces Pellicer's 1626 Spanish translation of the *Argenis*. Astioristes is Poliarchus's real name. For the reception of the *Argenis* in Spain, see Davis.

11 According to letter 159 to his publisher Peiresc on 19 April 1619, ct. Collignon 113, Barclay read the *Aethiopica*. For more on Barclay's use of Heliodorus for the *Argenis*, see Riley and Huber 26–30 and Plazenet 98–9; 308–12.

12 The *Argenis* is best known for being the first early modern political romance. It contains disquisitions on systems of government and was read as a political allegory, keys to the 'true' identities of people and places being published with the work almost immediately. It became a seminal text for the royalist romances of the English civil war and also inspired the heroical romance and roman à clef traditions in France and elsewhere. See Plazenet 308–12, Salzman 149–76, and Langford for the *Argenis*'s influence on early modern prose fiction. See also Smith's discussion of the varied political possibilities of romance in seventeenth-century England (234–9).

13 Grotius cites and discusses Barclay's father's views on sovereign authority in his *De jure belli* (*The Law of War and Peace*) 150, 157. Having put a new edition of his father's work on the topic into print for James I in 1609, Barclay echoed these views on absolute monarchy in his own political tract on the topic and, in revised form, in the *Argenis*'s political disquisitions.

14 The Canon, who excoriates chivalric romance, reveals he once had plans to write a romance, *DQ* 1, 48, that was perhaps the model for Cervantes's *Persiles*. For more on this see Forcione, *Cervantes, Aristotle* 169. Nicopompus's work is auto-referential, giving the historical reader a template for interpreting the *Argenis* and advising her on the preciseness of its political allegories. Whereas Nicopompus aims to intervene in a

political controversy (the rebellion in Sicily) rather than literary theory per se, the two situations are similar.

15 Barclay easily could have read the *Persiles*, which was first printed in 1617 and was quickly translated into French (1618) and English (1619).

16 Connors traces Ovidian myths in the *Argenis* in her exploration of its use of political metaphor. See esp. 251–8.

17 In the Ovidian context the reference was presumed to be to the tyranny of Dionysius I of Syracuse, who fought with Carthage over control of Sicily.

18 On Barclay's use of Ovidian myths about Sicily, see Connors 251–8. She notes numerous permutations of Zeus's mountain-hurling defeat of Typhoeus. Though she suggests that Apuleius is Barclay's model for 'this shift from a narrative register (Ovid has Galatea tell what happened to Acis) to an ecphrastic register (Barclay describes a fountain depicting the story)' (253), I believe that the Greek romance is Barclay's model for these ekphrastic transformations.

19 For more on the diptych and the way the two groups of three figures can be mapped on to the narrative, see Bartsch 55–62.

20 See Sedgwick, who uses this term to describe relationships of desire and denial between men that reinforce the bonds of patriarchal society and result in misogyny and homophobia.

21 For more on mimetic and triangulated desire, see Girard, who uses these terms to explore the literary and anthropological implications of love triangles that often result in violent rivalry.

22 In her study of the figure of the Moor in English drama, for instance, Bartels notes that in 'early modern representations, the Moor serves as a site where competing, always provisional axes of identity come dynamically into play, disrupting our ability, if not also our desire, to assign the Moor a color, religion, ethnicity, or any homogenizing trait' (7).

23 Poliarchus's and Timoclea's shock at Archombrotus's beauty does not consider his complexion, which is not mentioned, but their prejudice against African features fits well with Hall's claims about African blackness being judged as exclusive of beauty in the period. See *Things of Darkness*.

24 Floyd-Wilson argues that the European perception of African identity underwent a shift in this period, in part because of English anxieties about their own humoral imbalances as Northerners. Timoclea and Poliarchus seem to assume that Africans are cowardly and closed-minded, which fits with the view that their southern climate made them melancholic, and thus intelligent but weak of body.

25 The likeness between the descriptions of Greenwich and Lixa is just one of many conclusions that I came to independently before I had a chance to

read Connors's work, and I thank her for gently alerting me to her excellent essay on Barclay over a lovely dinner in the botanical gardens in Lisbon.

26 For other treatments of Hyanisbe's similarity to Elizabeth I, see Connors 264–5, and Riley and Huber 22–6, as well as their inclusion of a typical key to characters (45–50).

27 The well-documented and marvellous gardens at Nonsuch boasted six fountains as well as the grove of Diana, and the similarities to Hyanisbe's grove are striking. For more on Nonsuch gardens and their relation to Elizabeth, see Lees-Jeffries 255–78.

28 As Barroll has argued in *Anna of Denmark*, there is a strong case for referring to Queen Anne as Anna, which further supports my argument here, but which also might be a bit confusing to my readers if put into practice in this chapter.

29 Janus Nicius Erythraeus (Giovanni Vittorio Rossi), who knew Barclay, records his proclivity for gardening in his *Pinacotheca imaginum illustrium virorum*, vol. 3 (Cologne, 1643), 72–81, ct. Riley and Huber 11.

30 In Barclay's romance, Anna dies in childbirth after being betrothed to King Meleander, who met her in his travels in Africa. Her child is Archombrotus.

31 Though scholars put Barclay's arrival in England in the fall of 1605 (see Fleming, 'John Barclay: Neo-Latinist' 230), Barclay would not have had to see the performance in person to know about it, and could have read the printed version issued with the *Masque of Beauty* in 1608. Moreover, Jonson knew and admired Barclay's work, and he most likely executed the first (now lost) English translation of the *Argenis*. It was entered in the Stationers' Register on 2 October 1623, but Jonson lost the first three volumes of his translation in the fire that destroyed his library the next month. See Riley and Huber 30–1.

32 She was carrying Mary Stuart, who died age two.

33 In a letter describing the performance, Dudley Carlton remarks, 'Instead of Vizzards, their Faces, and Arms up to the Elbows, were painted black' (Jonson, *Complete Works* 448). Jonson attributes to Anne the idea of performing in black paint in the Preamble to his masque.

34 For more on Queen Anne's performance and female authority in the masque, see Andrea, 'Black Skin,' and for her creative influence, see Barroll 74–116. For a discussion of race and gender in the masque that takes its Heliodoran and Scottish valences into account, see Iyengar 80–102.

35 Here aemulation means rivalry, but its other meaning of emulation or imitation is also fitting.

36 See Dieckmann for an overview of the early modern understanding of hieroglyphics.

6. 'We are all picturd in that Piece': Lady Mary Wroth's *Urania*

1 The first part of *Urania* was published in London in 1621. References to this text come from the Roberts edition. The second half is a manuscript housed at the Newberry library and is difficult to date, though Wroth probably worked on it for many years. Citations from the second half are from the Roberts edition completed by Gossett and Mueller. For a recent critical biography of Wroth, see Hannay, *Mary Sidney, Lady Wroth*.

2 See Lamb, 'The Biopolitics,' and Beilin, 'Winning.'

3 One such episode is Wroth's story of the pirate Sandringal (I, 1, 29–32), who resembles Heliodorus's pirate Thyamis. The *Aethiopica* was available to Wroth in Underdowne's translation. Both pirates give first-person accounts of kidnapping a princess (Antissia in Wroth's text and Charicleia in Heliodorus's). Wroth refits her pirate to suit her times, casting him as a younger brother who resorts to piracy owing to penury.

4 Wroth's villain Clotorindus stages Meriana's decapitation (I, 1, 158), which resembles an episode in *Leucippe and Clitophon*, which Wroth could have read in Burton's translation. But this episode also resembles the false decapitations in Sidney's *NA*, making Tatius's influence uncertain.

5 Wroth mentions *Daphnis and Chloe* in the second volume of the *Urania* in the description of Drusio and Isabella (II, 2, 368), a couple whose side story could make up its own Greek romance. Wroth could have read Longus's romance in Angel Day's translation.

6 Along with the influence of Sidney's *Arcadia*, from which she borrows the name of her titular heroine, Wroth is indebted to Spenser's *Faerie Queene* and other Elizabethan romances. She was also influenced by Spanish prose fiction including *The Diana*, *Don Quijote*, and *Amadís de Gaula*. For her Iberian influences, see Hackett 162–6. Wroth could have read *Amadís* in Anthony Munday's 1618 translation.

7 See Roberts, 'Critical Introduction' xliv. She refers to Gerhard Mercator, *Atlas sive cosmographicae meditationes de fabrica mundi et fabricate figura* (Amsterdam, 1616). Ortelius had recently been translated into English: *Theatrum Orbis Terrarum: The Theatre of the Whole World* ... (London, 1606). See also Sandys, *A Relation of a journey*.

8 Gossett and Mueller note that 'a sixteenth-century map of the voyages of St. Paul provides the best illustration for Wroth's nomenclature' ('Textual Introduction' xxxiii). See also Andrea, who discusses Wroth's layering

of Greco-Roman and Ottoman-Islamic place names in *Women and Islam* 30–52.

9 Wroth's story of Seralius and his father-in-law mirrored the life of Denny and his son-in-law. For the similarities of the stories and of Denny's accusations with Wroth's rebuttals, see Roberts, 'Introduction,' *The Poems of Lady Mary Wroth* 31–5. Wroth also cloaks the Overbury affair of 1613; see Roberts, ibid. 35–6. Denny's accusations and Wroth's response can be found in ibid. 32–4.

10 For possible allusions to the marriage of Elizabeth Stuart and Frederic of Bohemia in the *Urania*, see Brennan, *The Sidneys* 133–48.

11 For Carlos V's use of imperial iconic portraiture, see Yates 1–22. She also examines Elizabethan and Valois uses of visual imagery in politics.

12 See Goldberg on James I's imperial pageants.

13 In Cervantes's *Persiles*, lovers fight over one of Auristela's portraits and haggle over another, episodes that create their own side stories and push the plot towards the marriage of the protagonists. Wroth could have been influenced by the *Persiles*, which was translated into English in 1619.

14 Pliny's descriptions of villas – see esp. 5.6 – constitute a form of ekphrasis. For more on this, see B. Bergmann.

15 On the emblematic frontispiece in England, see Corbett and Lightbown.

16 On the relationship between closets, sonnets, and the female subject in Wroth's work, see Andrea, 'Pamphilia's Cabinet.'

17 Murrey is Pamphilia's colour, both in the first half of the *Urania* (I, 1, 148), and in the second half (II, 1, 117). On murrey's connotation of constancy, see Linthicum 40.

18 As Roberts points out, Pamphilia's description 'contains a number of iconographical details typical of the portraits of Queen Elizabeth [...] The pearl, associated with purity and virginity, is prominent in both the Ermine and Rainbow portraits of Elizabeth at Hatfield House' (Wroth I, 736). On the iconography of the pearl in Elizabeth's portraits, see Beilin, 'Winning' 219, and Yates 215, 218.

19 The Family of Love or *familia caritatis* was an underground spiritualist Protestant sect based on the writings of the Dutch mystic Hendrick Niclaes that gained popularity in England in the sixteenth century. For more on the English Familists, see Halley. Wroth also makes what turns out to be ambiguous use of the figure of Venus holding a flaming heart in the first sonnet of *Pamphilia to Amphilanthus*.

20 The Battle of Lepanto (1571) was thought to be the greatest sea battle won by the Holy League against the Ottomans. Europeans idealized it as a decisive victory for Christianity, though within a year the Ottoman fleet regained its strength.

21 Roberts argues that Wroth uses Ortelius for her geography ('Critical Introduction' xliv). The theatre could, of course, also refer to playhouses or to memory theatres, which were used as mnemonic devices. See Bolzoni 196–203 on memory theatres.

22 Speculations about Amazons in the Americas abounded in Wroth's time. Musalina's connection with America is strengthened later on in the episode of the Hell of Deceit, where Pamphilia sees Musalina surrounded with severed body parts that are being thrown into a fire, suggesting cannibalism.

23 Along with the female allegorical representations of the continents on the title page, the first map or *Typus orbis terrarum* contains four stoical epigrams, two by Cicero and two by Seneca.

24 Like Pamela (*NA* 1, 176–81), Veralinda is attacked by a bear (Wroth I, 3, 426), and like Philoclea's flight from the lion (*NA* 1, 176–7), her sprint reveals her beautiful legs to Leonius (Wroth I, 3, 426), who saves her much as Musidorus and Pyrocles save Pamela and Philoclea from bear and lion. Leonius also adopts Amazon attire to seduce the girl as does Pyrocles. Thus, Veralinda functions as a composite Pamela-Philoclea and Leonius as a composite Pyrocles-Musidorus. For more on Wroth's imitation of Sidney's *Arcadia*, see Alexander, *Writing* 284–331.

25 The self-referential story-within-a-story and the machinations of mysterious enchanters (perhaps a figure for Wroth herself) resemble Cervantes's *Don Quijote*, a book that plays precisely on the inability of romance to function in reality. On the connections between Wroth and Cervantes, see Wall-Randell.

26 Hackett comments that the Hell of Deceit represents 'a striking inversion of Amoret's imprisonment by Busirane [...] Whereas the flames encompassing Busirane's castle can only be traversed by one as pure as Britomart, here only the unchaste can pass' (173).

27 Pamphilia's thwarted relationship with Amphilanthus is often also compared to Wroth's relationship with her cousin and lover, William Herbert. For a biographical reading of the construction of gender, see Waller.

28 For more on the *de praesenti* marriage in the *Urania*, see Roberts, '"The Knott Never to Bee Untide."'

29 Wroth's father, Robert Sidney, hosted Anthony and Robert Sherley in Flushing on their way to Persia, as recounted by Parry, *A New and Large Discourse*. For a study of the Sherleys' travel accounts and their attempts to gain social status through this medium, see Schleck, 'Writing Out Muslim Culture.'

30 See Andrea, *Women and Islam* 42–53.

31 This exoticization went both ways. While the English became fascinated with Persian costume and its representation in art as illustrated in the portrait reproduced in figure 6.3, Persians were also fascinated with English clothing and painting practices. Thomas Herbert notes the presence of several European painters in Persia, including a Dutch painter who Herbert alleges threatened the widowed Teresa Sherley over her husband's debts (125). Also, as Tavakoli-Targhi observes, 'during 1642–1643 Shah 'Abbas II, who appreciated European arts, dispatched a group of students to Rome to acquire Western painting techniques' (92). Paintings of the Sherleys in their English habits are still visible in Persian architectural painting on the façades of Safavi palaces in Iran today.

32 The Cloth of State or Cloth of Estate is presented specifically as a female sign of authority in the *Urania*.

33 As Gossett and Mueller point out in their commentary on this description, 'Costume books published in Wroth's time included illustrations of Persian dress' (Wroth II, 508).

34 The Lady's costume appears to be based on J. Boissard's depiction of a *Virgo Persica* (Persian Virgin) in his *Habitus variarum orbis gentium* (1581), reproduced in Ashelford 133. Strong suggests that the portrait was of Frances Walsingham, widow of Sir Philip Sidney and later of Essex.

35 The exchange between Pamphilia's court and Persia resembles ambassadorial exchanges involving the Sherleys. As Andrea explains, 'Sherlian discourse again comes to the fore [in the *Urania*] through a pair of embassies' (*Women and Islam* 51). One is sent from Europe to Persia and one from Persia to Europe. For more on the history of ambassadorial exchanges between Persia, Tartaria, and Europe, see Rubiés.

36 Ortelius's description of the Tartars reflects this ambiguity. He explains that because 'they inhabit large and vast countries far distant and remote from one another, they are similarly different in manners and way of life,' and while he admires their physical constitution, calling them 'well built' and 'strong and able-bodied and audacious,' with nomadic customs that include drinking horse-blood, he criticizes their alleged lawlessness and avarice, claiming, 'They observe no manner of justice or law. These people, especially the poorer ones, are very voracious and eager to take [someone else's] property.' Yet in the same breath he avers that '[t]hey have no use for gold or silver,' and he admires their military prowess and the construction of their cities. He comments in particular on 'Quinzai,' where 'the great Cham has a standing garrison of 12,000 soldiers continually resident. It is a wonderfully stately and pleasant city, which

is why it obtained the name of Quinzai by which they mean The city of Heaven' (105).

37 For more on how Rodomandro compares to some negative images of Tartaria, see Cavanagh, *Cherished Torment* 37–52. Like Andrea in 'Persia, Tartaria, and Pamphilia,' I argue that the depictions of Tartaria in the period were ambiguous, but Andrea goes into more detail on Tartaria and considers at length the relations between Persia and Tartaria as well.

38 See Hall, *Things of Darkness* 187–210.

39 Like Barclay, Wroth was doubtless influenced by Jonson's masques, having been herself one of the dancers in *The Masque of Blackness*. For more on Wroth's intellectual ties with Ben Jonson, see Brennan, 'A Sidney.'

40 For more on the similarities between Rodomandro and Othello, see N. Miller, 'Engendering Discourse.'

Conclusions

1 Negotiation of semantic and structural poles (in other words, content vs structure) dominates recent work on the chivalric romance. While Cooper's approach to the English chivalric romance has a semantic bent, she argues that its motifs of content function structurally like memes, 3–7. Robinson's assessment of books of chivalry, by contrast, emphasizes their temporal and spatial structure to comment on the semantics of their representations of Islam, 3–8.

2 The Zahir (a protean object that first appears as a coin) becomes a fetishistic obsession to its beholder, eventually excluding the possibility of its description and even of the perception of anything besides it. See Borges 105–16.

3 See Mitchell, *Picture Theory* 183–207.

Works Cited

Alexander, Gavin. 'Introduction.' *Sidney's 'Defence of Poesy' and Selected Renaissance Literary Criticism.* New York: Penguin, 2004. xvii–lxxix.

– *Writing after Sidney: The Literary Response to Sir Philip Sidney, 1586–1640.* New York: Oxford UP, 2006.

Allen, Michael J. *Icastes: Marsilio Ficino's Interpretation of Plato's Sophist.* Berkeley: U of California P, 1989.

Amyot, Jacques. 'Le Proesme du translateur.' *Romans Grecs.* Paris: Lefèvre, 1841. 105–10.

Andrea, Bernadette. 'Black Skin, The Queen's Masques: African Ambivalence and Feminine Author(ity) in the Masques of Blackness and Beauty.' *ELR* 29.3 (March 1999): 246–81.

– 'Lady Sherley: The "First" Persian in England?' *Muslim World* 95.2 (April 2005): 279–95.

– 'Pamphilia's Cabinet: Gendered Authorship and Empire in Lady Mary Wroth's *Urania*.' *ELH* 68.2 (2001): 335–58.

– 'Persia, Tartaria, and Pamphilia: Ideas of Asia in Mary Wroth's *The Countess of Montgomery's Urania, Part II*.' *The English Renaissance, Orientalism, and the Idea of Asia.* Ed. D. Johanyak and W. Lim. New York: Palgrave, 2010. 23–50.

– *Women and Islam in Early Modern English Literature.* New York: Cambridge UP, 2007.

Appiah, Kwame Anthony. *Cosmopolitanism: Ethics in a World of Strangers.* New York: Norton, 2006.

Aristotle. *On Rhetoric: A Theory of Civic Discourse.* Trans. G. Kennedy. New York: Oxford UP, 1991.

Ashelford, Jane. *Dress in the Age of Elizabeth I.* London: Batsford, 1999.

Bagley, Ayers. 'Hercules in Emblem Books and Schools.' *The Telling Image: Explorations in the Emblem*. Ed. A. Bagley, E.M. Griffin, and A. McLean. New York: AMS, 1996. 69–95.

– 'Some Pedagogical Uses of the Emblem in Sixteenth- and Seventeenth-Century England.' *Emblematica* 7 (1993): 39–60.

Bakhtin, M.M. *The Dialogic Imagination: Four Essays*. Ed. M. Holquist. Trans. C. Emerson and M. Holquist. Austin: U of Texas P, 1981.

Bal, Mieke. *Narratology: Introduction to the Theory of Narrative*. 2nd ed. Toronto: U of Toronto P, 1997.

– *'Rembrandt': Beyond the Word-Image Opposition*. Cambridge: Cambridge UP, 1991.

Barclay, John. *Argenis*. Ed. and trans. M. Riley and D. Pritchard Huber. 2 vols. Assen, Netherlands Royal Van Gorcum, 2004.

– *Argenis*. Trans. J. Pellicer y Salas de Tobar. Madrid: Luis Sanchez, 1626.

– *Euphormionis Lusinini Satyricon (Euphormio's Satyricon), 1605–1607*. Trans. and ed. D.A. Fleming. Nieuwkoop, Netherlands: Hes & de Graaf, 1973.

– *Icon animorum*. London: John Norton, 1614.

– *The Mirrour of Mindes or Barclay's Icon Animorum*. Trans. T. May. London: Printed by John Norton for Thomas Walkley, 1631.

Barkan, Leonard. 'Making Pictures Speak: Renaissance Art, Elizabethan Literature, Modern Scholarship.' *RQ* 48.2 (Summer 1995): 326–51.

– *Unearthing the Past: Archeology and Aesthetics in the Making of Renaissance Culture*. New Haven: Yale UP, 1999.

Barret, William, ed. *Heliodorus his Aethiopican History: done out of Greeke, and compared with other translations in diuers languages* ... London: Felix Kyngston, 1622.

Barroll, Leeds. *Anna of Denmark, Queen of England: A Cultural Biography*. Philidelphia: U of Pennsylvania P, 2000.

Bartels, Emily C. *Speaking of the Moor: From Alcazar to Othello*. Philadelphia: U of Pennsylvania P, 2008.

Bartsch, Shadi. *Decoding the Ancient Novel: The Reader and the Role of Description in Heliodorus and Achilles Tatius*. Princeton: Princeton UP, 1989.

Bataillon, Marcel. *Varia lección de clásicos españoles*. Madrid: Gredos, 1964.

Bath, Michael. *Speaking Pictures: English Emblem Books and Renaissance Culture*. New York: Longman, 1994.

Baxandall, Michael. *Painting and Experience in Fifteenth-Century Italy: A Primer in the Social History of Pictorial Style*. 2nd ed. New York: Oxford UP, 1988.

Bearden, Elizabeth B. 'Sidney's "mungrell tragy-comedie" and Anglo-Spanish Exchange in the *New Arcadia*.' *JEMCS* 10.1 (Spring 2010): 29–51.

Beaton, Roderick. *The Medieval Greek Romance*. 2nd ed. New York: Routledge, 1996.

Beaujour, Michel. 'Some Paradoxes of Description.' *Yale French Studies* 61 (1981): 27–59.

Behn, Aphra. *Oroonoko: An Authoritative Text, Historical Backgrounds, Criticism*. Ed. J. Lipking. New York: Norton, 1997.

Beilin, Elaine. *Redeeming Eve: Women Writers of the Renaissance*. Princeton: Princeton UP, 1987.

– 'Winning "the harts of the people": The Role of the Political Subject in the *Urania*.' *Pilgrimage for Love: Essays in Early Modern Literature in Honor of Josephine A. Roberts*. Ed. S. King. Tempe: Arizona Center for Medieval and Renaissance Studies, 1999. 1–18.

Benjamin, Walter. *Illuminations*. Ed. H. Arendt and trans. H. Zohn. New York: Schocken Books, 1968.

Bergmann, Bettina. 'Visualizing Pliny's Villas.' *Journal of Roman Archaeology* 8 (1995): 406–20.

Bergmann, Emily. *Art Inscribed: Essays on Ekphrasis in Spanish Golden Age Poetry*. Cambridge: Harvard UP, 1979.

Berry, Edward. 'Sidney's May Game for the Queen.' *Modern Philology* 86.3 (February 1989): 252–64.

Bhabha, Homi K. *The Location of Culture*. New York: Routledge, 1994.

Biester, James. '"A pleasant and terrible reverence": Maintanence of Majesty in Sidney's *New Arcadia*.' *Philological Quarterly* 72 (1993): 419–42.

Billault, Alain. 'Characterization in the Ancient Novel.' *The Novel in the Ancient World*. Ed. Schmeling. 115–29.

Bolla, Peter de. 'The Visibility of Visuality: Vauxhall Gardens and the Siting of the Viewer.' *Vision and Textuality*. Ed. S. Melville and B. Readings. Durham: Duke UP, 1995. 282–95.

Bolzoni, Lina. *The Gallery of Memory: Literary and Iconographic Models in the Age of the Printing Press*. Trans. J. Parzen. Toronto: U of Toronto P, 2001.

Boon, Elizabeth Hill. 'Pictorial Documents and Visual Thinking in Postconquest Mexico.' *Native Traditions in the Postconquest World*. Ed. E. Hill Boon and T. Cummins. Washington, DC: Dumbarton Oaks Research Library and Collection, 1998. 149–99.

Borges, Jorge Luis. *El Aleph*. Madrid: Alianza, 1995.

Brennan, Michael G. '"A Sidney, though un-named": Ben Jonson's Influence in the Manuscript and Print Circulation of Lady Mary Wroth's Writings.' *Sidney Journal* 17.1 (Spring 1999): 31–52.

– *The Sidneys of Penshurst and the Monarchy, 1550–1700*. Burlington, VT: Ashgate, 2006.

Brethes, Romain. 'How to Be a Man: Towards a Sexual Definition of Clitophon in Achilles Tatius' Novel *Leucippe and Clitophon*.' Crossroads in the Ancient Novel: Spaces, Frontiers, Intersections. International Conference on the Ancient Novel, CD ROM. Ed. M. Futre Pinheiro. Lisbon: 21–7 July 2008. 21 pages.

Brito Díaz, Carlos. '"Porque lo pide así la pintura": La escritura peregrina en el lienzo del *Persiles*.' *Cervantes* 17.2 (1997): 145–64.

Buxton, John. *Sir Philip Sidney in the English Renaissance*. New York: St Martin's, 1996.

Caldwell, Dorigen. 'Studies in Sixteenth-Century Italian Imprese.' *Emblematica* 11 (2001): 1–257.

Calvert, Laura, 'The Widowed Turtledove and Amorous Dove of Spanish Lyric Poetry: A Symbolic Interpretation.' *Journal of Medieval and Renaissance Studies* 3.2 (Fall 1973): 255–73.

Camerlingo, Rosanna. *From the Courtly World to the Infinite Universe: Sir Philip Sidney's Two Arcadias*. Alessandria, Italy: Orso, 1996.

Castiglione, Baldesar. *The Book of the Courtier: An Authoritative Text, Criticism*. Ed. D. Javitch and trans. C. Singleton. New York: Norton, 2002.

Castillo, David R. *(A)wry Views: Anamorphosis, Cervantes, and the Early Picaresque*. West Lafayette: Purdue UP, 2001.

Castillo, David R., and Nicholas Spadaccini. 'El antiutopismo en *Los trabajos de Persiles y Sigismunda*: Cervantes y el cervantismo actual.' *Cervantes* 20.1 (2000): 115–32.

Castro, Américo. *El pensamiento de Cervantes*. Madrid: Casa editorial Hernando, 1925.

Cavanagh, Sheila T. *Cherished Torment: The Emotional Geography of Lady Mary Wroth's Urania*. Pittsburgh: Duquesne UP, 2001.

– 'Prisoners of Love: Crosscultural and Supernatural Desires in Wroth's *Urania*.' *Prose Fiction and Early Modern Sexualities in England, 1570–1640*. Ed. Relihan and Stanivukovic. 93–112.

Cebes, of Thebes. *Cebes' Tablet: Facsimiles of the Greek Text, and of Selected Latin, French, English, Spanish, Italian, German, Dutch, and Polish Translations*. Ed. S. Sider. New York: Renaissance Society of America, 1979.

Cervantes Saavedra, Miguel de. *Don Quijote de la Mancha*. Ed. M. Riquer. 2 vols. Barcelona: Juventud, 1995.

– *Los trabajos de Persiles y Sigismunda: historia setentrional*. Ed. C. Romero Muñoz. Barcelona: Cátedra, 2004.

– *Novelas ejemplares*. Ed. J. Bautista Avalle-Arce. Vol 1. Madrid: Castalia, 1982.

– *The Trials of Persiles and Sigismunda: A Northern Story*. Trans. C. Richmond Weller and C.A. Colahan. Berkeley: U of California P, 1989.

Childers, William. *Transnational Cervantes*. Toronto: U of Toronto P, 2006.

Cicero, Marcus Tullius. *De natura deiorum; Academica*. Trans. H. Rackham. Loeb Classical Library. London: W. Heinemann, 1933.

– *De oratore*. Trans. E.W. Sutton and H. Rackham. 2 vols. Loeb Classical Library. Cambridge: Harvard UP, 1948.

Coles, Kimberly Anne. *Religion, Reform, and Women's Writing in Early Modern England*. New York: Cambridge UP, 2008.

Collignon, Albert. *Notes historiques, littéraires, et bibliographiques sur L'Argenis de Jean Barclay*. Nancy et Paris: Berger-Levrault & Cie, 1902.

Connors, Catherine. 'Metaphor and Politics in John Barclay's *Argenis*.' *Metaphor in the Ancient Novel*. Ed. S. Harrison, M. Paschalis, and S. Frangoulidis. Groningen: Barkhuis Publishing and Groningen University Library, 2005. 245–74.

Cooper, Helen. *The English Romance in Time: Transforming Motifs from Geoffrey of Monmouth to the Death of Shakespeare*. New York: Oxford UP, 2004.

Corbett, Margery, and Ronald Lightbown. *The Comely Frontispiece: The Emblematic Title-page in England, 1550–1560*. Boston: Routledge, 1979.

Correa Díaz, Luis. 'Cervantes in America: Between New World Chronicle and Chivalric Romance.' *A Twice Told Tale: Reinventing the Encounter in Iberian/Iberian American Literature and Film*. Ed. S. Juan-Navarro and T.R. Young. Newark: U of Delaware P, 2001. 210–24.

Cosgrove, Dennis. 'Globalism and Tolerance in Early Modern Geography.' *Annals of the Association of American Geographers* 93.4 (December 2003): 852–70.

Crawford, Julie. 'Sidney's Sapphics and the Role of Interpretive Communities.' *ELH* 69.4 (Winter 2002): 979–1007.

Crowley, Timothy D. 'Feigned Histories: Philip Sidney and the Poetics of Spanish Chivalric Romance.' PhD diss., U of Maryland, 2009.

Cummins, Thomas. 'From Lies to Truth: Colonial Ekphrasis and the Act of Crosscultural Translation.' *Reframing the Renaissance*. Ed. C. Farrago. New Haven: Yale UP, 1995. 152–75.

Curtius, Ernst R. *European Literature and the Latin Middle Ages*. Trans. W.R. Trask. New York: Harper and Row, 1953.

Daly, Peter M. *Literature in the Light of the Emblem: Structural Parallels between the Emblem and Literature in the Sixteenth and Seventeenth Centuries*. Toronto: U of Toronto P, 1979.

Daniel, Samuel, trans. *The vvorthy tract of Paulus Iouius, contayning a discourse of rare inuentions, both militarie and amorous called imprese...* By Paolo Giovio. London: Simon Waterson, 1585.

Davis, Charles J. 'Barclay and His *Argenis* in Spain.' *HL* 32 (1983): 28–34.

Deffis de Calvo, Emilia I. *Viajeros, peregrinos y enamorados: la novela española de peregrinación del siglo XVII*. Pamplona: Ediciones Universidad de Navarra, 1999.

Della Porta, Giovan Battista. *Ars reminiscendi aggiunta L'arte del ricordare tradotta da Dorandino Falcone da Gioia*. Ed. R. Sirri. Naples: Scientifiche Italiane, 1996.

Deyermond, Alan D. 'Narradora en la ficción sentimental: *Menina e Moça* y *Clareo y Florisea*.' *Tradiciones y puntos de vista en la ficción sentimental*. Mexico City: UNAM, 1993. 89–105.

Díaz del Castillo, Bernal. *Historia verdadera de la conquista de la Nueva España*. Ed. J. Ramírez Cabañas. Mexico City: Porrúa, 1968.

Dieckmann, Lisilotte. 'Renaissance Hieroglyphics.' *CL* 9.4 (Autumn 1957): 308–21.

Dolce, Ludovico. 'Amorosi ragionamenti.' *Historia de los amores de Clareo y Florisea y los trabajos de la sin ventura Isea*. By Alonso Núñez de Reinoso. 373–439.

Dolven, Jeff. *Scenes of Instruction in Renaissance Romance*. Chicago: U of Chicago P, 2007.

Doody, Margaret Anne. *The True Story of the Novel*. London: Fontana, 1996.

Drysdall, Dennis L. 'Occurrences of the Word "Emblema" in Printed Works before Alciato.' *Emblematica* 14 (2005): 299–325.

Duncan-Jones, Katherine. 'Sidney and Titian.' *English Renaissance Studies Presented to Dame Helen Gardner in Honor of Her Seventieth Birthday*. Ed. J. Carey. Oxford: Clarendon, 1980: 1–12.

– 'Sidney's Personal Imprese.' *Journal of the Warburg and Courtauld Institute* 33 (1970): 321–4.

– *Sir Philip Sidney: Courtier Poet*. New Haven: Yale UP, 1991.

Dundas, Judith. *Sidney and Junius on Poetry and Painting: From the Margins to the Center*. Newark: U of Delaware P, 2007.

Durán, Diego de. *Historia de las Indias de Nueva España y de islas de tierra firme*. Ed. A. María Garibay Kintana. 2 vols. Mexico City: Porrúa, 1967.

Egger, Brigit. 'Women and Marriage in the Greek Novels: The Boundaries of Romance.' *The Search for the Ancient Novel*. Ed. Tatum. 260–82.

Egido, Aurora. *Cervantes y las puertas del sueño: Estudios de La Galatea, El Quijote, y El Persiles*. Barcelona: Promociones y Publicaciones Universitarias, 1994.

Eisenberg, Daniel. *Romances of Chivalry in the Spanish Golden Age*. Newark, DE: Juan de la Cuesta, 1982.

El Saffar, Ruth. 'Fiction and the Androgyne in the Works of Cervantes.' *Cervantes* 3 (1983): 33–49.

Emery, Mary Lou. *Modernism, the Visual, and Caribbean Literature*. New York: Cambridge UP, 2007.

Erasmus, Desiderius. 'De Copia.' Trans. B. Knott and ed. C. Thomson. *Collected Works of Erasmus*. Vol. 24. Toronto: U of Toronto P, 1978.

– *Praise of Folly*. Trans. B. Radice. New York: Penguin, 1993.

Fernández, James D. 'The Bonds of Patrimony: Cervantes and the New World.' *PMLA* 109.5 (October 1994): 969–81.

Fleming, David A. 'Introduction.' *Euphormionis lusinini satyricon (Euphormio's Satyricon), 1605–1607*. By John Barclay. i–xxxvi.

– 'John Barclay: Neo-Latinist at the Jacobean Court.' *Renaissance News* 19.3 (Autumn 1966): 228–36.

Floyd-Wilson, Mary. *English Ethnicity and Race in Early Modern Drama*. New York: Cambridge UP, 2003.

Forcione, Alban K. *Cervantes, Aristotle, and the Persiles*. Princeton: Princeton UP, 1970.

– *Cervantes's Christian Romance: A Study of Persiles y Sigismunda*. Princeton: Princeton UP, 1972.

Foucault, Michel. *The Care of the Self: The History of Sexuality, Vol 3*. Trans. R. Hurley. London: Penguin, 1986.

– ['Des espaces autres.'] 'Of Other Spaces.' Trans. J. Miskowiec. *Diacritics* 16.1 (Spring 1986): 22–7.

Fraunce, Abraham. *Insignium, armorum, emblematum, hieroglyphorum, et symbolorum explicatio*. London, 1588.

– *Symbolicae philosophiae liber quartus et ultimus*. Ed. J. Manning and trans. E. Haan. New York: AMS, 1991.

– *The third part of the Countesse of Pembrokes Yuychurch Entitled, Amintas dale ...* . London: Thomas Woodcocke, 1592.

Freeman, Rosemary. *English Emblem Books*. 1948. New York: Octagon Books, 1966.

Freud, Sigmund. 'Creative Writers and Daydreaming.' Trans. I.F. Grant-Duff. The Critical Tradition: Classic Texts and Contemporary Trends. Ed. D.H. Richter. 3rd ed. Boston: Bedford St Martin's, 2007. 509–14.

Frye, Northrop. *Anatomy of Criticism: Four Essays*. Princeton: Princeton UP, 1957.

– *The Secular Scripture: A Study of the Structure of Romance*. Cambridge: Harvard UP, 1976.

Fuchs, Barbara. *Passing for Spain: Cervantes and the Fictions of Identity*. Champaign: U of Illinois P, 2003.

– *Romance*. New York: Routledge, 2004.

Fuchs, Barbara, and Brian Lockey, eds. *Anglo-Spanish Relations: Historical and Literary Perspectives on the Empires*. *JEMCS* 10.1 (Spring 2010).

Fumaroli, Marc. 'Jacques Amyot and the Clerical Polemic against the Chivalric Novel.' *RQ* 38.1 (Spring 1985): 22–40.
– 'A Scottish Voltaire: John Barclay and the Character of Nations.' Trans. M. Slater. *Times Literary Supplement* (19 January 1996): 16–17.
Fusillo, Massimo. 'How Novels End: Some Patterns of Closure in Ancient Narrative.' *Classical Closure: Reading the End in Greek and Latin Literature*. Ed. D.H. Roberts, F.M. Dunn, and D. Fowler. Princeton: Princeton UP, 1997. 209–27.
Galperín, Karina. 'Bernardim Ribeiro y Alonso Núñez de Reinoso: conversos, géneros y la emergencia de la voz feminina en la narrativa ibérica del Siglo de Oro.' PhD diss., Harvard U, 2002.
Garcés, María Antonia. *Cervantes in Algiers: A Captive's Tale*. Nashville: Vanderbilt UP, 2002.
Garrett, Martin, ed. *Sidney: The Critical Heritage*. New York: Routledge, 1996.
Gaylord, Mary M. 'Pulling Strings with Master Peter's Puppets: Fiction and History in *Don Quixote*.' *Cervantes* 18.2 (1998): 117–47.
Gilman, Ernest. *The Curious Perspective: Literary and Pictorial Wit in the Seventeenth Century*. New Haven: Yale UP, 1978.
Girard, René. *Mensonge romantique et vérité romanesque*. Paris: Grasset, 1961.
Goldberg, Jonathan. *James I and the Politics of Literature: Jonson, Shakespeare, Donne, and Their Contemporaries*. Baltimore: Johns Hopkins UP, 1983.
Goldhill, Simon. *Foucault's Virginity: Ancient Erotic Fiction and the History of Sexuality*. Cambridge: Cambridge UP, 1995.
– 'Genre.' *The Cambridge Companion to the Greek and Roman Novel*. Ed. Whitmarsh. 185–200.
– 'What Is Ekphrasis For?' *Classical Philology* 102.1 (January 2007): 1–19.
González Rovira, Javier. *La novella bizantina de la Edad de Oro*. Madrid: Gredos, 1996.
Gossett, Suzanne, and Janel Mueller. 'Textual Introduction.' *The Second Part of the Countess of Montgomery's Urania*. By Mary Wroth. xvii–xliv.
Graf, Eric C. 'Heliodorus, Cervantes, La Fayette: Ekphrasis and the Feminist Origins of the Novel.' *Ekphrasis in the Age of Cervantes*. Ed. de Armas. 175–201.
Greenblatt, Stephen. *Renaissance Self-Fashioning: From More to Shakespeare*. 2nd ed. Chicago: U of Chicago P, 2005.
Greene, Robert. *Morando, or the Tritameron of Love The first and second part ...* London: Printed by John Wolfe for Edward White, 1587. Modern spelling transcript by Nina Green, 2007. *The Oxford Authorship site*. http://www.oxford-shakespeare.com/new_files_jan_07/Morando%20(1587).pdf
Greenhalgh, Darlene. 'Love, Chastity, and Woman's Erotic Power: Greek Romance in Elizabethan and Jacobean Contexts.' *Prose Fiction and Early*

Modern Sexualities in England, 1570–1640. Ed. Relihan and Stanivukovic. 15–43.

Greer, Margaret R., Walter D. Mignolo, and Maureen Quilligan, eds. *Rereading the Black Legend: The Discourses of Religious and Racial Difference in the Renaissance Empires*. Chicago: U of Chicago P, 2007.

Greville, Fulke. 'The Life of the Renoun Sir Philip Sidney.' *The Works in Verse and Prose Complete of the Right Honourable Fulke Greville, Lord Brooke*. Ed. A. Grosart. Vol 4. New York: AMS, 1966. 1–224.

Grossberg, Benjamin Scott. 'Politics and Shifting Desire in Sidney's *New Arcadia*.' *SEL* 42.1 (Winter 2002): 63–83.

Grossman, Marshall. 'Subsequent Precedence: Milton's Materialistic Reading of Ficino and Tasso.' *Surfaces* 6 (1996): 5–25.

Grotius, Hugo. *[De jure belli ac pacis] The Law of War and Peace*. Trans. F.W. Kelsey et al. New York: Bobbs-Merrill, 1925.

Gruzinski, Serge. 'Images and Cultural Mestizaje in Colonial Mexico.' *Poetics Today* 16.1 (Spring 1995): 53–77.

– [*La colonisation de l'imaginaire*] *The Conquest of Mexico: The Incorporation of Indian Societies into the Western World, 16th–18th Centuries*. Trans. E. Corrigan. Cambridge: Polity, 1993.

– [*La pensée métisse*] *The Mestizo Mind: The Intellectual Dynamics of Colonization and Globalization*. Trans. D. Dusinberre. New York: Routledge, 2002.

– *Painting the Conquest: The Mexican Indians and the European Renaissance*. Trans. D. Dusinberre. Paris: UNESCO/Flammarion, 1992.

Guamán Poma de Ayala, Felipe. *Nueva Corónica y buen gobierno*. Ed. J. Murra and R. Adorno. Mexico City: Siglo XXI, 1980.

Hackett, Helen. *Women and Romance Fiction in the English Renaissance*. Cambridge: Cambridge UP, 2000.

Haedo, Fray Diego de. *Topografía e historia general de Argel*. Ed. I. Bauer y Landauer. 3 vols. Madrid: Sociedad de Bibliófilos Españoles, 1929.

Hager, Alan. *Dazzling Images: The Masks of Sir Philip Sidney*. Newark: U of Delaware P, 1991.

Hagg, Tomas. *The Novel in Antiquity*. Oxford: Basil Blackwell, 1983.

Hagstrum, Jean H. *The Sister Arts: The Tradition of Literary Pictorialism and English Poetry from Dryden to Gray*. Chicago: U of Chicago P, 1953.

Hall, Kim F. '"I Rather Would Wish to be a Black-Moor": Beauty, Race, and Rank in Lady Mary Wroth's *Urania*.' *Women, 'Race,' and Writing in the Early Modern Period*. Ed. M. Hendricks and P. Parker. London: Routledge, 1994. 178–94.

– *Things of Darkness: Economies of Race and Gender in Early Modern England*. Ithaca: Cornell UP, 1995.

Halley, Janet E. 'Heresy, Orthodoxy, and the Politics of Religious Discourse: The Case of the English Family of Love.' *Representations* 15 (Summer 1986): 98–120.

Hannay, Margaret P. *Mary Sidney, Lady Wroth*. Burlington, VT: Ashgate, 2010.

– *Philip's Phoenix: Mary Sidney Countess of Pembroke.* New York: Oxford UP, 1990.

Harlan, E.C. 'The Description of Paintings as a Literary Device and Its Application in Achilles Tatius.' PhD diss., Columbia U, 1965.

Harvey, Gabriel. 'A New Letter of Notable Contents.' *Sidney: The Critical Herritage*. Ed. Garrett. 131.

Heffernan, James. *The Museum of Words: The Poetics of Ekphrasis from Homer to Ashbery*. Chicago: U of Chicago P, 1994.

Heliodorus. *The Aethiopian History of Heliodorus*. Trans. N. Tate. London: Printed by J.L. for Edward Poole, 1686.

– *An Aethiopian History Written in Greek by Heliodorus and Englished by Thomas Underdowne Anno 1569*. Ed. C. Whibley. New York: AMS, 1967.

– *An Ethiopian Romance*. Trans. M. Hadas. Philadelphia: U of Pennsylvania P, 1957.

– *Historia etiópica de los amores de Teágenes y Cariclea traducida en romance por Fernando de Mena*. Ed. F. López Estrada. Madrid: Aldus, 1954.

Herbert, Sir Thomas. *A relation of some yeares trauaile begunne anno 1626 ...* . London: William Stansby and Jacob Bloome, 1634.

Hollander, John. 'The Poetics of Ekphrasis.' *Word & Image* 4 (1988): 209–19.

Holzberg, Niklas. 'The Genre: Novels Proper and the Fringe.' *The Novel in the Ancient World*. Ed. Schmeling. 11–28.

Homer. *Iliad*. Trans. R. Fagles. New York: Penguin, 1998.

Hulse, Clark. *The Rule of Art: Literature and Painting in the Renaissance.* Chicago: U of Chicago P, 1990.

IJsewijn, Jozef. 'John Barclay and His *Argenis*: A Scottish Neo-Latin Novelist.' *HL* 32 (1983): 1–27.

Iyengar, Sujata. *Shades of Difference: Mythologies of Skin Color in Early Modern England*. Philadelphia: U of Pennsylvania P, 2005.

Jameson, Fredric. 'Magical Narratives: Romance as Genre.' *NLH* 7 (Autumn 1975): 133–63.

– *The Political Unconscious: Narrative as a Socially Symbolic Act*. Ithaca: Cornell UP, 1981.

Javitch, Daniel. *Proclaiming a Classic: The Canonization of Orlando Furioso.* Princeton: Princeton UP, 1991.

Jonson, Ben. *Ben Jonson: Complete Works.* Vol. 10. Ed. C.H. Herford and P. Simpson. Oxford: Clarendon, 1941.

– *Ben Jonson: The Complete Masques*. Ed. S. Orgel. New Haven: Yale UP, 1969.
Kennedy, George A. *Classical Rhetoric and Its Christian and Secular Tradition from Ancient to Modern Times*. 2nd ed. Chapel Hill: U of North Carolina P, 1999.
Kennedy, George A., trans. and ed. *Progymnasmata: Greek Textbooks of Prose Composition and Rhetoric.* Boston: Brill, 2003.
Kim, Lawrence. 'Time.' *The Cambridge Companion to the Greek and Roman Novel*. Ed. Whitmarsh. 146–61.
Kinney, Clare. 'The Margins of Romance, at the Heart of the Matter: Revisionary Fabulation in Sidney's *New Arcadia*.' *Journal of Narrative Technique* 21.2 (Spring 1991): 143–51.
Konstan, David. *Sexual Symmetry: Love in the Ancient Novel and Related Genres.* Princeton: Princeton UP, 1994.
Krieger, Murray. *Ekphrasis: The Illusion of the Natural Sign*. Baltimore: Johns Hopkins UP, 1992.
Lamb, Mary Ellen. 'The Biopolitics of Romance in Mary Wroth's *The Countess of Montgomery's Urania*.' *ELR* 31.1 (Winter 2001): 107–30.
– 'Exhibiting Class and Displaying the Body in Sidney's *Countess of Pembroke's Arcadia*.' *SEL* 37.1 (1997): 55–68.
– *Gender and Authorship in the Sidney Circle*. Madison: U of Wisconsin P, 1990.
Langford, Jerald. 'John Barclay's *Argenis*: A Seminal Novel.' *Studies in English* 26 (1947): 59–76.
Lees-Jeffries, Hester. *England's Helicon: Fountains in Early Modern Literature and Culture*. New York: Oxford UP, 2007.
Leonard, Irving A. *Books of the Brave: Being an Account of Books and of Men in the Spanish Conquest and Settlement of the Sixteenth-Century New World*. Berkeley: U of California P, 1992.
Levin, Richard A. 'What? How?: Female-Female Desire in Sidney's *New Arcadia*.' *Criticism* 39.4 (Fall 1997): 463–87.
Linthicum, M. Channing. *Costume in the Drama of Shakespeare and His Contemporaries.* Oxford: Oxford UP, 1936.
Lockey, Brian C. *Law and Empire in English Renaissance Literature*. New York: Cambridge UP, 2006.
Longus. *Daphnis and Chloe ...* Trans. A. Daye. London: Robert Walde-grave, 1587.
López de Gómara, Francisco. [*Historia general de las Indias* vol. 2], *Cortes: The Life of the Conqueror by his Secretary Francisco López de Gómara*. Trans. and ed. L. Byrd Simpson. Berkeley: U of California P, 1964.
López Estrada, Francisco. 'Prólogo.' *Historia etiópica de los amores de Teágenes y Cariclea traducido en romance por Fernando de Mena*. By Heliodorus. i–lxxxv.

López Pinciano, Alonso. *Philosophia antigua poética*. Ed. A. Carballo Picazo. 3 vols. Madrid: Consejo Superior de Investigaciones Científicas, Instituto Miguel de Cervantes, 1953.

Lozano Rinieblas, Isabel. *Cervantes y el mundo del Persiles*. Alcalá de Henares: Centro de Estudios Cervantinos, 1998.

Lucian of Samosata. *The Works of Lucian of Samosata*. Trans. H.W. Fowler and F.G. Fowler. Vol 4. Oxford: Clarendon, 1905.

Maravall, José Antonio. *La cultura del barroco: análisis de una estructura histórica*. Barcelona: Ariel, 1980.

Mariscal, George. 'Persiles and the Remaking of Spanish Culture.' *Cervantes* 10.1 (1990): 93–102.

Maslen, Robert W. *Elizabethan Fictions: Espionage, Counter-espionage and the Duplicity of Early Elizabethan Prose Narratives*. New York: Oxford UP, 1997.

Matar, Nabil. *Turks, Moors, and Englishmen in the Age of Discovery*. New York: Columbia UP, 1999.

Mattessich, Stefan. *Lines of Flight: Discursive Time and Countercultural Desire in the Work of Thomas Pynchon*. Durham: Duke UP, 2002.

McCoy, Richard C. *Sir Philip Sidney: Rebellion in Arcadia*. New Brunswick, NJ: Rutgers UP, 1979.

Melville, Herman. *Moby-Dick or the Whale*. Ed. H. Hayford and H. Parker. New York: Norton, 2002.

Menéndez y Pelayo, Marcelino. *Orígenes de la novela*. Ed. D. Enrique Sánchez. Vol. 1. Santander: Aldus, 1943.

Mentz, Steven. *Romance for Sale in Early Modern England: The Rise of Prose Fiction*. New York: Ashgate, 2006.

– 'The Thigh and the Sword: Gender, Genre, and Sexy Dressing in Sidney's *New Arcadia*.' *Prose Fiction and Early Modern Sexualities in England, 1570–1640*. Ed. Relihan and Stanivukovic. 77–91.

Miller, Naomi J. 'Engendering Discourse: Women's Voices in Wroth's *Urania* and Shakespeare's Plays.' *Reading Mary Wroth: Representing Alternatives in Early Modern England*. Ed. Miller and Waller. 35–66.

Miller, Naomi J., and Gary Waller, eds. *Reading Mary Wroth: Representing Alternatives in Early Modern England*. Knoxville: U of Tennessee P, 1991.

Miller, Shannon. 'Constructing the Female Self: Architectural Structures in Mary Wroth's *Urania*.' *Renaissance Culture and the Everyday*. Ed. P. Fumerton and S. Hunt. Philadelphia: U of Pennsylvania P, 1999. 139–61.

Milton, John. *The Collected Works of John Milton*. Vol. 3. Ed. D. Wolfe et al. New Haven: Yale UP, 1952.

Mitchell, W.J. Thomas. *Picture Theory: Essays on Verbal and Visual Representation*. Chicago: U of Chicago P, 1994.
– 'Translator Translated (Interview with Cultural Theorist Homi Bhabha) by W.J.T. Mitchell.' *Artforum* 33.7 (March 1995): 80–4.
Mitsi, Efterpi. 'Writing against Pictures: A Study of Ekphrasis in Epics by Homer, Virgil, Ariosto, Tasso and Spenser.' PhD diss., NYU, 1991.
Morales, Helen. 'Introduction.' *Leucippe and Clitophon*. By Achilles Tatius. Trans. Whitmarsh. viii–xxxii.
– 'The History of Sexuality.' *The Cambridge Companion to the Greek and Roman Novel*. Ed. Whitmarsh. 39–55.
– *Vision and Narrative in Achilles Tatius' Leucippe and Clitophon*. Cambridge: Cambridge UP, 2004.
Most, Glenn W. 'The Stranger's Stratagem: Self-Disclosure and Self-Sufficiency in Greek Culture.' *Journal of Hellenic Studies* 109 (1989): 114–33.
Muñoz Camargo, Diego. *Descripción de la ciudad y provincia de Tlaxcala de las indias y del mar océano para el buen gobierno y ennoblecimiento dellas*. Ed. R. Acuña. Mexico City: UNAM, 1981.
Newcomb, Lori Humphrey. *Reading Popular Romance in Early Modern England*. New York: Columbia UP, 2002.
Oliveira e Silva, Jose de. 'Sir Philip Sidney and the Castilian Tongue.' *CL* 34.2 (Spring 1982): 130–45.
Orgel, Stephen. 'The Poetics of Spectacle.' *NLH* 2.3 (Spring 1971): 367–89.
Orgel, Stephen, and Roy Strong. *Inigo Jones: The Theatre of the Stuart Court*. London: Sotheby Parke Bernet, 1973.
Ortelius, Abraham. *Theatrum Orbis Terrarum: The Theatre of the Whole World: Set Forth by that Excellent Geographer Abraham Ortelius*. London: John Norton, 1606.
Ovid. *Metamorphoses*. Ed. H. Magnus. Gotha, Germany: Friedr. Andr. Perthes, 1892.
Parker, Patricia A. *Inescapable Romance: Studies in the Poetics of a Mode*. Princeton: Princeton UP, 1979.
Parry, William. *A New and Large Discourse on the Travels of Sir Anthony Sherley, Knight, ...* . London: Valentine Simmes for Felix Norton. 1601.
'Passibility.' Def. 1 and 2. *Oxford English Dictionary*. 2nd ed. Oxford: Oxford UP, 1989.
Perkins, Judith. 'An Ancient "Passing" Novel: Heliodorus's *Aethiopika*.' *Arethusa* 32 (1999): 197–214.
Perry, Ben Edwin. *The Ancient Romances: A Literary-Historical Account of Their Origins*. Berkeley: U of California P, 1967.

Petrarca, Francesco. *Petrarch's Africa*. Trans. T.G. Bergin and A.S. Wilson. New Haven: Yale UP, 1977.

Philostratus, The Elder and The Younger. *Imagines: Callistratus Descriptions.* Reprint ed. and trans. A. Fairbanks. Loeb Classical Library. Cambridge: Harvard UP, 1979.

Plazenet, Laurence. *L'ébahissement et la delectation: Réception comparee et poétiques du roman grec en France et en Angleterre aux XVIe et XVIIe siècles.* Paris: Honoré Champion, 1997.

Plepelits, Karl. 'Achilles Tatius.' *The Novel in the Ancient World*. Ed. Schmeling. 387–416.

Plutarch. 'De gloria Atheniensium.' *Moralia*. Trans. F.C. Babbit. Vol. 4. Cambridge: Harvard UP, 1936. 489–527.

Pratt, Mary Louise. *Imperial Eyes: Travel Writing and Transculturation*. New York: Routledge, 1992.

Praz, Mario. *Studies in Seventeenth-Century Imagery.* 2nd ed. Rome: Edizioni di storia e letteratura, 1964.

Puttenham, George. *The Art of English Poesie*. Menston: Scolar Press, 1968.

Pynchon, Thomas. *The Crying of Lot 49*. New York: Perennial Classics, 1999.

Quintilian. *The Institutio Oratoria of Quintilian.* Trans. H.E. Butler. Loeb Classical Library. Cambridge: Harvard UP, 1954.

Reardon, Bryan P. *The Form of Greek Romance.* Princeton: Princeton UP, 1991.

Reeve, Michael. 'The Re-emergence of Ancient Novels in Western Europe, 1300–1810.' *The Cambridge Companion to the Greek and Roman Novel*. Ed. Whitmarsh. 282–98.

Reinoso, Alonso Núñez de. *Historia de los amores de Clareo y Florisea y los trabajos de la sin ventura Isea*. Ed. J. Jiménez Ruiz. Málaga: Universidad de Málaga, 1997.

Reiss, Timothy J. *Against Autonomy: Global Dialectics of Cultural Exchange.* Stanford: Stanford UP, 2002.

– *Mirages of the Self: Patterns of Personhood in Ancient and Early Modern Europe.* Stanford: Stanford UP, 2002.

– *The Uncertainty of Analysis: Problems in Truth, Meaning, and Culture*. Ithaca: Cornell UP, 1988.

Relihan, Constance C. *Cosmographical Glasses: Geographic Discourse, Gender, and Elizabethan Fiction*. Kent, OH: Kent State UP, 2004.

Relihan, Constance C., and Goran V. Stanivukovic, eds. *Prose Fiction and Early Modern Sexualities in England, 1570–1640*. New York: Palgrave Macmillan, 2003.

Rendall, Steven. 'Introduction.' *Astrea (L'Astrée).* By Honoré d'Urfé. vii–xxviii.

Riley, Edward C. *Cervantes's Theory of the Novel*. Newark, NJ: Juan de la Cuesta, 1992.

Riley, Mark, and Dorothy Pritchard Huber. 'Introduction.' *Argenis*. By John Barclay. Vol. 1. 3–92.

Roberts, Josephine A. 'Critical Introduction.' *The First Part of The Countess of Montgomery's Urania*. By Mary Wroth. xv–xcviii.

– 'Introduction.' *The Poems of Lady Mary Wroth*. By Mary Wroth. 1–84.

– '"The Knott Never to Bee Untide": The Controversy Regarding Marriage in Mary Wroth's Urania.' *Reading Mary Wroth: Representing Alternatives in Early Modern England*. Ed. Miller and Waller. 109–32.

Robinson, Benedict S. *Islam and Early Modern English Literature: The Politics of Romance from Spenser to Milton*. New York: Palgrave Macmillan, 2007.

Rohde, Erwin. *Der griechische Roman und seine Vorläufer*. Liepzig: 1876. Ed. W. Schmid. Darmstadt: Wissenschaftliche Buchgesellschaft, 1974.

Romm, James. 'Travel.' *The Cambridge Companion to the Greek and Roman Novel*. Ed. Whitmarsh. 109–26.

Rosand, David. '*Ut Pitor Poeta*: Meaning in Titian's Poesie.' *NLH* 3 (1971–2): 527–46.

Rose, Constance Hubbard. *Alonso Núñez de Reinoso: Lament of a Sixteenth-Century Exile*. Rutherford, NJ: Fairleigh Dickinson UP, 1971.

Rubiés, Joan-Pau. 'Late Medieval Ambassadors and the Practice of Cross-Cultural Encounters, 1250–1500.' *The Book of Travels: Genre, Ethnology and Pilgrimage, 1250–1700*. Ed. P. Brummett. Boston: Brill, 2009. 37–113.

Ruiz Gito, Jesús M. *La tabla de Cebes: Historia de un texto griego en el humanismo y educación europea*. Madrid: Ediciones Clásicas, 1997.

Russell, Daniel S. *The Emblem and Device in France*. Lexington: French Forum, 1985.

Sacchetti, María Alberta. *Cervantes' Los trabajos de Persiles y Sigismunda: A Study of Genre*. London: Tamesis, 2001.

Salomón, Hermán Prins. 'Mendes, Benveniste, De Luna, Micas, Nasci: The State of the Art (1532–1558).' *Jewish Quarterly Review* 88.3–4 (January–April 1998): 135–211.

Salzman, Paul. *English Prose Fiction 1580–1700: A Critical History*. Oxford: Clarendon, 1985.

Sandys, George. *A Relation of a journey begun An: Dom: 1610 ...* . London: Printed by Richard Field for W. Barrett, 1615.

Scaliger, Julio Cesare. *Poetices libri septem*. 1561. Facsim. Ed. A. Buck. Stuttgart Bad: Cannstatt, 1964.

Scanlon, Patrick M. 'Emblematic Narrative in the Argument of Love in Sidney's *Arcadia*.' *Journal of Narrative Technique* 15.3 (Fall 1985): 219–33.

Schleck, Julia. 'Writing Out Muslim Culture: Genre, Narrative and Truth in Early Modern Travel and News Reports from Persia and the Levant, 1565–1630.' PhD diss., NYU, 2006.

Schmeling, Gareth, ed. *The Novel in the Ancient World*. Leiden: Brill, 1996.

Sedgwick, Eve Kosovsky. *Between Men: English Literature and Male Homosocial Desire*. New York: Columbia UP, 1985.

Selden, Daniel. 'Genre of Genre.' *The Search for the Ancient Novel*. Ed. Tatum. 39–66.

Sider, Sandra. 'Introduction.' *Cebes' Tablet*. By Cebes of Thebes. 4–18.

Sidney, Sir Philip. *The Countess of Pembroke's Arcadia*. Ed. M. Evans. New York: Penguin, 1987.

– *The Countess of Pembroke's Arcadia (The New Arcadia)*. Ed. V. Skretkowicz. Oxford: Clarendon, 1987.

– *The Countess of Pembroke's Arcadia* (*The Old Arcadia*). Ed. K. Duncan-Jones. New York: Oxford UP, 1999.

– *Sir Philip Sidney: The Major Works*. Ed. K. Duncan-Jones. New York: Oxford UP, 2002.

Skretkowicz, Victor. 'Building Sidney's Reputation: Texts and Editors of the *Arcadia*.' *Sir Philip Sidney: 1586 and the Creation of a Legend*. Ed. J. Van Dorsten, D. Baker-Smith, and A.F. Kinney. Leiden: Brill, 1986. 111–24.

– 'Devices and Their Narrative Function in Sidney's *Arcadia*.' *Emblematica* 1 (1986): 177–82.

– 'Hercules in Sidney and Spenser.' *Notes & Queries* 27 (1980): 306–10.

– 'Sir Philip Sidney and the Elizabethan Literary Device.' *Emblematica* 2 (1988): 171–9.

Smith, Nigel. *Anglia Rediviva: Literature and Revolution in England, 1640–1660*. New Haven: Yale UP, 1994.

Spenser, Edmund. *The Faerie Queene*. 2nd ed. Ed. A.C. Hamilton, H. Yamashita, T. Suzuki, and S. Fukuda. New York: Longman, 2006.

Spitzer, Leo. 'Perspectivismo lingüístico en El Quijote.' *Lingüística e historia literaria*. Madrid: Gredos, 1955. 135–87.

Steiner, Wendy. *Pictures of Romance: Form against Context in Painting and Literature*. Chicago: U of Chicago P, 1988.

Stephens, Susan. 'Cultural Identity.' *The Cambridge Companion to the Greek and Roman Novel*. Ed. Whitmarsh. 56–71.

Stephens, Walter. 'Tasso's Heliodorus and the World of Romance.' *The Search for the Ancient Novel*. Ed. Tatum. 67–87.

Stewart, Alan. *Philip Sidney: A Double Life*. New York: St Martin's, 2001.

Stillman, Robert E. *Philip Sidney and the Poetics of Renaissance Cosmopolitanism.* Burlington, VT: Ashgate, 2008.

Strong, Roy. *Splendour at Court: Renaissance Spectacle and Illusion.* London: Weidenfeld and Nicolson, 1973.

Tasso, Torquato. *Discourses on the Heroic Poem.* Trans. M. Cavalchini and I. Samuel. Oxford: Clarendon, 1973 .

– *Le lettere di Torquato Tasso.* Ed. C. Guasti. Vol. 1. Florence: Felice le Monnier, 1854.

Tatius, Achilles. *Leucippe and Clitophon.* Introd. H. Morales and trans. T. Whitmarsh. New York: Oxford UP, 2001.

– *The Loves of Clitophon and Leucippe. A most Elegant History: and Now Englished.* Trans. A. Hodges. Oxford: Printed by William Turner for Iohn Allam, 1638.

– *The most delectable and pleasaunt history of Clitiphon and Leucippe ...* . Trans. W. Burton. London: Thomas Creede for William Mattes, 1597.

Tatum, James, ed. *The Search for the Ancient Novel.* Baltimore: Johns Hopkins UP, 1994.

Tavakoli-Targhi, Mohamad. 'Persianate Europology.' *Refashioning Iran: Orientalism, Occidentalism, and Nationalist Historiography.* New York: Palgrave Macmillan, 2001. 83–114.

Teijeiro Fuentes, Miguel Ángel. '*Clareo y Florisea* o la historia de una mentira.' *Anuario de estudios filologicos* 7 (1984): 353–9.

– *La novela bizantina española: apuntes para una revision del genero.* Cáceres: Ediciones Universidad de Extremadura, 1988.

Tucker, George Hugo. *Homo Viator: Itineraries of Exile, Displacement and Writing in Renaissance Europe.* Geneva: Droz, 2003.

Urfé, Honoré d'. *Astrea (L'Astrée), by Honoré d'Urfé.* Trans. S. Rendall. Vol. 1. 1607. Binghamton: State U of New York P, 1995.

– *L'Astrée.* Ed. M. Hugues Vaganay. Vol 1. Strasbourg: Heitz, 1920.

Valadés, Fray Diego. *Retorica Cristiana* [*Rhetorica Christiana.* 1579]. Trans. T. Herrera Zapién et al. Mexico City: Fondo de Cultura Económica, 1989.

Vasaly, Ann. *Representations: Images of the World in Ciceronian Oratory.* Berkeley: U of California P, 1993.

Vaught, Jennifer C. *Masculinity and Emotion in Early Modern Literature.* Burlington, VT: Ashgate, 2008.

Vilborg, Ebbe, ed. *Achilles Tatius: Leucippe and Clitophon.* 2 vols. Stockholm: Almqvist and Wiksell, 1955.

Vinaver, Eugène. *The Rise of Romance.* New York: Oxford UP, 1971.

Virgil. *Aeneid.* Trans. R. Fitzgerald. New York: Random House, 1990.

– *Bucolics, Aeneid, and Georgics of Virgil.* Boston: Ginn & Co., 1900.

Wall-Randell, Sarah E. 'Imagining the Book in Early Modern England: The Romance of Reading in the Age of Print.' PhD diss., Harvard U, 2005.

Waller, Gary F. *The Sidney Family Romance: Mary Wroth, William Herbert, and the Early Modern Construction of Gender.* Detroit: Wayne State UP, 1993.

Webb, Ruth. *Ekphrasis, Imagination and Persuasion in Ancient Rhetorical Theory and Practice.* Burlington, VT: Ashgate, 2009.

Whitmarsh, Tim, ed. *The Cambridge Companion to the Greek and Roman Novel.* Cambridge: Cambridge UP, 2008.

Whitmarsh, Tim, and Shadi Bartsch. 'Narrative.' *The Cambridge Companion to the Greek and Roman Novel.* Ed. Whitmarsh. 237–57.

Wiesenthal, Christine, and Brad Bucknell. 'Essays into the Imagetext: An Interview with W.J.T. Mitchell.' *Mosaic* 33.2 (June 2000): 1–23.

Wilson, Diana de Armas. *Allegories of Love: Cervantes's Persiles and Sigismunda.* Princeton: Princeton UP, 1991.

– 'Cervantes and the New World.' *The Cambridge Companion to Cervantes*. Ed. A.J. Cascardi. Cambridge: Cambridge UP, 2002. 206–25.

– *Cervantes, the Novel, and the New World*. New York: Oxford UP, 2000.

Winkler, John J., trans. *Leucippe and Clitophon*. By Achilles Tatius. *Collected Ancient Greek Novels*. Ed. B.P. Rearden. Berkeley: U of California P, 1989. 170–284.

Wolff, Samuel L. *The Greek Romance in Elizabethan Prose Fiction.* New York: Columbia UP, 1912.

Woolf, Virginia. *The Second Common Reader*. 1932. Ed. and introd. A. McNeillie. New York: Harcourt, 1986.

Worden, Blair. *The Sound of Virtue: Philip Sidney's Arcadia and Elizabethan Politics*. New Haven: Yale UP, 1996.

Wroth, Lady Mary. *The First Part of The Countess of Montgomery's Urania*. Ed. J.A. Roberts. Binghamton: Center for Medieval and Early Renaissance Studies, State U of New York P, 1995.

– *The Poems of Lady Mary Wroth*. Ed. J.A. Roberts. Baton Rouge: Louisiana State UP, 1983.

– *The Second Part of the Countess of Montgomery's Urania*. Ed. J.A. Roberts, S. Gossett, and J. Mueller. Tempe: English Renaissance Texts Society and Arizona Center for Medieval and Renaissance Studies, 1999.

Yates, Frances A. *Astraea: The Imperial Theme in the Sixteenth Century.* London: Routledge and Kegan Paul, 1975.

Zandvoort, Reinard W. *Sidney's Arcadia: A Comparison between the Two Versions.* Amsterdam: N.V. Swets and Zeitlinger, 1929.

Zeitlin, Froma. *Playing the Other: Gender and Society in Classical Greek Literature.* Chicago: U of Chicago P, 1996.

Zeitlin, Froma, David Halperin, and J.J. Winkler eds. *Before Sexuality: Structures of Erotic Experience in the Ancient Greek World*. Princeton: Princeton UP, 1990.

Zeitlin, Judith Francis, and Lillian Thomas. 'Spanish Justice and the Indian Cacique: Disjunctive Political Systems in Sixteenth-Century Tehuantepec.' *Ethnohistory* 39.3 (Summer 1992): 285–315.

Zimic, Stanislav. 'Alonso Núñez de Reinoso, traductor de *Leucipe y Clitofonte*.' *Symposium* 21 (Summer 1967): 166–74.

– '*Leucipe y Clitofonte* y *Clareo y Florisea* en el *Persiles* de Cervantes.' *Anales Cervantinos* 13–14 (1974–5): 37–58.

Index